D. J. ENRIGHT taught literature in Egypt, ~~~~~~ ~~~~~ Far East, and was Professor of English at the University of Singapore between 1960 and 1970. He then worked for the publishing house Chatto and Windus until retiring in 1982. A book of autobiography and travel, *Memoirs of a Mendicant Professor*, appeared in 1969, and in addition he has published four novels, three novels for children, and most recently, his *Collected Poems* (1981), *A Mania for Sentences* (essays on language and literature, 1983) and *Instant Chronicles* (poems, 1985). He has also edited *The Oxford Book of Contemporary Verse 1945–1980* (1980) and *The Oxford Book of Death* (1983). In 1981 he received the Queen's Gold Medal for Poetry.

ANTHONY THWAITE was born in 1930. Since he left Oxford in 1955, he has varied his career between literary editing (on the *Listener*, the *New Statesman* and, since 1973, on *Encounter*) and teaching English abroad: from 1955 to 1957 at Tokyo University, from 1965 to 1967 at the University of Libya, and since then for shorter visiting appointments and tours, sometimes for the British Council, in many European countries and in Kuwait, Iraq, Pakistan, India, China, and Argentina. He published his *Poems 1953–1983* in 1984, and in the same year *Six Centuries of Verse,* based on his television series for Channel 4. He is spending part of 1985–6 in Japan.

D. J. ENRIGHT

Academic Year

A Novel

—◆—

INTRODUCED BY
ANTHONY THWAITE

Oxford   New York
OXFORD UNIVERSITY PRESS
1985

Oxford University Press, Walton Street, Oxford OX2 6DP

London New York Toronto
Delhi Bombay Calcutta Madras Karachi
Kuala Lumpur Singapore Hong Kong Tokyo
Nairobi Dar es Salaam Cape Town
Melbourne Auckland

and associated companies in
Beirut Berlin Ibadan Mexico City Nicosia

Oxford is a trade mark of Oxford University Press

First published 1955 by Martin Secker & Warburg Ltd.
First issued, with Anthony Thwaite's introduction, as an
Oxford University Press paperback 1985

British Library Cataloguing in Publication Data

Enright, D. J.
Academic year : a novel.—(Twentieth-century classics)
I. Title   II. Series
823'.914[F]   PR6009.N6

ISBN 0-19-281876-7

Library of Congress Cataloging in Publication Data

Enright, D. J. (Dennis Joseph), 1920–Academic year.
(Twentieth-century classics)
First published: London : Secker & Warburg, 1955.
I. Title.   II. Series.
PR6009.N6A64 1985   823'.914   85-262

ISBN 0-19-281876-7 (pbk.)

Printed in Great Britain by
Richard Clay (The Chaucer Press) Ltd,
Bungay, Suffolk

INTRODUCTION

BY ANTHONY THWAITE

NOT so many years ago as it sometimes seems, it was possible for literate British persons with qualifications that could hardly be called 'specialist' (and sometimes with very few qualifications at all) to find jobs in universities all over the world as teachers of English Literature. This was before the exacting days of TEFL, TESOP, of ESP and EAP; an innocent epoch, when it would have been unlikely for a British professor to make (or at any rate to make in public) such a bizarre remark as 'literature is useful even in language learning'. Nowadays the display advertisements for English-teaching posts abroad demand a thorough apprenticeship working on the linguistic interface. Experts like Dr Petworth in Malcolm Bradbury's novel *Rates of Exchange* pick up their briefcases and circle the globe carrying with them this 'ideal British product, needing no workers and no work, no assembly lines and no assembly, no spare parts and very little servicing'—the English language.

But until about the mid-1960s, the situation was not like that at all. True, English has been an international language for a long time, but until roughly twenty years ago it was seen to have a close relationship with, if not actually to be embodied in, something called English Literature. In Ankara and Athens, from China to Peru, exported teachers expounded the Great Tradition and the Common Pursuit, the plays of Shakespeare and Shaw, the novels of Dickens and George Eliot, the poems of everyone from Langland to Larkin. Why? One answer has been supplied by the author of the novel you are about to read: 'we teach literature because there is as yet no substitute for it'.

In his essay 'The Daffodil Transplanted', from which those words are quoted, D. J. Enright draws on his wide experience of teaching English Literature abroad. He began with three years in Egypt, the setting of *Academic Year*, and went on for varying periods to Japan, Germany, Thailand, and Singapore. These experiences have fed his poems and novels for almost forty years: some of them have been relayed more directly but no less entertainingly in one of the sharpest and funniest autobiographies of our time, *Memoirs of a Mendicant Professor* (1969). If we add to these the several books of critical essays Enright has published over the years, we see a consistent, distinct, and remarkable individual. At the end of his *Memoirs*, he calls them 'the animadversions of a disillusioned liberal'; but he continues:

Disillusioned—and yet with no superior illusion in view, and so perhaps not to be accurately called 'disillusioned'. 'Chastened' let us rather say. What you have not deified cannot fail you so utterly. As for 'liberal', I don't think it will ever come to seem a dirty word to me.

*

That is very much the standpoint of *Academic Year*, written some fifteen years earlier. Enright, born in 1920 into a poor Anglo-Irish family in the Midlands, won his way through scholarships to grammar school and Cambridge. At Cambridge in the late 1930s he was a pupil of F. R. Leavis at Downing College—an experience which neither made him a Leavisite parrot nor turned him into a contemptuous apostate. He contributed to *Scrutiny* while still an undergraduate, which might make one suppose that a conventional and successful domestic academic career lay in front of him. But he has maintained, in an essay in *Conspirators and Poets* (1966), that for a candidate for home university posts immediately after the war—let alone earlier— to have appeared in the pages of *Scrutiny* was considerably more disadvantageous than to have appeared in no pages at all. Some of us went abroad in the first case . . . simply because foreign universities were less particular or (perhaps through backwardness) less prejudiced against *Scrutiny*'s minor fry.

So in 1947 Enright began his profession of English Literature as a lecturer in what was the Farouk I University, later to be the University of Alexandria. British teachers had long been employed in Egyptian universities. In 1926 Robert Graves was appointed Professor of English Literature at the newly-founded Egyptian University in Cairo. He was promised (and received) 'a very high salary' and was assured 'there was little work to do' ('I found that I was expected to give two lectures a week, but the dean soon decided that if the students were ever to dispense with the interpreters they must be given special instruction in French—which reduced the time for lectures, so that I had only one a week to give. This one was pandemonium'). Graves stayed in Egypt for a year, and was succeeded by Bonamy Dobrée who, presumably treating the place with less arrant contempt, survived three years. Among others in the university roll-call, particularly during the Second World War, were Robin Fedden, Robert Liddell, P. H. Newby, Bernard Spencer, and Terence Tiller.

But the post-war Egypt in which the young Enright arrived was no longer the curiously Bohemian place of temporary intellectual exile conjured up by these names (to which one could add the non-university-based but associated ones of Keith Douglas, Lawrence Durrell, Olivia Manning, R. D. Smith, and several others). These were the last years of Farouk's corrupt and decadent régime. It was a country on the edge of extreme and violent change. In *Academic Year* Enright reflects its mixture of anarchy and repression, nihilism and nerves: riots and rumours of riots and of *coups d'état*, as well as the more customary student strikes. The end of the British Mandate in Palestine in 1948 and the foundation of the state of Israel resulted in the first Arab–Israeli war, and the humiliation, in particular of Egypt, in the subsequent defeat. In 1952, two years after Enright left Egypt, Farouk was forced to abdicate. Though he ostensibly handed over the throne to his infant son, the real power became Neguib and his military council and, behind Neguib, Nasser.

It was a time of apprehension, and of a different kind of scrutiny from that which Enright had experienced at Cambridge. Farouk's Secret Police and so-called Moral Police were everywhere. (Enright casually brings in mention of a member of the latter in Chapter 2.) In an incident which one feels could easily have involved Packet and Bacon in *Academic Year*, but which in fact had to wait to be commemorated in *Memoirs of a Mendicant Professor*, Enright tells of walking along the Corniche with an Irish colleague on their way to take tea with one of the university professors. Enright remarked jokingly to his friend that they were approaching an anti-aircraft gun, newly installed to protect Alexandria against Israeli attacks; so that, although no attempt had been made to camouflage it, they would be well advised not to stare at it as they passed:

We fixed our tactful gaze in front of us, perhaps a little too fixedly, for some bystander, bored with the long Sunday afternoon, conceived the thrilling notion that we might be Jewish spies. Quickly a crowd gathered, and cries of 'Yahudi!', some questioning and some answering, broke the calm of the Corniche.

A policeman having appeared, Enright and his friend were taken to the nearest police station ('a little squalid hell of its own, smelling of urine'), where a lieutenant roared 'When did you swim ashore from that Jewish ship?' Fortunately the interrogation was curtailed by the chance intervention of a coffee-drinking chum of the assembled policemen. He turned out to be a clerk in the university administration who recognised Enright and vouched for his identity and respectability, 'and everybody smiled and exclaimed and congratulated everybody else':

I suggested hesitantly that since the police had made us late for our appointment, they might like to stand us a taxi. That was the funniest joke of all. We stumbled past the prostrate women and the quarrelling policemen with laughter exploding at our heels. Drama had turned to comedy, and that was the next best thing on a boring Sunday at the police station.

*

In *Academic Year*, drama often turns to comedy, and vice versa. When the novel was first published in 1955, it was greeted with genial praise, but almost wholly as a comedy, if not actually a farce. It followed close on the heels of John Wain's *Hurry On Down* and Kingsley Amis's *Lucky Jim*, and it was in their terms that it was praised: the *Daily Telegraph*, in fact, called it 'an Alexandrian *Lucky Jim*'. The *Star* thought it 'should give the right-minded reader many a laugh and not a few reminiscent chuckles later on'. The *New Statesman* called it 'splendidly seedy'—'a phrase which' (thinks Packet, in the opening pages of *Academic Year*'s sequel, *Heaven Knows Where*) 'might be taken to connote one shelf above the consciously pornographic'. Certainly it is a great deal funnier than that other, vaster literary memorial to Alexandria of modern times, Durrell's *Alexandria Quartet*, the first volume of which (*Justine*) appeared two years after *Academic Year*, in 1957. Nothing could be more different than these two poets' treatment of the city and its inhabitants. But rereading Enright's novel almost thirty years after its first appearance, I found that my memory had played tricks.

I too had remembered it as much more of a comic turn, much more a slice of farcial picaresque, than in fact is the case. I had forgotten how, among the jokes and the flippant observations, the book has a strong vein of melancholy, disgust, and even tragedy.

Its three central performers can be seen (as William Walsh has pointed out, in *D. J. Enright: Poet of Humanism*) as embodiments of 'the experienced, the ardent, and the intolerant in the English character, and present a kind of English solidity in the face of the aspiring and impalpable Egyptian sensibility'. There is Bacon, an oldish lecturer at the university, 'that Egyptianised *pagliaccio*', as he is described, an affable and boozy cynic; Packet, a younger lecturer and in some sense Enright's mouthpiece (though it is Bacon who, in Chapter 5, delivers what is in fact an early Enright poem, 'Children, Beggars and Schoolteachers'); and there is Brett, a young prig newly arrived and employed at the Cultural Centre.

In the course of the academic year Packet has his hopeless affair with Sylvie, the kind but worldly-wise westernized Syrian; Brett witnesses a small boy shot dead in the act of looting a shop; Bacon, threatened by ruffians pretending to avenge a family debt of honour, is killed with a knife. This is not really the stuff of comedy, certainly not of farce. The apophthegms and definitions are witty and sardonic, but they are not lightweight: 'The terror of lawlessness had been succeeded by the terrorism of law. And the latter was more dangerous in a way, because it was more organised and better armed and it had less of a sense of humour.' And perhaps more pervasive than any of the characters is the city itself, that 'vast account book: debit and credit side by side, and sizeable sums in each column', the city which 'itself was a colossal lie', grandiosely ennobled with the name of its great founder, and by the late 1940s a polyglot sprawl of Greeks, French, Jews, Italians, ranged against the Egyptians and all the other Levantine mixtures of races and creeds.

Of course it *is* a book full of hilarious passages and persons as well. Anyone who has ever taught in a Middle Eastern university will recognise with delight the duplicating machine for the printing of examination papers installed in the lavatory, and the stunningly unmarkable answers written during the feverish exam rituals ('Dickens' father was not successful in his marriage and he had ten children'). Enright's command of Arab student English (beseeching, charming, ingratiating, insolent) is superb: 'We all honour you, sir, you are our teacher. But we cannot work today—it is Down with Britain day, if you will excuse it, sir.' One wouldn't want to do without Sylvie's effusively Frenchified relative, Madame Nader—or her dog.

But alongside the fun and frolics there is much of what the Japanese have come to call the Enrightenment: the sense that 'There had been too much politics over the past twenty years: we had almost forgotten what it was to be merely human.' The sheer precariousness of life is the novel's uninsisted centre, 'made up of short violences and short calms, brief sorrows and brief joys'. One is grateful that, things being what they were and his background being what it was, Enright chose in 1947 to embark on his career as peripatetic teacher of literature. His learning and his liberality of spirit made him a good teacher; his acute and mordant observation and wit made him a good poet and novelist; his restlessness—and his apparent capacity for putting his foot into official quagmires—made him keep moving on. Egypt was a fortunate first place for his gifts. At one point in *Academic Year*, the avuncular Bacon suggests to Packet that he 'could write a novel about our Alexandrian revels. Why not make some use of those crammed notebooks?' Young Packet/Enright did; and the result was and is a modern classic not just of mendicant professorialism or campus japes slightly west of Suez, but of surprising sharpness and seriousness.

Academic Year

ACKNOWLEDGEMENTS

The lines by Cavafy come from *The Poems of C. P. Cavafy*, translated by John Mavrogordato (The Hogarth Press); and the chapter headings are taken from Rodwell's translation of the *Koran* (Everyman's Library).

To the ex-Egyptian P. I.
and University staff

CONTENTS

Chapter 1

ENTER YE EGYPT, IF GOD WILL, SECURE

PACKET gazed into the noxious strip of oily water, struck with a kind of awe. How relieved, how glad he was to be . . . to be . . . well, yes, home ! And almost more surprised to find the word ' home ' rising in his mind.

On the other side of the boat lay the true blues of the Mediterranean. In front of him, seemingly hysterical men were hurling ropes at each other, yelling in a medley of Italian, Arabic and nautical English. Somewhere over there —beyond the forgotten crates, the fallen barriers and the anonymous customs sheds—lay his flat, his bank, his friends, his lecture-room—and, of course, all that dust and dirt and noise which, it seemed, was less than unforgivable.

He had spent the greater part of his leave in England, a little sad and more than a little wet, and then a week in Paris, less sad but more expensive. And then he had travelled down to Naples to pick up an Italian boat bound for Alexandria. Unhappily the franc had devalued at the very moment he crossed the border, while the coyer lira had hesitated to follow suit. Spending the end of a vacation in Naples without money was at least an appetizer for the beginning of a fresh academic year. One meal of spaghetti a day, standing in embarrassing fashion against a white marble ledge affixed to a white tiled wall in a workmen's eating-house—and a nameless bed in an unnamed *albergo*. There had been no Capri for him—and when he sacrificed his day's spaghetti for a third-class ticket to Pompeii, he still lacked the small change which would have opened to him the doors of the more notable houses. For him, in short, only the dark side of Naples : dust, dirt and noise, tubercular beggars, desolate women in their hot dusty black dresses, whipped horses galloping painfully in front of monstrous iron loads, a rancid air circulating through too many desperately tenacious lungs.

And so he had looked forward eagerly to boarding the ship, expecting no luxury—a commodity which aroused obscure misgivings in him. But simply sufficient food for the stomach, sufficient air for the lungs. He was travelling third-class, however, and the dark side of Naples followed him into the boat. His narrow cabin was crowded with a sort of banditti who sprawled all day on their bunks, dressed only in long grey woollen underpants which they hauled up to roll black cigarettes on their brown thighs. For the first two days he had felt from their furtive glances and sinister mutterings that they were plotting against his life. It transpired that they were merely deliberating whether or not to offer the shy Englishman one of their cigarettes. In the end they did. Packet smoked it through then and there, encircled by their stern and vigilant faces—and only a smart rush to the deck saved him. As for the long-awaited food —what flavour it occasionally possessed was provided, he suspected, by the cockroaches which fell from the air at the ship's slightest stagger.

With a sharp jolt the boat ground against the landing-stage. A tense pack of porters, licensed and otherwise, seethed behind a harbour policeman. What strong, diseased, underfed, powerful brutes they were, Packet reflected comfortably. They did not wait for any gangway to be dropped, but hurled the policeman aside and threw themselves against the ship. Somehow or other, by grabbing at portholes or

8

snatching at bits of odd rope, most of them managed to gain the deck. Without mercy they swept into the helpless flock of passengers, tearing away suitcases, bags, hat-boxes from Paris, tennis rackets and camouflaged chianti flasks. ' Nummer feefteen, missie ! ' And an emigrant's battered tin trunk was tossed on top of the hat-box. There seemed to be rather more porters than passengers : they fought among themselves for the remaining scraps of luggage, to the sound of breaking handles and snapping straps. Packet pulled a sympathetic face. This time he was travelling light, he was no man's prey. Tugging his suitcase out of the claws of a furious latecomer, he was the first to run down the gangway, the first through the jaded customs and the first to reach the waiting taxis. Should he go straight to his flat (the summer tenants would have left for the capital yesterday) ? No, first of all let him say hello, with a new and unexpected appreciation, to Alexandria. ' *Mahatta Ramleh,*' he directed the driver.

The centre of town was already thronged. He recognized with pleasure a number of the local characters as they stalked or stumbled past. A horse trudged up the incline where Alexander's tomb was said to lie, pulling a monstrous load of cotton : but at least no-one expected it to gallop, least of all the somnolent driver. Packet walked happily up and down, dropped in at the book-shops to announce his return, beamed at a student who had given him inordinate trouble the previous year, scattered a few piastres among the old familiar beggars, and stared appreciatively at the girls in their pretty summer frocks—they were all, he felt sure, either past or future pupils of his. And then, in this state of mild intoxication, he strolled towards the sea. Home? he asked himself. Well, it would do nicely for the time being. And soon he would see Bacon again, and that would be good, too.

At that moment his hungry eyes fell on a well-dressed, well-groomed young man, hunched up on a bench. Undoubtedly

English, he was about Packet's age, perhaps a couple of years younger—a stranger, by the look of it, and apparently under some kind of cloud. Packet was strongly inclined to speak to him, but averted his gaze and walked past. It had happened before now that in his zeal to help some hot and bothered tourist from his own country he had been taken for a tout. He looked back, however. The young man seemed rapt in some deep-seated kind of disapproval. After all, he might be in trouble, Packet thought, walking back to the bench.

'I say.' In spite of himself, shyness contributed a tint of toutishness to his voice. 'You're English, aren't you? New here?—I don't remember seeing you before.'

There was a rather frigid silence, until the young man noticed the ship's label on Packet's suit-case.

'I came on from Port Said yesterday,' he admitted somewhat stiffly, and then added in a shocked tone, 'I've already been robbed of my fountain-pen.'

Feeling very relieved, Packet sat down on the bench. ' My name's Packet—I teach at the university here. What's yours? Brett? Tell me how it happened,' he suggested paternally, an old hand.

An hour or so earlier, Brian Brett had walked out of his hotel, wearing that particular look of confidence, business-like and yet tolerant, which is often seen on the faces of Englishmen in the East. At any rate during their first two or three days in the East. Breakfast at his rather expensive hotel had happily combined the seriousness of England with the smoothness of France. It was a Jewish-owned establishment, with a French name which conveniently was also English, sheltering behind a Syrian manager ; and it owed its efficiency to a Jewish staff—rather well educated and all of them reasonably proficient in four or five languages—so blatantly underpaid that it was obviously only the impossibility of finding other employment which discouraged them from resigning.

The air was full of a fantastic good will ; the sun forbore to oppress ; there was a gentle motion of warm breath. The streets were pleasantly moist, the little shops neat and tidy. The hotel receptionist had already registered his complaint : his *baccalauréat* . . . writing names in a book and recommending travel agencies . . . the new company laws against non-Egyptians . . . Brett had found it altogether deplorable, and even said so. However, he told himself, we shall see about it later, summing up and evaluation would follow in due course. In any case, he was still on holiday, since the Cultural Centre to which he had been posted was not opening until the beginning of the next week.

At the bottom of the street he could see the Mediterranean —or rather a long white balustrade, with someone sleeping untidily on top of it, and then the sea, deep blue breaking into an almost cruel silver. He must pay his respects to this historical accumulation of water. Oh dear, that really was off-putting : he had very nearly tripped over what remained of a beggar's leg which, from the amount of blood on the filthy bandages, appeared to have been recently amputated. Red ink, in all probability, or from a butcher's shop, sheep's blood or something of that sort. Of course the leglessness couldn't have been faked. But they did it on purpose: some little village south of the city, he had heard, specialized in turning out cripples, who then came up to ply their trade, like Irish emigrating to join the American police. The capital outlay was rather heavy—but they were better off than he was, he imagined.

A stranger's first impression of the city is that he is looking at a vast account book : debit and credit side by side, and sizeable sums in each column. For at first there seem to be only two things which, whirling, colliding, shoving one against the other, make up its life. Beggars in various stages of incompleteness, and large American cars fitted with that Middle East speciality, a type of klaxon modelled on the cinema organ. The breeze was growing fainter, Brett felt, the sun less kindly, the silver knives of the sea were glinting more sharply ; and the little noises which he had found so jolly when he stepped out of the hotel were now merging into one long continuous roar.

But of course it was only the stranger who noticed the beggars and the automobiles. The inhabitant's more sub-tilized eye was for different things : Henry Miller set up by drunken Swedes and erratically impressed upon inferior toilet paper, the gentleman driving into the desert with the wife of another gentleman, the latest phase in the war between Coca-Coca and Cola-Cola, the new sambas in the Columbia Music Store (the first word painted out ever since the window was smashed after Colombia's representative at United Nations had voted against an Egyptian motion), the gleam-ing and often incomprehensible toilet accessories culled from a dozen countries, the level to which the jewellers' shutters were raised—a good barometer of the city's political tempera-ture—or the price of olives. According to one's taste. As for beggars and bashas, they were like the wallpaper in a house. One soon ceased to notice them, and one rarely asked what degree of moral or æsthetic hardening that obliviousness implied.

Brett was a stranger, however, and the wallpaper proved a little too loud for his stomach. He turned into a com-paratively quiet side-street, past a minute grocery crammed with hundreds of tins and dozens of barrels, into another little street, and down to the promenade, the Corniche. The nearer sea no longer glittered so keenly ; it rippled slowly and luxuriously under the full sun, it beamed hugely at him, a quite personal welcome, the arms wide open. For a moment, such was its impact upon him, he could not think, or not of anything else. This great mass of liquid, of various blues and greens and bluish-greens, static and yet in continuous motion, formless and yet never for one instant without innumerable forms, filled his mind, and his mind began to drown in it. Swim? For how long? It was too large. He could not believe that it ever slept—that you could catch it then, tie it into a neat bundle, and find out all about it. It was always awake, always changing shape, and so you could never comprehend it, only drown in it.

But the light poured down on him, a passing taxi sounded its horn, and in slight panic he shook his head briskly. Idle day-dreaming was no habit of his. And remembering who he was, he reflected with fresh pleasure that he was here, in a sense, to provide what the sea, the sun and the menu had left out—access to English social restraint, to the rocky culture of Britain. The poetry of Shakespeare, Milton, Shelley, Eliot, the novels of George Eliot and Charles Dickens—all that great literature of conscience which set out to measure the demands of the individual against his duty towards God or the rest of humanity. The East was lacking in that—it knew only of sudden unthinking death and of dark impossible beauties playing dulcimers. . . .

He walked contentedly along the side of the sea, divided from it only by a thin strip of dry and brittle sand, thinking vaguely of discussion groups in East London, poetry readings in the Black Country, seeds which flourished in those stony, smoky places. . . . And now the fertile soil of the Nile, and a sun so brilliant that it forced a way into every hole and corner. Surely something more impressive than crocodiles could be hatched out of that rich mud. For he was of a rather earnest cast of mind, and had the firm intention of earning his not ungenerous salary.

A gangling middle-aged Egyptian surged up towards him from his rear. With an intensely surreptitious glance about him, he unfolded a large piece of paper to reveal a whisky bottle.

' English whisky !   Only half-pound to you.   Vair' good, sair ! ' He grinned knowingly and licked his lips.   Brett smiled scornfully : he knew all about that, a trick played on tourists—the innocent paid his half-pound for a bottle of cold tea.   Why, you could even see an occasional tea-leaf floating round, though he had to admit that the bottle was sealed very skilfully.   He studied the proposition with a kind of professional disdain, and then waved his arm contemptuously.

' *Yallah !* '   His basic Arabic was coming in useful already. ' Go away ! '   A second Egyptian surged up in his *gallabieh* from the other side, proffering a generous sheaf of miscel- laneous reading, *News of the World*, *Digest Sexuel*, *Sex Appeal* and others.   That, Brett knew, was another old trick—the papers were weeks old, salvaged from trams and hotel baskets.   The vendor waved his sheaf in front of Brett's nose—a little too near—with a graceful fan-like gesture. The other once again elevated his precious bottle in its tattered wrappings.   It was quite a little ballet.   But Brett felt that it had gone far enough ; he gave voice to a further and more masterful '*Yallah !* ' and the two retreated, smiling still and apparently quite satisfied with their failure.   He walked on, more amused than irritated.   One had to treat them like children—that was what they were, over-grown children, always up to the same old tricks, the same old lies.   All that was needed was a little firmness.   He glanced behind : why, they had already disappeared.

Petrol fumes had begun to invade the Corniche, and he was already feeling thirsty.   The little fishing boats with their ragged white sails, rocking exaggeratedly on the gentle swell, reminded him that he ought to send off cards to his relatives.   He had bought some at the hotel : pictures of other hotels, of the World Health Organization, the *Lycée Français*, the British Club, the splendid Greek Hospital, and the Water Company Offices—nothing Egyptian in the romantic sense. This was a modern city ; and, what was more, he would not be teaching poetry and anomalous finites either to pharaohs or to *fellahin*. . . . Sitting on a bench, he felt for his pen. It had been in his pocket when he left the hotel. He remembered fingering it when he almost fell over the beggar on the pavement. But now it had gone—along with the cold tea and the old magazines.

' Might have been worse,' Packet commented cheerfully. ' Now, in Naples . . . but what about a drink of some kind ?—do you good.'

But Brett's only desire was to return to his hotel, that remote-seeming haven of peace, of respectability and respectfulness. Before parting, they arranged to meet on an evening in the near future.

' I'll introduce you to Bacon,' Packet promised by way of consolation, ' a colleague of mine—and so of yours, too, really. He's been here for donkey's years. Very good man —and *the* authority, I should say. You weren't told anything about him in London ? Well, he's a—a rather unofficial kind of man.'

Chapter 2

OUR WORKS FOR US AND YOUR
WORKS FOR YOU

'BRETT should be here soon. I told you about him—remember? He'd had his pen stolen.'

It was about nine in the evening, and the two men were sitting in a reasonably respectable Greek bar called Nicola's. The elder, whose rather knobbly features emerged from a fell of greying hair, sighed gently.

'A new boy? Cotton, currency, consular or cultural?'

'New man at the Cultural Centre. A young man with what is called a good family background.' Packet sighed gently, too. 'Earnest, you might say, but not simple. I bet he'll never lose another pen. No, I'll have beer. *Ena zibib, meya biera, se parakallo.* Why is beer a feminine noun? —all the women I know drink whisky.'

'Except Sourayah, my dear Packet, and if you'd known her as long as I have, you'd appreciate how much cheaper coffee is, in bulk, than whisky. She's visiting friends who occupy a hut behind the abattoir, so we shan't see her tonight.'

'Perhaps it's just as well. I mean,' he continued soothingly, 'it's better not to spring Sourayah on people, not when they've just come out from England . . .'

'Spick and span in a government kit allowance, with the *Seven Pillars* in one pocket and the *Seven Types* in the other, and the respect—if modified—of the Cottontots . . .'

' Well, Bacon, she is a type of ambiguity not taught in the book, you know. Ah, this beer is beautifully cold. What an important thing temperature is, when you come to think of it ! ' He had never thought about it himself until that moment.

' I love to watch you discovering the great platitudes,' his friend smiled. ' This one deserves expanding. In the so-called temperate zones—may I take over from you ?—temperature has become an outcast from human experience. In England, for instance, the beer is neither warmed nor iced : it is, like the temperature, temperate. A long greyness without perceptible change, and so man too ends by losing his seasons. He becomes temperate in his outward garb but intemperate in his surmisings, wild and hectic in his thoughts. Mark my words, young man '—he emptied his glass and brought it down sharply on the table—' the end of the world will begin in the temperate zones, and a gentleman in tennis shoes carrying a mackintosh will inaugurate it.'

Bacon had been teaching in Egypt for more than twenty years. His first post after graduating had been in a primitive school in Upper Egypt, and he was one of the first to be appointed to the new state universities. He married during his first leave, but his wife had long since attached herself to a well-spoken bank manager, who was then about to be transferred to a tourist centre in Switzerland. Bacon had survived this blow, with the help of alcohol, an interest in poetry and food, and a large and diverse acquaintance. A year or so later he had unaccountably set up house with a wholly uncelebrated and otherwise unremarkable dancer. Sourayah had rescued him from some thieves who waylaid him late one night outside the little cabaret where her functions were to sing the more genteel kinds of song, dance with the more sober customers and encourage them to drink. She was bored with this life and very ready to abandon dancing and singing and inciting to drink. In a country where rough diamonds do not always display hearts of gold in their dealings with other races, this behaviour of Bacon's alarmed his friends—and even his employers, for all their ability to turn a blind eye on European eccentricities, had not known which way to stare. Contrary to public expectation, the two had settled down comfortably enough. Sourayah appreciated the security and (in her eyes) the largeness of Bacon's salary, and in running his household she protected him against a hostile world and dishonest trades-people in a fashion both ferocious and efficient. The years had only increased her fidelity, along with her bulk, and among her own people she enjoyed considerable prestige of a kind not generally allowed to women. She had bought another small piece of land—she informed Bacon from time to time—or paid some minor debt for one of her brothers, or invested in a goat or so. And he looked forward to the day when she would endow her village with a school hall or perhaps a public urinal.

Meanwhile he flourished gently under her management. He never left Egypt, but spent a good deal of his free time working on a mysterious enquiry into the nature, means and utility of education, which his friends too easily assumed to be a delayed doctoral thesis. He talked considerably, was acquainted with all the people one was supposed to be acquainted with (though met them infrequently), drank a fair amount—Sourayah grew more severe on this point as the years passed—and had a great following among the students, who always warned him in advance of a proposed strike. ' Down with Britain—but not you, sir, you are our father. And there will not be any work for three days, sir.' In fact, his life was comfortable, reasonably full, and —the few who knew him well suspected—might turn out to be valuable. He thought so too : a urinal here, fresh milk there, two or three human beings temporarily freed from debt.

'Talking about women,' Packet said to him, 'I went round last night to a dingy little shack just out of town that the savage-looking weight-lifter in the third year told me about—you know, the one who said that Philip Sidney wrote a novel called *Sir Charles' Grandson*. I came across a woman who looked quite clean and intelligent . . . and even not unattractive . . . in the half-light, and took her back to the flat. She wasn't not unattractive, however.' His voice betrayed an involuntary regret. Two-thirds of his mind insisted that such women should be as squalid in appearance and bearing as possible ; the other third hoped for a lush and enigmatic Lilith. 'I asked the old Greek gentleman who lives below to interpret. It seemed a good idea, and I thought she'd welcome the change. So we started with the obvious questions—where she came from, her family, how she took up her present occupation. But she was furious—the old Greek seemed quite embarrassed, though he was eager to help—he's rather fond of me, I think. And when I took out a notebook and pencil, she was positively shocked—not used to observation at all— even tried to take her clothes off.'

Having caught their attention, Mr. Nicola bowed with reverent gratification. Englishmen—other than sailors— gave tone to his establishment ; and these were professors. They might help to get his nephew into one of the English schools.

'Continue,' said Bacon grimly.

'The old Greek was very upset—doesn't seem used to women. So I opened a bottle of gin—English, too—and she drank half of it in hurt silence. She got more cheerful then. It seems that a friend of hers was working as a servant somewhere here and sent for her to take a similar job. She was fifteen years old, and the family paid her a pound a month. She began going with men to make up her wages, so she got the sack and had to go with more men. But she remained a cook at heart. It was all quite dispassionate, until she asked me how much I paid my servant. Then she fell into a fury again and shouted that he was a thief and she'd cook for me for half as much. Things got out of hand at that point, unfortunately, because Sonya insisted on preparing a specimen meal. She tore through the kitchen —you should have seen her——'

'No thanks.'

'—dressed in a flowered frock, with an inch of lipstick on her mouth and her hair bubbling with oil, amok among the saucepans. Finally she got something stewing—at least there was a peculiar smell—and the old gentleman remembered an appointment. I was trying to open a window when the end came—the primus blew up. She was in a state—paraffin over her Sunday best, bits of meat on the ceiling—it was quite alarming——'

'How dangerously you live, Packet! You might have caught her fleas.'

'—but I led her back to the gin, and she got hiccups— something very homely about that, I felt—and then fell asleep. It was midnight by then, and I had to take her back to the house by taxi. She had long black hairs growing on her wrists. We carried her into the passage—it was very dark—only an oil lamp and a broken chair and some dirty coffee cups. They were very respectful—the taxi-driver and the one-legged man who opened the door—during the day he sells papers at the tram station. Neither of them tried to swindle me.'

'That's the fourth time you've done that, Packet, and they always tell you the same story. "To Beg I am Ashamed" —pfui, do you think you'll find one of those highbrow prostitutes here, to give you the inside story for one of the serious weeklies! Your miserable Sonya—she's like the rest of her class, and that's about three-quarters of the Egyptian nation—she doesn't know what is going on. She doesn't look forward, not further than the next meal, the next night in gaol—and she can't look backward. Mohamed taught these people to live in a crafty, dishonest unself-conscious little dream—and, ever since, the bashas have prospered and grown fat. And yet,' he threw up his hand urgently, ' the dream mightn't have been crafty and dishonest if the West hadn't interfered. " We have set before man an Arabic Koran, free from ambiguous wording, that they may fear God." Mohamed couldn't be expected to foresee stock exchanges and blocks of flats, and how ambiguous his words might come to be.' He paused for a drink. ' Have you ever asked yourself, Packet, how precisely you are earning the money—admittedly a pittance—that Egypt pays you ? '

' I teach the set books of English literature in accordance with the regulations of the university as laid down in Arabic and French.'

' Quite. I haven't found a better answer than that. I've run up and down the gamut of the political emotions, I've known them all at their most extreme—the rage of the Communist and the nervousness of the Tory—and even now I feel them still, all together. And so—one teaches the set books. But that woman of yours . . .'

Bacon was losing his normal equanimity, and Packet signed to the waiter to bring another round.

' She ought to have stuck a knife in you, instead of trying to cook the supper. " And how does it feel to be a whore, Miss Sonya ? "—she only told you that story to repay you for the gin. It's a continuous war, Packet, and no-one has bothered to tell them what it's about, they only know that it's each of them against everybody else. These people don't know the word " introspection " : they are the psycho-analyst's nightmare, just as they're the Communist's dream. The highest infant mortality rate in the world, and the lowest suicide rate. Why, the nervous breakdown didn't exist until the first school was opened—then a schoolteacher discovered it. Afterwards the universities were opened, and the complaint became common. And you, my dear young man——'

Packet was some eighteen years younger than his companion : he had seen nothing of those halcyon years between the wars when Englishmen in the Middle East enjoyed considerable respect and lived in a certain style, even though they were teachers. It is silly to cry over spilt milk that one has never tasted, Packet reckoned. Things being what they were, one was lucky if one didn't get one's head knocked off. And since human exports had been mostly military for so long, the civilian jolly well ought to go around and see what it is really like and be seen for what he is really like. Soldiers had to correct the mistakes of civilians, and then civilians had to correct the mistakes of soldiers. The vicious circle had to be broken, he reasoned, and it would never be broken by large pronouncements and sitting committees. A thoughtful person, his chief interest was what he called amateur sociology—'but it all is,' Bacon had objected on first hearing the confession—and he had not found England a very fruitful field. ' Everyone is watching from behind his little curtain—but just you try to twitch the curtain aside and look in at him ! ' Stimulated by the idea that emotions as found in the hotter climates of the Middle East, in their pure forms and free from any kind of unscientific reserve, would offer more copious material, he had come out as a junior lecturer at the university. Three years of baring his head beneath the storm of emotions which at once poured down upon it had modified his enthusiasm for sociology and even imperilled his affection for humanity. Emotions, he discovered, were generous and uninhibited and public enough—but they were nearly always the same emotions. Greek, Egyptian, Syrian, Lebanese, Armenian, Jewish, the seedy little bars and the expensive restaurants, the complaints after the lecture and the con-

fidences on the dance floor—oh dear, he was beginning to
conceive a nostalgia for the little curtain that must not be
disturbed.

'—tip-toeing in like a Brains Trust and asking the poor
girl what it's all about ! Just for the files. And then you
send her home like an unsuccessful applicant for a job, and
in all probability drunker than she's ever been before.
You'd better not let Sourayah hear of your antics.'

Packet hung his head. ' Never again, I promise. Hassan
was extremely displeased when he found the mess waiting
for him this morning. I told him that there'd been a beginning of term party for the students—he'd believe anything
of students. Oh, here we are. Won't you sit down ?
Mr. Brett, Mr. Bacon . . .'

' How do you do,' the neat young man said. ' Awfully
sorry I'm late—there's an exiled royalty of some sort at my
hotel, and I became involved with him over dinner. But I
see that you've been wetting your whistles.' His voice was
perhaps just a little too clear ; there was an effect of naked-
ness about it, something almost indecent—though, Packet
reflected, it was somehow the person addressed who felt
guilty of the indecency. One heard too completely what
he said ; yet the young man was so obviously decent, and
not at all immodest.

Bacon, who had not yet recovered from his outburst over
Packet's scientific activities, answered rather ungraciously.
' Wetting what ? Oh, I beg your pardon. An English
idiom, of course. One is getting out of touch, Packet, one
is losing the thread. A little fresh blood will be welcome.'
He managed a welcoming smile.

' We teach a little grammar from time to time, you see,
Brett,' put in the other tactfully, ' out of a very popular book
called *Ulliphont's Graded Exercises*. It's taught us quite a
number of most exotic idioms. Johnny Crapaud, for
instance—it means a Frenchman, and better skip the exercise

23

if you have any French people in your class at the Centre. We call them White Ulliphonts, that kind. But we seem to have forgotten the ones they use in England.'

'What—as perhaps they say—is your poison, Brett?' asked Bacon. The waiter cleared away the glasses, the ashtray, the scraps of grated cabbage and fried octopus.

The band was assembling. There was an ancient gentleman, bald and Neronic of feature, in a green frock-coat, who played the lyra; a fat-faced person who played a piano-accordion with his eyes closed so fixedly that he seemed to be asleep; a guitarist whose noble and even poetic appearance was marred only by bad teeth; a small man of villainous mien who attacked his violin with unrelenting malice; a boy, obviously under heavy American influence, who doubled on clarinet and *bouzouki* and sang the Western numbers; and lastly a middle-aged girl with an enormous mouth and kittenish manners, who sang Greek songs in an extraordinarily penetrative and zestful voice. Mostly they played the popular music of their own country, expressive of powerful emotions, colossally unsuccessful love, nostalgia, the superiority of drunkenness, an immense cynicism kept in check by irresponsible cheerfulness. They were packed into a narrow stall at the bend of the bar, between the inadequate little lavatory and Madame Rose, the large cashier; artificial vines and wax grapes were twined about a trellis above their heads. The noise of their playing swept through the small room and out into the street.

As if drawn by it, three unlikely customers swaggered timidly into the bar. They wore soiled *gallabiehs*; one, rather tall, was sadly wall-eyed, another limped badly on a twisted foot. They inspired little confidence in Mr. Nicola's Egyptian waiters. Dropping their obsequiousness, the latter attempted to shoo the newcomers away—Nicola's was not a fashionable establishment, but all the same . . . But they

refused to budge, though clearly intimidated by the foreign
music and the snowy robes of the waiters. After much
muttering they ordered a Coca-Cola and three glasses of water.
Mr. Nicola, who had been following the incident closely
from his little dais, nodded slightly, and the indignant waiters
dispersed. The tall Egyptian caught at one of them and
asked him something, pointing in the direction of the
Englishmen. '*Mush arif*,' the waiter said contemptuously :
no tip, no information. The man cursed him quietly.

The door swung open smartly, and a short round man
dressed in an expensive overcoat bounced in. Not, emphatically, the kind of person one would think of calling Tubby,
however.

'Oh look !' Bacon exclaimed. 'Marcel Haggernetti !
How nice—now should one or should one not offer him a
drink ? Which way does the wind blow ?'

Marcel glided over to them, clearly glad to see them and
just as clearly ill-at-ease. 'Charmed !' he cried sweetly.
'Charmed, I am sure ! Bacon ?' He nodded : no need
for words there. 'And Packet, dear boy—enjoyed the
vacation ?' A momentary tenderness shone in his large
eyes. 'Oh, someone I don't know.' This was remedied.
And Marcel gazed intently at Brett for a moment, gave a
consciously cryptic sigh and caused his heavily veined lids to
slide tragically over the eyes.

'All this,' he straightened up and waved a hand round
the room, 'is a thing of the past for me. The Past.' His
gaze flickered from Packet to Brett and rested, more comfortably, on Bacon. 'So do not bother to offer me anything. I've come purely to ask after Madame Rose's health
—an old acquaintance—did you know she was my father's
cook, long ago ? I was a '—he cast about for the precise
term—' a mere stripling then.' Inclining his head solemnly
he left them.

The three unwelcome customers, defiantly thrusting out

Chapter 2

their legs, passed round the bottle of Coca-Cola. As Marcel was on his way out, they stopped him. And a moment later, on the pretext of a last word with Madame Rose, he called back at the English table.

'What queer followers you have, Bacon! Those cut-throats near the door asked me if you weren't the teacher, Bacon Effendi—to be on the safe side I told them you were the British Ambassador incognito,' he tittered. 'One can't be too careful—but how many times have I told you that! Well, adieu—may not see you for some time,' he added in a discouraging tone. 'My life these days is not my own.'

'It never was,' Bacon grunted after him, *sotto voce*.

There was another little scene at the door as the Egyptians left, complaining loudly that they had been overcharged. At Mr. Nicola's nodded hint the band played more strenuously than ever.

'I suppose this music serves the same purpose as the salted chips,' Packet remarked. 'Still, it's a sight more impressive than English café music. Oh the melancholy eyes of the cellist, the sad spirituality of the violinist! I knew some of them in Leamington once—foul-mouthed lot in private life, used to rush away and get drunk as soon as the café closed.'

'How embarrassing it must be, when the music stops and everyone is caught roaring out his secrets,' said Brett with a disapproving look at the yelling, gesticulating groups about him. He was nervously aware of the accumulation of price-slips in the mustard pot beside them, too.

'The Greeks know the rhythm of their music too well for that.' Some people had queer ideas about pleasure, Brett reminded himself. 'There seems to be an awful quarrel going on behind us.'

'Tut, no,' Bacon said. 'They're probably arranging a trip to the desert on Sunday. You can tell a real quarrel by the silence which surrounds it.'

'I can see why they play Greek stuff,' he conceded, ' but why must they inflict this on us ? '

It was a heavily theatricalized rendering of ' Irish Eyes '; and the Greek eyes of the singer rolled desperately, ingratiatingly, and in the direction of their table.

' It must be for your benefit, Brett. The exiled Englishman is always supposed to find relief in the memory of Irish eyes or Scottish bluebells. We shall have to stand the musicians a pot of beer. In the meanwhile let us try to look moved somewhat.'

A special occasion. The music swept lusciously to its close. The players smiled and bowed very consciously towards the foreigners. The Greeks, feeling that here at any rate they themselves were at home, turned to look at the exiles, smiling and nodding sympathetically. There was something approaching a respectful silence. Brett blushed with irritation : now if it had been ' Greensleeves '. . . ' *Pollee kallah !* ' shouted Packet. The Greeks murmured approvingly. And with an air of relief the band went on to an uproariously merry song about a drunkard whose wife had stolen his life's savings and eloped with a taxi-driver. The hubbub of conversation mounted again. Bacon snapped his fingers at a waiter and pointed to the band. Mr. Nicola beamed and bowed like a successful author taking his curtain call.

Two young men, in appearance rather like barrow boys, were performing the handkerchief dance in a narrow space between the tables while the others clapped rhythmically. They had suddenly left the table where their friends were still talking, one had produced a greyish handkerchief, and conversation merged into dancing like a change of topic. Brett was heard to murmur something about English pubs.

' The average English pub,' Bacon stated regretfully, ' as I remember it, resembles the ante-room to a gas chamber. A stupefied silence alternates with bursts of hysterical laughter.

Shame is the keynote. Thou shalt not drink, but if thou dost, thou shalt be exceeding uncomfortable and exceeding brief.'

'Oh come now,' Brett protested—was this the spirit in which to convey the English way of life ? 'There's something about the English public house which you can't find anywhere else. A kind of security, something essentially homely——'

'If I had a home, I should take better care of it,' but Bacon did not feel that the point deserved pressing. 'I hear, by the way, that you've already encountered one of the mysteries of the East—the disappearing fountain-pen ?'

'I was really shocked—my very first day here ! But I've written a strong letter of protest to the Commandant of Police.'

Packet tittered. '*Maalish*, Brett, *maalish*. If we walk along the street outside we shall find five or six fellows selling stolen pens, and you can pick up a posh American model for a few shillings. As for writing to the Commandant, you've wasted a stamp.'

'Let's hope you've only wasted a stamp. It will be most embarrassing if the Commandant takes you seriously,' Bacon said. 'I remember an incident which happened many years ago. I hadn't been long in Egypt then, I was married, it was in another part of the country. It's a rather long story . . .' He told it to them.

The ice-box was leaking slightly, and of course the news spread through the neighbourhood. One day a huge ruffian, in patched trousers, an oily vest and a yellow scarf, turned up with the intention of mending it. Their servant refused to let him in on the grounds that he was a 'bad man'. The truth, Bacon suspected, was that the servant had promised the job to one of his brothers-in-law. The following day, at an hour when Bacon was away teaching and the servant had gone to the market, the same ugly customer forced his way into the house, pushed Bacon's wife roughly aside, hammered at the ice-box for a few minutes and then demanded ten shillings. On his return Bacon found his wife very upset and the ice-box leaking twice as quickly as before. It was an unpleasant situation : the man now knew when to find Mrs. Bacon alone in the house. Apart from his irritation at having been so arrantly swindled, Bacon felt it hardly the time for *maalish*. He rang up the father of one of his pupils—something of an Anglophile and an important official in the Moral Police—who wrote a letter in Arabic on government note-paper and sent it along by his chauffeur. Early the next morning Bacon took the letter to the *caracol*, the local police station. The guard at the gate read it very slowly and then called a corporal who also read it very slowly and then called in a sergeant. Some twenty minutes later Bacon achieved the presence of the captain, who spoke English. The signature of the letter baffled him, but obviously he felt that it might be an important one. He bit his nails, yelled abuse at a young *shawish* who had fallen over a rifle left propped against a chair, ordered a coffee. Finally he came to a decision. A serious crime had been committed (but was the gentleman sure that the bad scoundrel had not done anything bad to the English lady ? Ah well, never mind), and Bacon would have to report it to another and bigger *caracol* two kilometres away. One of his men would accompany him. ' So pleased to be of service '—he was even more pleased to pass the Englishman and his letter on.

The *shawish* insisted on taking a taxi ; he had probably never been in one before. On arrival at the *caracol* the driver demanded an outrageous sum ; he had no meter, to begin with—and a policeman standing by. The impudence of it utterly maddened Bacon ; he cursed in vile English ; the *shawish* tut-tutted in horror, and then intervened. ' *Maalish, ya effendi*'—he took Bacon's wallet, paid the driver roughly two-thirds of what he was asking, pocketed the other third and returned the wallet. He wore the expression of an angel.

In the *caracol* they passed through the hands of an ascending hierarchy, repeating the whole story at each step. The place stank, Bacon felt sticky, his nerves were raw. It had seemed so simple and clear-cut, this question : right versus wrong, the defence of the weaker sex : it ought to have been obvious to anyone. It began with a leaking ice-box . . . but Bacon was ceasing to believe in his own story. Eventually the captain invited him to make a formal statement. Name, address, age, passport number, date of entry into Egypt, occupation, relationship to signatory of accompanying letter, date of incident, age of wife, condition of ice-box before and after treatment, number of children (none ? how long had he been married ?), age of wife again, would he take a coffee ? . . . They had collected the usual crowd of spectators ; all were agog.

'It is necessary that you tell me exactly what this man did to Madame.'

'He used threatening language. He didn't *do* anything.'

No-one attempted to conceal disappointment ; several of the bystanders even drifted away. But the captain was too polite—or too nervous of the letter—to ask Bacon what on earth he was complaining about in that case.

'To get rid of this man my wife was compelled to give him fifty piastres.' A fresh ripple of interest ran through the crowd : a clever man, this mender of ice-boxes : how much more profitable than being a mere *shawish* ! The captain's natural sympathies, too, were with the culprit. An Englishman can easily afford fifty piastres. First the ice-box leaks dreep-dreep and now it leaks drip-drip-drip. The effendi has a servant of course ? Then the servant will wipe up the water, *mush kidda* ? But once again the signature, deciphered as that of a bey of the second class, prevailed.

A guard would be placed outside Bacon's house and in the end, he was assured, this bad man would be caught.

In the street—it was tea-time by then—he found his private *shawish* chatting affably with the same taxi-driver. The latter yelled at him, ' Take you home, Mister—very cheap ! ' He swore at them and hurried away.

' So much for my pen ! ' Brett commented. ' You can't expect to find justice in a country like this.'

' Justice?—ah, but my story isn't ended yet.' Bacon caught the eye of Mohamed, the plump and prosperous oyster-seller, as he stuck his head into the bar in search of custom. ' For three, *ya bey*? At once.'

' Packet, dear boy, do please take your note-book off the table and make room for the oysters. A shilling a dozen, Brett, let them console you for the lost pen. Excellent, Mohamed, and now could you persuade the patron to find us a lemon ? '

The man called Mohamed was not as clean as he might have been, Brett felt ; but after all, oysters were very fashionable ; his opinion of Bacon rose ; the oysters even tasted rather pleasant.

' No, alas, my story is only beginning. Another round ? I think so.'

Early the following day two policemen took up their station outside Bacon's house ; they slept much of the time, or fraternized with the local servants or passing tradesmen. But each time Bacon and his wife entered or left, they grabbed their rifles and scrutinized them menacingly. This, Bacon realized later, was only to prove their fidelity and efficiency. It continued for over a week, until he asked his influential acquaintance to have them taken off. Soon afterwards— early one Sunday morning—he was dragged out of bed by two *shawish* who requested his immediate presence at the *caracol*. There he found the 'bad man', as big and ugly as his wife had described him, but otherwise how different! His head was bowed, he and his very pregnant wife were both in tears. They were surrounded by a mob of chattering policemen, relatives and inquisitive passers-by. The captain greeted Bacon triumphantly, 'We have found him, as I have promised to you!'

By this time the ice-box had been repaired by the servant's brother-in-law and had begun to leak afresh. But Bacon clung to his principle: this man, at least, was guilty; there was no doubt about that; for once justice should be done, in however small a way, and at whatever cost to himself. Who knew what effect it might not have on the whole shabby system? The woman wailed beseechingly at him, but he knew next to no Arabic in those days, and his heart remained comparatively whole. The man was an altogether contemptible object: one would have thought that he faced the gallows.

'And now that we have caught him, what do you want that we should do?' Bacon was aghast. On the way to the *caracol* he had thought up some pretty compliments to pay the captain and some noble and scorching things to say to the prisoner. But he hadn't prepared an answer to that question. The captain turned to the man and—as far as Bacon could tell—spoke to him in the accents of a proud father rebuking a high-spirited boy.

'He tells you that he is sorry for the bad thing he has done in your house.' The spectators watched Bacon expectantly. He felt his grip on the situation, on himself, slipping rapidly. 'That is not enough,' he brought out desperately, 'the man must be punished.'

'What does the effendi wish that we should do to him?' Bacon stuttered at the captain: the nature of the punishment was not his concern—he was only the victim—or rather his wife was—or might have been. He even asked, with too obvious a sarcasm, whether the laws of Egypt made no provision for the punishment of proved offenders.

' We ask you,' repeated the captain with determined politeness, ' what you wish.'

Bacon's temper gave out. It was a hot day : a sizeable horde of policemen, minor criminals and others had pressed into a very small room. He had not expected to find himself at such close quarters with the ice-box mender and his wife : the only other occasion on which he had been confronted with a criminal was at the age of fourteen when he attended court to recognize a bicycle lamp stolen by some unfortunate half-wit—and the whole length of an English court-room had stood between them.

' Hang him then ! ' he shouted. The captain simply waited, as if Bacon had said nothing, his face and body completely motionless.

' Well, put him in prison for a night ! '

The captain smiled coldly. And it struck Bacon that only the rather important person's letter stood between him and a very unpleasant scene.

' He is sorry for what he has done,' the captain remarked.

The cause of the trouble gaped uncomprehendingly at them. His wife, squatting on the floor, swayed from side to side, moaning without pause.

' Well, at least,' Bacon was at his last gasp, ' make him give me back the fifty piastres.'

The captain talked this over with the company. The Englishman remained inexorable : but his last proposal had the advantage of being practical. It also appealed to their sense of humour. The thief was informed, he and his wife immediately burst into wild lament—their worst fears had been realized : the death penalty had been invoked. He had no money, he swore, not a piastre. A big *shawish* clawed through his pockets and found a bundle of small banknotes. The captain then counted out twenty piastres and gave them to Bacon with the air of one bestowing a more than adequate gratuity. The prisoner wailed : he had only made thirty piastres, then. Bacon could have wailed : thirty piastres was more than he received for an hour's private tuition in those days. But it was no longer a case of saving justice—simply of saving his face. Feeling that it was his turn to indulge in histrionics, he waved the dirty notes at the captain, requesting him loftily to divide them among the policemen responsible for making the arrest. Bacon did not realize at the time that he was avenging himself on the captain's dreadful blandness in the only way open to him. The captain couldn't refuse the money—his men had gathered what was afoot, and their eyes were gleaming—and he couldn't bring himself to take the money from the Englishman's hands.

' I cannot touch this money,' he said after a pause, ' but you can give it to them.' He added a few words in Arabic, and the *shawish* surged forward, about a dozen of them. Bacon pushed the banknotes into the hands of the biggest, and took to flight. The news had travelled even faster, and as he passed them, the two guards at the *caracol* gate whispered shyly at him, ' *Baksheesh ?* ' Why, he asked himself bitterly, should they be left out of it ? And then he had just enough money to take a tram home : it was well after lunch-time.

' Justice . . .' Bacon concluded. ' Give me a drink.' He was reflecting that it was very soon after that little incident that his wife had left him. Bacon must have been rather a nice husband to have, Packet was thinking. While Brett, with pained misgiving, noticed the arrival of a further musician. In the midst of a riotously tragic song the band shuffled up closer to each other, and their colleague crawled precariously under the dangling vines. A small nondescript man of middle age, he bent over the *bouzouki*, plucking at it avidly, like someone doing up his boot-laces in an emergency. The orchestra was now properly balanced, Packet remarked. But Brett was aware only of an increased tinniness ; he ought to go back to the hotel, to read up Forster's guide to the city, which an aunt had given him before he sailed. But Packet was talking—impossible to hear more than half of what the fellow said.

'. . . they all know when it's someone's first day here— just as surely as if you were carrying a placard : " I'm new here : rob me." Very sensitive people, the poorer Egyptians.'

'I lost my brief-case on my first day,' Bacon joined in. ' Packet here lost an envelope full of human data collected on the voyage. It's remarkable—that kind of sensibility which reads your character and by which they regulate their approach to you. In theory, our job has been to turn it towards the appreciation of good literature—pardon me if I sound like a syllabus—and then, of course towards—whatever lies behind good literature. But in practice most of the time it dies on us. Pedagogic brutality ? I don't think so. It lives naturally in the streets—where a large proportion of the race still lives—but sickens as soon as it crosses an educational threshold. How few of our students, Packet, can be described as either sensitive or crafty in any very interesting sense of the words ! '

Bacon was slightly drunk ; and in no mood to receive Brett's remarks on the right way to educate Egyptians.

' With all due respect to your long experience in the field but aren't we, as it were, engineers who have been sent on a mission——'

' You were sent,' Bacon commented. ' I just came . . . sorry.'

'—simply to do a particular job—build a bridge or excavate a canal ? I mean to say, all we're supposed to do is offer our knowledge and taste. They take what they want to, and they must abide by the consequences.'

'Good God.' Bacon's voice rose above the distressful shrieks of the love-lorn Greek lady. 'Have a proper respect for metaphor, please! Engineers study the terrain before they get out their picks and shovels. Academic—worse than academic—like holding a sick child in front of a pharmaceutical counter and inviting it to choose a bottle for itself. Which does it choose?'

'I'll have another beer,' said Packet. 'The same for you two?' A waiter was hovering nervously nearby. Englishmen must be terrible when they quarrelled, he was thinking.

'The biggest and brightest, of course,' Bacon continued. 'Sartre or Monsieur Despair—Lawrence or Mr. Sex—Kafka or Herr Too-good-for-this-world. Trouble is that there's no literary tradition in this country. No tradition at all, one might gather. Look at the tourist picking his way fastidiously through an over-crowded and decaying village to get at the spacious and polished antiquities on the other side! Nothing ties up. Most of our students are profoundly ashamed of anything at all old—it reminds them of their grandparents who were *fellahin*. Ignorant and superstitious old people who might well have built temples and pyramids. No, for them social life began with the milkbar, cultural life began with having a university to go to, and political life began with having a university to stay away from.'

Packet gave a kind of laugh, to indicate to Brett that of course his friend was exaggerating a little.

'If you believe that, how have you managed to spend so long here as a teacher?' Brett thought it rather disgusting that anyone should foul his own nest in such a way and still continue to live in it.

'A teacher is like a Jewish mother—he always hopes to have something to do with the new Messiah's arrival. I wonder whether it's so different in Europe? One goes on, in the hope of opening for someone that obscure and narrow door which is there—somewhere there—hidden between the two immense portals of Art for Art's sake and Art for the sake of Message. And once in a while, for all the muddled directions one gives him, somebody finds the door.'

'I know what you mean, I think,' Packet said. 'But is this the time and place? Look at the country—it's a very big door of some kind that's wanted. I hate to think that I might be pursuing a luxury trade!' Brett began to listen to the music: it was, he felt, at any rate less affected than this conversation.

'There are plenty of people proclaiming themselves the gate-keepers of some or other Heaven,' Bacon answered, 'and not so many willing to do our little job of work. It's a long term policy, of course. I've only been here twenty years as yet.' He pointed to the wall behind them. Two rough murals, executed by the patron himself, depicted with gusto a number of happy Greek peasants stretched out on the ground with large tankards of *retsina*: in the middle distance their infuriated wives could be seen wrangling with the host. Incongruously placed between the murals was a glamorous piece of publicity, two cupid's bows, bearing the caption, '*le* rouge baiser *permet le baiser*'.

'Oh well,' he said, 'if you want to go in for an obviously useful job, try for something like that.'

The three teachers suddenly realized that the music had stopped. Everyone else, in dead silence, had turned towards a thin, long-faced and melancholy man who was raising himself precariously on to the rostrum of the band. He dipped down abruptly, retrieved his tarbush from beneath the chair and stuck it crookedly on his head. Bacon groaned softly. The patron grinned uncertainly, the musicians fidgeted with their instruments, the lady singer edged towards the further side of the platform. And then the Egyptian gentleman began to shout. The words poured out at the speed of Morse, in a tone of malignance, near to hysteria at times, at times coarse and bullying. The waiters stood transfixed, the vast bulk of Madame Rose was paralysed. The customers, twisting round in their chairs, had set their glasses quietly down ; looking towards the orator with curiously neutral expressions, all individuality had drained from their faces, their bodies. The children, all of them awake now except for a baby pressed to its mother's breast, were silent and motionless, as if having their photographs taken. Not a clink from a glass, not the rattle of a fork. The dancers stood where they were, their hands on their hips, the handkerchief still dangling from the fingers of one of them.

The voice stormed on. Packet and Bacon looked embarrassed. Brett was quite in the dark, he felt only a slight fear mixed with an inexplicable shame and considerable curiosity. What was the man going on about ? A bad actor declaiming some diabolical Arab Shakespeare ? He shivered slightly. Yet it was less boring than that Greek music, and not much noisier. The voice passed rapidly from one tone to another, never relaxing its intensity . . . intense rage, intense indignation, intense pleading, intense insinuation, intense sorrow, intense pathos, with now and then a hint of exasperated uncertainty, and then back to intense rage and menacing brutality.

'What on earth's the matter ? ' he whispered. Bacon seemed to have fallen into an unpleasant dream. Packet whispered back, ' He's complaining that they've played Greek music, and French, and Spanish and Italian and Irish —everything except Egyptian music. This great country permits them to live here, and they betray it by playing foreign music—I can't understand everything he says . . . '

' But he's obviously drunk—why don't they throw him out—or send for the police to do it ? '

Bacon made a sour face. ' The police might side with

their compatriot. Especially if they imagine he's someone
of importance. Perhaps he is. Who knows? But Mr.
Nicola is a clever man. He won't insist on justice being
done.'

One of the servants who had been dispatched at the
beginning of the incident now returned with a well-dressed
sober Egyptian whom he had found in the street. The
patron and the newcomer held a wordy and ceremonious
colloquy over the orator, who had now subsided into a
chair, grumbling half-heartedly about foreign music. His
tarbush was still aloft, the dissipated narrow face seemed to
be crumbling under its brightness and weight. Mr. Nicola
tore the little pack of bills across with a large gesture. Both
the newcomer and, more dimly, the orator were impressed
by this action. The former harangued the latter in tones of
sweet encouragement while Mr. Nicola, standing a few feet
away, a fixed smile on his plump wary face, winked and
nodded knowingly. Finally the orator was hauled to his
feet very gently by a couple of dark servants, he was weeping
tears of sentimental self-pity now, still laved by an unending
flow of soothing and admonitory words. The stranger
swallowed a whisky and soda presented by the patron, hands
were shaken all round, compliments flew, head-shakings and
understanding smiles filled the air, and the four of them,
backed up closely by Mr. Nicola, lurched towards the door
—the patriot, the two boys, the good samaritan, bound
together in a cocoon of dark arms and honied noises, out
through the swing doors, into a taxi.

Tension relaxed inside the bar. A nervous murmur arose
from the Greeks as they gradually resumed their normal
personalities and their bodies returned to their normal shapes.
Then, saying goodnight to Mr. Nicola in restrained tones as
if he had suffered a bereavement, they too disappeared into
the street. The musicians finished up their beer and began
to pack their instruments.

' Let's go,' Bacon said. ' *Finie la musique*—until the same time tomorrow.'

Mr. Nicola came in person to collect their money, began to apologize for the unseemly incident, and said the things which he always said to Englishmen on such occasions. They made further soothing noises. The doors swung to behind them. Silence within and without.

Chapter 3

THE INFIDELS CAVIL WITH VAIN WORDS

PACKET was walking along the Corniche on a late October evening. Anything but salty, he reflected, gazing into the sea : no nymphs, no satyrs, no peanut vendors. A pronounced air of retired well-being hung over it : at the same time a light but constant agitation suggested that it could lose its temper at any minute. Honey or wine, Coca-Cola or corrosive acid, but never salty. Never bitter. It was, as the tourist agencies in Europe sang, an eminently pleasurable sea. We have no sympathy but what is propagated by pleasure—the poet's words came into his head— pleasure enlarges the imagination, and the imagination is the great instrument of moral good. And no doubt of moral evil. The proposition soothed him. He tried to repeat it, became confused, and looked into the sea instead.

Packet had been born into a sort of Methodist family, of narrow means. He had grown up in that last period of time when it was possible for respectable people, in full employment, to be what one has to call poor. He deviated from the norm, but only in ways so common as to need little elaboration. A succession of scholarships, none of which was quite sufficient, had taken him to a secondary school, after much heart-searching, and, after more heart-searching, to a university. At every step up the ladder so heavy a load of financial worry and care of conscience had accumulated that now—at the dizzy top of the ladder, or at the bottom of another one—he found himself wellnigh incapacitated for enjoying the view. For the good of whom was it that a progressive but nonetheless precise country had put enough money into his pocket to buy the books which would tell him which books he ought to buy? A yellow bar, the reflection of the moon, lay across the water like a shaky ladder. Two policemen slouched by, turning on him the curious but mild and impersonal stare which poverty bestows on certain wealth.

Margarine is very tolerable, until some specious benefactor gives you a taste of butter. It was the spiritual margarine on which he had been reared that, in one way or another, had preoccupied him ever since. In his early days, like all young men of his kind, he had reacted against the damp foggy morality of his environment, sharply enough to gain for himself, along with a vague name for cleverness, something of a bad reputation. Quite undeservedly, for he had never possessed money enough or charm or even inclination to be more than verbal in his bad ways. His relatives were rarely able to give reasons, either convincing or otherwise, for what they did or supposed—he had shown a considerable talent for adducing reasons, whether good or bad, for doing exactly the opposite. And then, having been hung for it, he would fail to start to do it. He had only meant to rebuke their narrowness, to indicate how there might be, in all worthiness, an exception or two to their unwritten laws. He was, in fact, with the quixotry of the Sixth Form, only standing up for the underdog—usually a mythical one who, if he had ever found himself at the mercy of this unmethodical Methodism, might have experienced some slight and passing inconvenience. Unfortunately he who stands up for imaginary underdogs may only too easily find himself the thing he has imagined. And so, repetitive arguments, hot harangues and cold silences.

Packet's very beginnings had inspired him with a rebellious

and deliberate respect for pleasure : unhappily they had also left him in complete darkness as to what kind of thing pleasure was and whereabouts it resided. By the others it was taken for granted that pleasure, if not exactly a shady procedure, was certainly a negligible accessory ; the faces in the street confirmed this view. For, first and foremost, pleasure dwelt in other streets, in the broad leafy avenues where the business men lived and kept their cars. And there it should be left, quite without reproach, as long as the owner paid his income tax and did not exceed the speed limit, quite right and proper. (What gloating, however, if he defaulted or was found driving under the influence of drink !) There was nothing puritanical about this attitude. (That was left to Packet.) Simply, margarine is good enough for us, it doesn't really taste much different, some people prefer it. Indeed, the word ' pleasure ' was heard in Packet's street as infrequently as the word 'God'. The residents were God-fearing people, in a mild unself-conscious way : they had never asked themselves, or been asked by anyone to whom it would have been necessary to give an honest answer, whether they believed in God—but that was another matter. And they feared the name of pleasure, too, though in the same tepid and impersonal way. Nothing was good, exactly ; nothing was bad, precisely. This was the world of which the near poles were the nice and the nasty. The margarine was neither one nor the other, and in that it resembled most of the other things which Packet grew up among.

Then, when he had grown up a little—at the time when most of his contemporaries were earning just enough to think of marriage—he had come to see all this as the direct result of certain unequivocal evils, the popular press, cheap novels, hypocritical church-going. And he instituted a protracted campaign—nasty remarks about the library books which came into the house, insinuations as to the vicar's lack of intimacy with the gospels as written, grumbled attempts to get the newspaper changed (which might have succeeded had his nominee not cost twice as much). What an academic giant-killer he was in those days ! Would any of them, tired out by a long day of margarine-winning, have derived anything in the way of betterment—he would not himself have used the word 'pleasure' then—from *Ulysses* or *To the Lighthouse*? *A Passage to India* would have taken his father back to a very different country from the one he had known as a soldier. And what interest could they have found in a superior headline-less journal which boasted of its disinterestedness, and whose advertisements were so plainly directed towards a cruelly different income-group? What good would it have done them to quarrel with an over-worked clergyman who hardly knew of their existence, when he commended rearmament in the parish magazine which no-one read—for he was equitable in dividing the harvest offerings among the poorer streets? What an odd knight errant he had been, Packet thought. Of the kind who pushes the lost and weary damsel into the giant's castle, on principle, so that he may fight the good fight on her behalf—and then discovers that the giant cannot be bothered to come out into the open and that his castle is quite impregnable and stocked with dainties. So that, with an undignified gesture like spitting into the moat, all he can do is turn his mule round and ride away, consoling himself that the damsel anyway was too exhausted to go any further, and quite probably related in some way to the giant.

Spitting into the sea, Packet considered, of all the unpleasant characters in literature, Stephen Dedalus was the worst. 'I go to forge in the smithy of my soul the un-created conscience of my race.' And he ended flat on his back in the red light district. Packet felt that he preferred men who forged cheques without any conscience at all, or even men like Brett, those buds of well-manured stock,

44

who forged nothing—except, calmly and unquestioningly, their way ahead.

So much to unlearn, so much to learn, and so little time to do it in. First all the years and weariness of combating that muggy 'goodness', the unwritten and shapeless but desperately clung-to conception of 'the proper' and 'like everyone else'. At first fighting only shadows—but then, as he became old enough to be unmistakably 'unpleasant' and 'queer' even to those who would be hard pressed to define the pleasant and the normal, fighting very real things, real people —this had shocked him since, in spite of appearances, he was too modest to suppose that people took what he said seriously. Real people, affronted by the sight of a foolish boy questioning in so unprepossessing a manner what was in fact sometimes good and right, though not always. People, some of them kindly souls who had helped or would have helped or, in spite of their misgivings, sometimes continued to help him.

First, then, all the years of unlearning—in a most conscientious and even scholarly way—everything he had absorbed along with his mother's milk, along with the hissing of the gas mantles, the deliberately careful and muffled tread of boots and slippers on shared staircases, the margarine that was always on the point of being finished up and the crusts of bread that had to be.

And then, the years of testing the contraries which, sometimes without thinking, he had let himself in for : of finding out what, in this brave new world into which he had clawed and buffeted and scraped his way, had any significance over and above that of being the opposite of something in the world out of which he had so painfully dug and ripped his way. Of exploring other and more portentous evasions of pleasure, other proprieties, written down this time and fully glossed, in a variety of editions. And consequently trying to re-learn some part of what he had unlearned : like a Prodigal Son who hesitates in the middle distance, while at his back the swine make merry on his husks and in front of him stands his father coldly proffering —for all the world as if he had never noticed his son's absence —a plate of bread and margarine. The taint of Methodism, he told himself—its God is such a mean priggish little creature, smelling of bread and watered milk, that you throw yourself into the arms of its Devil, a mean cynical little creature who smells of stale alcohol. In that world the difference was only that the good man relieved himself in the chapel while the bad man relieved himself outside, against the chapel wall.

'And I'm only now finding out that there is a world elsewhere !' he very nearly shouted, in mixed fury and excitement. 'Me—supposed to have been a bright boy, winning scholarships and prizes, accounted a worthy recipient of public monies—and only now, on the way to my thirties, realizing that doors are opened by turning the knob and not by kicking them down—and that if one door is locked there's generally another that's open !' He must really tell Bacon about it. 'My dear Bacon, you see before you a classic case of retarded development.' But Bacon would probably reply, 'So is everyone else who develops. Don't flatter yourself, Packet.' And of course he would be right again. Classic cases only existed in the textbooks—or in his notebooks, which were full of cases, each one if possible more classic than the last. But all the same Packet refused to take too much for granted : the scholastic habit died hard, and he would fill up his notebooks just in case. It doesn't hurt to take your umbrella, even if the sun is shining. Though he was, and it made him feel almost ten years younger, becoming increasingly certain that—just as very little was got into people by lecturing to them—so very little was got out of them by inviting them to lecture about themselves.

He oughtn't to have spat into the sea. It was unchivalrous, considering how female, how warm and generous and delicate-skinned she seemed at the moment. The sea shivered

pleasurably, and winked and blinked, and whispered back
at him : if he enjoyed spitting into it, then spit he should
—but wasn't it time he moved along, hadn't he forgotten
that he was going to a party, to enjoy himself ? He had.

It was a smart party, and so there were not many English
at it. And indeed if there were any Egyptians at all—with
the one exception of Said Mohamed Said—then they passed
off as Syrian or Lebanese. At the moment behaviour was
as tasteful and restrained as their apparel, among the men,
the women, and the others who glided up and down, drinking with quiet greed and ostentatiously making notes about
hats and gowns for the gossip columns which they contributed
to the local press. It was advisable to keep on the right side
of them if one's wife desired to feature as ' the charming '
or ' the chic ', but fortunately they displayed active malice
only towards their friends and their friends' friends.

The language in general use was French, of course. English
is not considered quite the thing in high Egyptian society—
in high society in Egypt, that is to say. It has its sordid uses
in business, and fragmentarily it manifests its barbarous
intonations in almost every form of outdoor sport. One
hears it occasionally, a legacy of the British army, on the
lips of road-sweepers or dustmen who have been driven too
far ; and from time to time one hears it, after some doubt
as to what one is hearing, rasped out on the trams by boys
from the British schools. But oneself, one speaks French.
Rumour has it that above this already high society is yet a
more exalted and exclusive circle in which nothing but
English is heard, but as none of Packet's acquaintance had
soared so far we must be content to regard it as one of those
unnerving myths endemic to a rarefied social atmosphere.

Packet stood at the buffet with a French colleague on
whose suggestion, though he did not know it, he had been
invited. Monsieur Martin was a cheerful and simple soul,

a specialist in phonetics, who had once been a champion amateur boxer. A huge fellow, whom uninformed beggars and whisky-sellers avoided with care, he had immense fists and dangling arms and a face like that of a backward but benign cod. He liked cars and swimming and women, he had a heart so soft that it impelled him to pursue terrified mendicants with charitable intentions, and he was fashionable only by virtue of being undeniably French in a society that yearned to be. Even so, Packet had already collected several telephone numbers from smart and brittle young ladies— blessed with everything in the world except a reliable passport —who had discovered that he danced quite well ('*pour un Anglais*'). Packet enjoyed formal flirtations of this sort : it was entertaining to guess what they would expect the 'Anglais' to do or say next, and then not do or say it. He had an eye on his notebooks, too—a special section.

'She is the wife of the Cypriot who makes gin and brandy —very rich—she with the red hairs,' pointed out Martin. Packet recalled some war-time story of the fleet, alarmed by an epidemic of delirium tremens, emptying the gentleman's consignments into the unlucky Mediterranean. The lady was surrounded by a swaying circle of slightly corrupt-looking young men, the sons of Greek importers and Arab business houses. Her voice rose for a moment above the mounting din. 'I have been everywhere in the world. I have seen everything in the world. It is all quite the same.' The young men tittered cynically.

'One would say that she has been drinking her husband's gin,' Martin remarked, laying his huge fist on a bottle of Scotch. One of the young men led the bright, ageing lady off to the adjoining room where, under lights so dim that they seemed on the point of extinction, dancing was in progress.

Packet detected a conversation going on in English a little way off and, edging towards it, was rather surprised to find

Brett there, extremely elegant, chatting with some gently inebriated painters. The young man appeared to have arrived rather quickly, but then, he was employed by an institution which, in spite of the fact that they rarely if ever entered its doors, commanded a certain respect among these people. If one works for some kind of foreign cultural body one is already more than a teacher, one is an *attaché* ; but if one works for the Egyptian government, worst of all for the Egyptian Ministry of Education, then one must be down and out, financially and morally.

'But my digs are very decent—can't grumble you know,' Brett was saying. 'One can't have everything.'

'Digs? But you are an *archaéologue*, then ? '

'Good gracious no. I mean where I put up—that's to say, my hotel.'

'Ah, I excuse myself. We are not accustomed to speak English, you see. *A bientôt . . .* ' They moved off in some embarrassment. '*A quoi bon apprendre l'anglais* ? ' Packet heard one saying to the other in disgruntled tones.

'Hallo, Packet, fancy seeing you here ! Do you know our host ?—a charming man. You know Mr. Packet, of the university, Robert ? ' As it happened, Robert El Hamama did know Packet, slightly. He was in his early forties, a figure in the social world and doctor to a large proportion of the resident and transitional royalties. 'An Alexandrian leprachaun who lives on finesse instead of grass ', Bacon had once described him. He was small, with a short and precise beard and large soft eyes and an incredibly gentle voice—as it were, a Toulouse-Lautrec whom nature had treated more kindly and who would certainly never dream of addressing a chorus girl. He had an old black servant from the Sudan, who was even smaller (and perhaps, had one known, equally refined). And he also had—though the verb was scarcely apt—a small but savage wife, whom it was both necessary and dangerous to know, as she dwelt near the summit of the twin peaks of culture and fashion and guarded them both fiercely. It was no doubt an odious thing in this company to be thought to love a wife or husband, but it might be felt that these two went rather far in their concern to avoid any such suspicion. But they were both so brilliant, sophisticated and susceptible that few gatherings would be likely to survive the strain of their combined presence.

' I am very pleased to meet you again, Mr. Packet. One has heard so much of your sociological studies. You still like people? I do not . . . ' Packet felt called upon to feel sorry for people, not merely because Dr. El Hamama did not like them, but because he failed to like them with such a Christ-like gentleness that it was hard to conceive of any mistake having occurred.

' Please help yourself to whisky, Mr. Packet,' he continued, rather unnecessarily, ' and feel that you are *chez vous*. You will not find any *people* here, I fear, but there are some charming and interesting *persons*.' He added, ' You must dine with me one evening soon, when we shall have more time together, and you will tell me about your poet T. S. Eliot—I should love to know what you feel about his *Conversation Galante*.' Oh dear me, Packet thought, *Conversation Galante*, it must be one of the French pieces. Oh no, ' our sentimental friend the moon '.

' I think I feel more about *The Waste Land*,' he replied, hoping to heaven that he didn't sound superior. He couldn't regulate the tone of his voice when he was wondering feverishly how much longer he could keep his hand inert, held loosely in the host's, without twitching his fingers madly.

' *The Waste Land*? Really? But don't you find it just a little vulgar? And so very long . . . ' Smiling intimately, he dropped Packet's hand and glided away to save an unfortunate lady from his immense persian cat, an animal of uncertain temper.

'Robert is a poet,' Brett remarked in a voice which betrayed pride and awe mixed with the feeling that after all Packet might not be ignorant of the fact.

'Well, yes,' Packet made an effort not to niggle over the literary status of the man whose whisky he was consuming. 'But so is everybody else here—they all write or paint or something.'

'It's very cosmopolitan. And so exciting. I begin to enjoy Egypt.'

'Still, this isn't Egypt, you know—this is Dr. El Hamama's salon.' There I go again, Packet told himself, always censuring, always putting people right. 'You're right, though. It is interesting. In England, a set-up as social as this wouldn't be arty, and a set-up as arty wouldn't be social. In fact, if you want to be accepted here, you really need to have a finger in some artistic pie or other, though you needn't push it in very far. It's the French influence, no doubt.' He helped Brett and himself to more Scotch. 'Bacon says there isn't much to choose between business men pretending to be writers in order to succeed socially and writers pretending to be business men for the same reason.'

'Have you seen his books?—I mean Robert's.'

'They're printed on lovely thick paper—like a courtesan's mattress, as Bacon puts it, and bound in calf-skin. Bacon calls his copies the fatted calves, because when you get inside there are only about a dozen poems, all very short. But the margins are very beautiful.'

'Does he write in French?'

'Don't insult him by supposing that he writes in Arabic! Mind you, Arabic is such a difficult language to write in that it's just as well it's unfashionable.'

Packet knew little about El Hamama apart from what Bacon had told him. The latter had taken the poet as an example of one who erred in the opposite direction from his young colleague. El Hamama, he said, had published a book of poems (" *100 exemplaires numérotés, dont 75 hors commerce* ") containing not a single allusion, subtle or otherwise, to beggars, dust, dirt, desert, palm trees, lizards, policemen, diseases of the eye, illiteracy, education, *gallabiehs* or automobiles.

' What *does* he write about then ? ' Packet had asked.

' He doesn't write *about*. Sensibility, refinement, and money : when one has all that, one does not write *about* —one just writes. Subject matter, El Hamama would say, is the betrayal of style : it should be left to journalists, who need it to conceal their lack of style. El Hamama sets out to create what didn't exist beforehand, in any sense, and is quite useless when it does exist. And he'd even object to the word " create ", I expect, on the grounds that it suggested manual labour or the pyramids. You, on the other hand— as sociologist, I mean—concentrate on the subject matter of other people's lives to the exclusion of their style of living. And you are so afraid of creating what doesn't exist that you carry a notebook in which to jot down the facts as soon as observed. You count the number of beggars in a given street as carefully as El Hamama discounts them.'

Packet had found this a little hard. He assured Bacon very earnestly that the older he grew the more careful he was not to assume that statistical carefulness could be a substitute for caring. Bacon congratulated him on his mastery of words. ' It makes one happy to know,' he concluded, ' that El Hamama for financial reasons has to devote most of his time to medicine and you most of yours to teaching.'

But Bacon was a Character. Packet was very attached to him, but the fact remained that he had never found him very useful for study. Characters, he supposed, had too much personality : they were not amenable to generalization : one ended up with a mass of footnotes and precious little text.

' I shouldn't trust Bacon's opinions too far,' Brett demurred, apropos of the former's comments on El Hamama. ' He's way out of the stream. I mean, there's something awfully nineteenth century about him, isn't there ? You know, the high-minded and benevolent sahib.' An uncouth specimen, too, he added to himself.

The one open and undisputed Egyptian national present at the party was even a bey, of a minor order. But in these circles and under these conditions he featured as what a Greek journalist had first called him : the Egyptian Renoir. The title carried a good deal of honour with it in a society for whom abstract art had soon proved uncongenial (it smelt of the engine rooms which had no part in their myth of Europe), while surrealism carried unacceptable political and unacceptably naïve implications.

Packet noticed a group of noisy males near the decanters ; his rate of drinking (where on earth had this sudden thirst come from ?) would be less likely to attract attention over there, he felt. He manœuvred his way towards them. The subject of outcry appeared to be painting. Said Mohamed Said was one of the few painters whose work Packet could be sure of recognizing in the numerous local exhibitions. Indeed, it would be difficult to mistake a Said Mohamed Said after you had encountered your first. He specialized in large fleshy women, good enough to eat, if you were very fond of milk chocolate. Chocolate done up in enticing wrappers, too, for his was in an unashamed way something of a touristic art—his native women wore fantastically brilliant and multi-coloured garments of a type never seen in the East since the Thousand and One Nights. Give him a baggy slut or an emaciated sexless young hag, and he ended with a ripe and melting odalisque. If, like Renoir's, his flesh erred on the side of vulgar plenty, it showed no signs of beating or of child-bearing, and it was wholly free from the flavour of garlic. His art, except for the hard look in his women's eyes, was a hashish dream. The King, indeed, had purchased a number of Said Mohamed Said's canvases, and not merely in a spirit of encouraging national art. Nor did the painter have to rely upon his sales, since he was by profession a judge in the Egyptian courts. In that he had not put brush to canvas before the age of forty, one might have expected something more ' primitive ' from him ; but a judge is as different from a *douanier* as Frenchness-in-exile is from France.

At present Said Mohamed Said was contentedly playing the fool for his less prosperous fellow artists, El Hamama quietly at his elbow, refilling the Egyptian Renoir's glass as the occasion arose. They were both small in stature, the host resembling an over-delicate gazelle and the painter a jovial but potentially indelicate ape.

' Tell us, *maître*, how do you manage that dull leaden glint, so suggestive of recent sinfulness, on your breasts and bellies ? '

' He stirs in a little cheap icing sugar ! '

' So what ? My clients know that one cannot judge a cake by its icing.'

' They go for the plums underneath ! Is it true, *maître*, that you are to be made a pasha for your services to Egyptian womanhood ? '

' That's a reason for making him king ! ' A ripple of uneasiness ran through the bystanders. The only Egyptian came to the rescue.

' Alas, I am in disgrace ! One of my best clients—his walls palpitate with my pictures—has been taken queer. He ran away to Suez—with an English girl, all skin and bones. His wife, who has a full figure '—he knocked a plate of minute sandwiches out of El Hamama's hand—' blames me for it ! ' He noticed the thin young Englishman who, unusually enough, had the beginnings of a sense of humour ; and he turned over to English, a language which he pretended to speak rather badly.

' Ah yes—but you, if my memoirs are correct, are Scottish —or is it Irish? I too have been privileged. I had an Irish governor—governoress?—*ma première amante*—what a woman! How well I can recall lacing her—how do they call themselves? *Baleines*—whales?—oh yes, stays!' He put his foot against the table and pushed, heaving at the cloth with mimic violence; several small bottles of soda fell to the ground.

This was a good party, Packet told himself. 'You must meet a friend of mine—man called Debrett—Brett, I mean —if you haven't already met him,' he heard himself saying rather thickly. 'He had a governess, too.' He looked fiercely about and eventually detected him; but Brett was in earnest and intimate conversation with a Russian prince.

The party was warming up. People who were not in the habit of speaking English suddenly began to show great idiomatic prowess; people who spoke nothing else suddenly developed miraculous linguistic powers. Brett, who had once read part of the *Inferno* in a bilingual edition, could be heard discoursing on Italian films to an aged Italian countess. She nodded patiently: how nice were the *Inghlesi* when they delivered themselves in a foreign tongue, how unperfidious! She replied in a slow and immaculate French, gratified to hear of all the wonders her countrymen were accomplishing in celluloid. The truth was that she had not lived in Italy since her childhood, and as for films—her servants frequently went to the cinema, she believed. Verdi, she remarked, remembering that after all she was some kind of contessa, and that something should be said in return to this agreeable and striving young man—Verdi, one of the greatest of Italy's sons, were these new Italian artists making films of his great operas? She hoped that they would not forget Verdi.

The large formal groups of guests were breaking up. Said

Chapter 3

Mohamed Said was eloquently pretending to try to persuade the Belgian consul's stout wife to sit for his next nude, while the consul gave himself to sympathetic discussion of the Koran with a bewildered and rather hurt Lebanese free-thinker whom he had taken for an Egyptian. El Hamama was carrying on an intensely spiritual flirtation with a rather attractive Syrian girl ; her thin intelligent face wore a polite and barely sceptical expression and her responses were moderate ; Packet waited impatiently for El Hamama to finish. At last he delicately communicated to her—handed, Packet thought irritably, was not the word, and gave was hopelessly crude—his slim *plaquette* of poems and modestly turned away to inspect the buffet. Oh good evening, said Packet casually, would she like to dance perhaps ? With pleasure, she replied, tucking the book away.

Conversation was yielding to the less strenuous delights of the dance floor. Even those who had never danced before in their lives, who hated it, who despised it, were contriving to shuffle, to stand still, to roll back and forth on their toes. Which was the most that was asked of them. Brett was engaged with the daughter of the Belgian consul, a good tennis player but extremely plain ; she wielded him as if he were a racket. If these people had possessed local accents, Packet reflected, this was the moment when they would rear themselves, the vowels would broaden, the h's would begin to be dropped, just as the smart ladies were beginning to drop their hard masks ever so slightly, in favour of softer ones. I don't have to conceal my accent, he thought, as he talked carelessly to the girl in a haphazard mixture of French and English : everyone here assumes that what I speak is King's English, except Brett, who actually does speak it.

A Syrian damsel, with jet black hair, white skin, good high cheekbones. Is it that, he began formally—could she tell him whether there was a recognizably Syrian way of speaking French—he meant, did Syrian French differ from

French French at all ? Yes, she smiled, or so the French said.
He smiled back sternly : the French were really a bit too
self-righteous and supercilious about their precious language.
He dismissed the *Académie Française* with a lift of the shoulders
—they should be only too proud that such an attractive
Syrian girl deigned to speak their language at all.

They danced, retired for refreshment, and danced again.
Packet was immensely taken with Sylvie : here, he told
himself, was an occasion on which one should concentrate
one's forces, such as they were. She had a beautiful name,
he told her, it suited her (guiltily remembering an old family
row when he had attacked Sylvia, his sister's name, as a vulgar
and pretentious appellation, a shop-girl name, pseudo-literary).
Sylvie, sylphide. The poor girl was certainly on the thin
side. There was something worthy about thinness, he felt ;
it was a sort of guarantee of something or other. The fatter
types were more amusing, but . . . like Marcel, for instance.
Did Arab girls of the better class necessarily get fat later in
life ? Were the Syrians Arabs ? But he kept those questions
to himself. In any case there were plenty of other things
to talk about. I am becoming quite a good talker, he thought
with pride and pleasure ; though in fact he was rather
proving a good listener. But whatever their relationship,
they were both enjoying it, in a somewhat sad and noble
manner, melancholy calling eagerly to melancholy. That
was the keynote of their mutual bearing, though how it came
to be struck was difficult to say.

Packet attached himself to Sylvie quite savagely, advising
Brett, when he came up with sociable intentions, to seek out
a quite imaginary Spanish duchess, ' standing by the buffet,
in a black mantilla, with gigantic pearls, waiting for someone
to dance with her '. And more than once he steered her out
of the way of their host, as he approached with the determined
smile of one who intends to talk about poetry in general and

his own in particular. ' He has known you for years, Sylvie, whereas I only feel as if I had.' The pretty compliment warmed his heart so much that he went on to make others, until a look of slight alarm came into her face.

But then, disastrously, she was whipped off by Said Mohamed Said, whose short violent figure arrived with less warning than a torpedo. He would try to persuade her to sit for him, thin as she was, Packet told himself scornfully. What a chance ! The record came to an end and he set out to reclaim her as tactfully as possible, but firmly. Alas, someone else, some interfering little man with a face like a monkey, had reached her first : he greeted her as if they were old family friends, and the next record began to play—a slow and sorrowful tango, exactly the sort Packet would have enjoyed dancing with her. He felt suddenly ill at ease, staring around him at these slowly swaying foreign bodies. What was he doing at this party ? No-one took the slightest interest in him any longer. He felt horribly sober. Seeking out the figure of Sylvie dancing in the dim mass, he ground his teeth softly ; the sound cheered him up, and he turned quickly and marched into the other room, brilliantly lighted, but a little disgusting under the dissolving remnants of the feast, the pools of spilt liquids and the overflowing ash-trays.

Ahmed, the small servant, had given up the unequal battle and stood with a respectful but bored expression, asleep on his feet, safely behind the buffet. Packet felt a rush of affection for the old man. ' *Ezayak, Ahmed ?* ' he shouted jovially, patting him gently on the shoulder. The old man jerked his head, opened his eyes and in the same movement seized and lifted a bottle. ' Wheeskey, effendi ? ' he remarked wearily. Packet's Arabic was inadequate to explain what he had meant by the pat on the shoulder ; even in English he would not have found it easy. How sad that the old fellow should think he had been yelled at and pushed by an

intoxicated young man greedily hunting for more alcohol !
But it was all too complicated, so he only smiled and held
out a glass.

'Have you lost your girl friend, old boy ?' The voice,
as precise and clear as ever, belonged to Brett who was standing in the corner with a glamorous creature, all mouth and
eyes, nestling beneath a black silk shawl. 'Come and be
introduced to my fascinating new friend, Packet.'

Packet turned a smile on Ahmed, heavy with such
frustrated affection that the old man might have been alarmed
had he not already closed his eyes again.

'Packet teaches the Gippos all about Wordsworth and his
daffodils,' Brett instructed his friend in what was not quite
an undertone. Turning to Packet, he added, 'She's no
duchess, old chap, but you were right about her being
Spanish—her father runs the Bank of Spain in Cairo. I've
always wanted to visit Madrid . . .' But Packet was listening for the end of the tango : if he wasn't nippy that Don
Juan from the French Department would collar her. He
smiled sourly at the couple : what were they looking so
smug about ?

He was lucky this time and, moreover, some understanding
person had put another tango on. They had almost started
to dance before he realized that he was holding his empty
glass. It seemed to him that they took up the conversation
exactly where they had left off. Musing on the happiness of
it, on the awful precariousness of happiness, for a few seconds
he failed to take in what she was saying. She was married,
she was saying, and then, that she had a daughter, three years
old, living with some relative, in some part of the world.
He felt a sudden chilliness, almost shivering with it. What
was he doing at this party ? The vague shapes around him
turned into actual human figures once again, sharp elbows
and assertive feet and insidious buttocks. Not the misty

background to sad mythological lovers, but human bodies, hot and twisted and ungainly, in the grip of some surreptitious and under-lighted activity. The hum of conversation, which had washed over the music like a gentle sea, broke into harsh splinters ; the intonations of malice, of vulgar and spurious surprise, the unmeaning ejaculations of loosened and strange tongues. It had been a *mariage de convenance*, she was saying and her hand tightened gently on his shoulder, she had never quite loved her husband, nor—she spoke with less certainty —had he loved her. The main achievement of their marriage had been to keep money in the family.

Packet felt a welcome warmth trickling back into his veins, a warmth of indignation. He was still prone to indignation : for years he had had little else to warm himself by. Life seemed increasingly less simple, however, and he could think of nothing very cogent to say ; he grunted on two notes, expressive of sympathy and then of decent anger. Her husband had a mistress, she remarked dispassionately, and she was free to do as she wanted, to apply for a divorce if she wished—no one would mind very much, business was business (the family exported onions and imported coal), and if a transaction fell through, then one wrote it off.

' You must divorce, then,' he stated firmly. It was the only thing.

' Probably,' she replied, too casually he felt, ' but it is not urgent. How should it be ? Remarriage—with another of these men ? One of them—that small man, like a monkey, dancing over there—I tell you this in confidence, of course— offered me a hundred pounds to live with him for a week.'

Packet's indignant grunt was louder this time, and more genuine. It was shameful, a nice girl like this (and she seemed to like him, too), left to fend for herself in this plausible and predatory society. The vague bodies and the confused tongues took more precise shape : Said Mohamed Said the connoisseur of flesh with his insidious frankness (though perhaps Packet was the only person in the room for whom frankness could be said to be that), El Hamama the soul-sucker with his long tentacular fingers and his parasitical *plaquette* (but what a noble forehead the man had !), Monkey-face with his cheque book and ready pen, and even Packet's own compatriot who apparently possessed a special genea-logical sense and had in little more than a month mastered the sanctions of this world. Packet's fierce eyes pierced the gloom in all directions. If this twilight were not to be noble and revelatory and sad, then it should not exist. Lights ho ! But he could still think of nothing very appropriate to say to the girl, except ' What a brazen scoundrel ! A hundred pounds ! ' And to that she only replied, ' It is what happens in this world when a woman leaves her lord and master . . . *tout de même*, I have to think of the child. Should I not make a home for her ? '

' You would be much happier in France, I should think, or,' he continued with less conviction, ' in England. At any rate England is a fine place for children—they are, you might say, the *spécialité de la maison* . . . ' They had tacitly agreed that the medium of their intercourse should be basically English, French to be used when necessary.

' How should I ever live in England ? '

The various circumstances had combined to enlarge and heighten his sense of pathos. The tango seemed enormously tragic. Another powerful wave of glamorous sadness swept over him, and he also felt, with gratified surprise, a distinct savagery in his breast. Sylvie looked pale and mysterious in the quarter-light and rather fragile though, he had to admit, not excessively so. Her story took on dimensions in his mind which could never have been contained in his fat yellow notebooks (*Cahiers le Roi* they were called). I've been wasting time, he told himself. They bumped against another couple, jarring his sense of the fit : it was the monkey-faced gentleman. Packet's muscles tensed and he heard himself growling softly. But his partner only smiled and said 'Pardon'.

The next dance was a samba and Packet at once suggested that they should go and find a drink. It was not that he felt silly when dancing the samba—indeed, at the moment, he was totally incapable of feeling silly—but such gay abandon, or at least such jiggling of the legs, did not consort with his emotions. 'Ce n'est pas pour nous,' he whispered grimly to his lady, taking refuge from his enfeebled but persistent sense of humour in the unaccustomed language. 'Nous—nous allons boire.' Sylvie didn't seem to comprehend. The fact was that she quite liked sambas, they had the advantage of being athletic. He supposed that his accent was not up to the mark. 'Whisky!' He intoned the word in her ear ominously, yearningly, imperatively, and holding her tightly by the hand—actually by the little finger, which must have given her some pain—he jerked her off the dance floor and towards a chair, and then strode decisively in the direction of the bar.

Surveying the bottles and decanters, he was aware of a great lack of enthusiasm. He had better not drink any more; it was not as if he were alone; he should take his new responsibilities seriously. Nor should Sylvie drink any more; not that she showed the slightest sign of intoxication, he had to admit, but he didn't want her to get muddled about that hundred pounds . . . He came back to her carrying two large glasses of chilled pineapple juice.

'This will be good for you,' he said, a little too paternally.

'But I am not ill! However, I shall drink it, with pleasure,' she smiled, 'because I like it, not because it will be good for me.'

Without stopping to argue that point, he hastened back to the buffet and, after much gesticulation, persuaded Ahmed to fetch some olives from the refrigerator. The truth was, he felt rather unsteady on his legs and there was an odd distant humming in his ears, and the best way to take care of himself was to take care of someone else. Whether they needed it or not. In an access of the old puritanism he sniffed disapprovingly at a recumbent painter, reciting Baudelaire to the twitching cat.

'Look what I've found for you,' he told Sylvie with pride, 'fresh from the refrigerator!' A pity that he staggered noticeably. All the same, he thought, on the whole he compared well with the rest of the male guests. They were increasingly noisy; drinks were being spilt freely, and at frequent intervals came the tinkle of a breaking glass. Even Brett, in a corner with the Spanish heiress, the Romanoff ex-royalty and a young gossip-columnist, had relaxed sufficiently to slap a well-dressed back or two.

An outburst of ironical cheering indicated a new arrival. He stepped into the centre of the room, dispensing a general but carefully qualified smile, and stated by way of apology, 'I have been with the Patriarch.'

'Good old Marcel!' exclaimed Packet. He was always glad to see Marcel again, at any rate for a short time; and certainly Marcel would offer no serious threat to his possession of the young lady.

'Do you know Marcel Haggernetti?' she asked in some surprise.

'Oh yes . . . not intimately, perhaps,' he felt a silly blush rising, 'but for a long time.'

Marcel was getting on in years, but his continuous though varying enthusiasm, and the fact that his father (a tremendously shrewd and wealthy business man who had been lorded a generation ago) was still alive and active, endowed him with a general impression of comparative youthfulness. In physical appearance, however, he was far from youthful, being short and broad, with a slightly hunched back, a fleshy nose and a low and wrinkled brow. At times he could look more corrupt than one would have thought possible, outside the films—especially when wearing his beret and his sensuous and cynically understanding smile and hurrying down the street with nose lowered, in a perceptibly effeminate waddle, like an ignoble but determined bird of prey.

What was his nationality? He had an Egyptian passport, of course, and he was received in, though he did not frequent, the circles of the bashas. But he had once confided to Packet, in what he had hoped was the beginning of their intimacy, that his family had earlier held British passports and, while their patronym was distinctly Syrian, the distaff side was strongly Italian. But one did not think of him as a citizen, of whatever country. He carried his own world round with him, a world of miserliness, dubious mannerisms, temptations rarely overcome, a sporadic itch for respectability, complicated intrigues, a vast ambitiousness, and a multitude of enthusiasms.

It had not taken Packet long to discover that, beneath everything else, Marcel owned a shocking reputation. He moved in the highest circles without comment, and in the less high; but in the night streets, in the little bars with their long memories, he was an outcast. They would hardly lower themselves to serve him, even those who catered largely for whores, pimps and dope-pedlars. Once—it was in a very middling sort of bar—Packet had been warned in the strongest of terms against his friend, temporarily absent. 'Your friend no —— good,' the waiter had a certain fluency in colloquial English, 'he very bad man . . .' and some anecdotes involving shoe-blacks and newspaper-sellers had followed. 'Don't worry about me,' Packet assured him, but thereafter the waiter greeted him less warmly than of old, and soon he had ceased to go there.

But that was two years ago. Packet had soon come to terms with Marcel; they had agreed to meet from time to time, they had agreed to differ on other points. And now, though perhaps not as a result of his friend's good influence, Marcel was in the very middle of his most respectable period.

He had reformed (the word for him had no moral connotation, precisely). He had taken up the Church, or the Churches rather, and his house on the edge of the desert, formerly the scene of artistic and other salons, was now full of priests.

'Marcel is making quite a reputation for himself these days, isn't he?' Packet remarked to Sylvie. She had, she replied vaguely, heard talk about his lectures on the Desert Fathers.

Marcel had in fact discovered some neglected Egyptian saint—Packet couldn't remember the name, though Marcel had bored him enough with the story—St. Angostura, something of that kind—and had written and printed a monograph on the subject. The Church—or rather the Churches —had welcomed this unexpected ally with open arms. And Marcel's acquaintance thereupon became largely ecclesiastical. Even Packet had been tacitly excluded, not because he represented a link with any muddy past but merely on the grounds of his inveterate secularity. And the affair which was working up was emphatically not an English one, in any case: it was oriental, it was—Marcel liked the word very much—Byzantine. In the first instance, that was to say: afterwards it would be international, and even English.

For Marcel was not resting content with his corner in the obscure desert saint. He had something larger in mind. The novel he had been finishing—half as long again as *Forever Amber*, it dealt with a certain ancient Egyptian queen whose life and times made Cleopatra's court seem Victorian, and he had already half-secured a film contract for it—the great novel which had preoccupied him for the previous eighteen months was put aside. It also was too secular. And he no longer took the slightest interest in the Film as an Art Form or in the latest excitations of *Les Temps Modernes*. The politest bars received his meagre tips no more. And the only contributions he made to the local newspapers were of a severely ecclesiastical nature, accompanied perhaps by a photograph of himself, with head reverently bowed, shaking the hand of some bearded dignitary, or posed against the ruins of a Coptic monastery and wearing the modest but resolute expression of a master builder.

No, his latest was his greatest : something that would make the name of Haggernetti live as long as Christianity—and Christianity, under Marcel's auspices, was going to live a very long time. The union of the churches—nothing less. In this pursuit his late set of acquaintances could be of little use : writers, painters, teachers, publishers, film producers —they did not seem to realize that the churches were disunited. But they could easily be spared. Whatever Marcel's mission, two things remained constant—the energy he devoted to it, and the large number of people, all important in their way, which it involved. Packet had often reflected on his own lack of importance, his inability to be of use to Marcel in any of his careers ; he was not unaware that in the uncharitable public mind this fact relegated him to a disreputable category. However, never since their early days had Marcel reproached him for being neither fish nor flesh. The truth was that he liked to have just one disinterested and as it were neutral friend, a person who could be relied upon to express the decently orthodox point of view—one with which Marcel was keen to keep in touch—and in no unduly censorious spirit. As for Packet, he found the older man an amusing companion, in short doses, and felt that from him he was learning a good deal which it would not hurt him to know. His reaction against the debased puritanism of his upbringing did not persuade him to cast himself headlong into the depths of unconventionality, and he could not find perversions glamorous in themselves. They suffered from all the drawbacks of the usual thing and on top of that were so dreadfully vulnerable to even the most guarded and sympathetic sense of humour. What had surprised Packet was that Marcel could be, at times, such a good fellow.

And so, apart from temporary maudlinness, he greeted him warmly. Marcel shook his hand, with that short manly grip which characterized his periods of respectability, asked after Bacon and, lifting his eyebrows shortly, bowed ceremoniously to Sylvie. He was popular with the ladies, because he went out of his way to amuse and flatter them ; this he imposed upon himself as a special discipline, rather like a man who insists on garaging his car half a mile from home for the sake of the exercise. He took much of the virtue out of the bow, however, by remarking that he oughtn't to be there, really : the Patriarch was a broad-minded man, a man of the world as you might say, but all the same . . . He secured their forgiveness by the unregenerate grin with which he ended.

'You are attracting much attention these days,' Sylvie repaid the compliment. He shrugged his shoulders in a manner which Packet had from the first found almost seductive. 'The work was waiting for me. I simply happened to come along. Why has no-one done it before ? It's possible, you know—more than that, it's probable. We all have so much in common. All that's needed is the right kind of—what shall I say ?—catalyst : an intermediary who is trusted by all . . .'

Packet found this modesty definitely irritating. What the churches had in common, presumably, was a belief in God, and he doubted whether Marcel really shared that belief. But one couldn't mention such a doubt to him, one would only seem jealous. Packet was losing his iconoclastic tendencies. And perhaps, he thought, to be an efficient catalyst necessitated no more than a belief in oneself.

'How is it going ?' he merely asked therefore, rather inaptly. Marcel lowered his voice : the subject was sacred, and these surroundings indubitably profane. 'Very well, very well indeed. You understand that I cannot talk about the matter freely—it has reached a delicate stage, when the interference of men of ill will could still ruin everything. And there are such men,' he whispered, ' oh yes, you would be surprised. But you will be hearing great news soon, oh yes !'

He turned smartly away, in search of the host, who was an important man too, in his way. And his two admirers returned to their pineapple juice and their profane interests.

They were both tired ; they both felt it was time to leave, but neither liked to mention it to the other. In the next room the painters were singing ' Chevaliers de la Table Ronde'. The other guests were leaking away gradually, and Packet kept a close guard on his new friend.

Marcel, putting on his coat, tripped over to them again. His eyes were glittering, the barrel-shaped body seemed about to explode with excitement. He pinned them against the wall, breathing heavily into their faces.

' What *do* you think has happened, my dears ? Incredible ! '—this was the old Marcel, Packet remarked to himself —' El Hamama's sister left a huge flask of terribly expensive perfume in the bathroom, unopened—and it's gone ! Nothing left but the wrappings ! ' He tittered wickedly. ' She's awfully upset, quite hysterical . . . ' Then he remembered himself, his present self, the awfully disunited churches. He tightened his coat about his middle and re-set his face into sterner lines. Glancing quickly round the room to make sure that no-one else had witnessed the lapse, he bade them a curt farewell : ' I must go. I should never have come, of course . . . '

They could hear in the distance the voice of El Hamama cooingly consoling his sister. The painters had stopped singing, they sensed that something was amiss, they insisted loudly on sharing the awful secret, but their host was too polite to disclose the matter. It was undoubtedly time to go.

' I'll look for a taxi,' Packet offered.

'If you are not too tired after all the dancing we can walk. My flat is in town, not far from here. It will be pleasant by the sea. But perhaps you are tired?'

'No, not at all,' he replied, so weary that he could hardly stand. 'It will be *very* pleasant to walk by the sea.' The breeze would clear his head, at any rate. And there was something mournful and lovely about the waves breaking along the Corniche at night, in a whiteness that suddenly appeared out of nowhere and burned against the black night. And perhaps he could save her from some passing blackguard. He no longer felt tired in the least.

'But you live a long way out, don't you?' she said, 'so you must promise me to take a taxi back from town.'

Chapter 4

I AM NO APOSTLE OF NEW DOCTRINES

IT had been a grey week. A flurrying wind along the streets, not enough rain to lay the dust, and a persistent eddying draught which threw up scraps of paper and cigarette packets into one's lap and spirals of sand into the eyes. The cold sea was broken everywhere with angry bobbing short waves. It was the precise kind of weather, Packet grumbled, for which the city had not been intended, neither the *malayas* of the women, whipping against their sad splashed legs, nor the windows of his flat, which let in draughts at every joint. His servant had turned up in the morning with a swollen face and a foul temper, and Packet had sent him home with a stock of aspirin. He had cooked himself a rudimentary lunch on the defective primus stove. And now, in the early evening, he was waiting for Bacon to join him for a large dish of something in a gaunt but generous Greek restaurant.

Bacon was late. But Packet felt that he was using his time well. A couple at the next table were wrangling desultorily in a debased English. Neither was exactly English, but possibly both belonged to that outcast category which the English abroad were scrupulous to avoid, the British. The woman, little with small malevolent features and intensely black hair and eyes, might have been Maltese. The man, a good twenty years older, had thinning sandy hair and watery blue eyes. His accent eluded Packet : the product

of a Scottish-Egyptian union perhaps ? What could he be ?
A foreman in some factory ? Manager of one of the smaller
petrol stations ? Someone left behind after some war had
ended, who would never be at home anywhere ; possibly
married, with three or four scruffy children, all speaking
three or four languages badly, and a fat bullying wife who
had hoped for something better. Distrusted by the police,
the butt of the passport office, cringing to malicious little
officials who thumbed through his passport with its flippant
unicorn and inappropriate lion, each time he went to renew
his visa. Always talking about emigrating to Australia,
away from these dirty wogs, but secretly terrified by the
idea.

The woman offered less room for speculation. At the
moment she was making her companion's life very difficult.
Packet was at first alarmed by her careless use of words which
the English themselves rarely allow to pass beyond the lips.
He reminded himself that expressing oneself in a foreign
language often brought a freedom from conventional pres-
sures : he had said some remarkable things to Sylvie in
French, though not remarkable in the same way. Rather
self-consciously, like someone smoking against doctor's orders,
he pulled out his notebook.

'What's the matter ?' the man whined. 'Didn't I give
you a pair of stockings last week ?'

'That was last week. Take your hands off me. I must
go back to the club. They're expecting me.'

'I'll come too and wait till you're finished.' If he had
possessed a tail, he would have been wagging it hopelessly.
She was a hard one, Packet thought, she didn't make the
slightest attempt to conceal her opinion of him. Really,
what a charming girl Sylvie was—especially when one
considered what some girls were like. Sylvie : he wrote
her name ornately in the notebook.

'He'll be mad. Says it puts the customers off. Anyway,

who are you?' She looked at him as if she really didn't know. 'Are you my father?'

Clearly he made no pretensions to that status. 'I don't want to go home.'

'Pooh, you're drunk. You stink of it. Why don't you go and find yourself some rich sloppy widow. Do yourself some good.'

'You're the only friend I have.' The man pulled out his handkerchief.

Packet began to feel angry. They shouldn't go on like that, not in English, it was horrifying : the homely words carried such a black load of contempt and squalor. Shall I intervene, he thought. But he was interested as well. Good lord, he said to himself, this is the first trace of middle class social life that I've come across in Egypt, at least the first I could follow. Palaces of sin in plenty, and only too many wretched hovels. But this was exotic : they were talking neither of art, nor of sport, nor of business, nor of politics : it reminded him of home. However, he coughed loudly in the accepted manner and pulled out a copy of *The Times* which he spread ostentatiously over his table : they ought to be warned that he could understand them. Had he pulled out a Union Jack and swathed himself in it, it would have made no difference.

'Don't be silly. Mimi is very fond of you. Why don't you dance with her?'

'I don't like dancing, you know that. I want someone to take care of me.' Good God, Packet wondered, what language did they use when they weren't going on like this? They must have another language, a kind of native tongue, for everyday use. Or perhaps they didn't usually talk at all.

'Go to England !' Her voice thudded against the wilting wretch like a boot against a dog's side. 'Go and find your precious relatives—if you can !'

'I shall be nice to you, why aren't you nice to me?'

' Shut your mouth. I have a headache, I'm bleeding . . .
don't you believe me ? And I've gotta dance till midnight.
Don't you believe me ? . . . ' And so forth. Packet was
reading *The Times* quite avidly when Bacon at last arrived.

He was out of breath. No, he couldn't sit down—he
ordered a speedy beer—a most unfortunate thing had
happened. The building in which he lived was in chaos :
the police had raided one of the apartments, they had found
some dubious literature—three or four old Left Book Club
issues and—of course they couldn't read the title—a copy
of Plato's *Republic* in Greek. These they had carefully taken
away, and, less carefully, their owner, a serious young Greek,
about seventeen years old. His mother, a widow who
doted on her son, was almost mad with fear ; and Bacon, as
a government employee, had offered to go to the *caracol* and
see what could be done at once, while consular officials began
the slower procedure of intervention at a higher level.
Packet readily offered to go with him—action would take
the taste of the sordid couple out of his mouth, and he had
already lost his appetite—so they dashed out and into the
waiting taxi.

On the way Bacon explained that, apart from mere
humanity, he felt obliged to take a hand—young Andrea,
a pleasant studious boy, was keen on improving his English
and so Bacon had passed on to him the Left Book Club
volumes ages ago, together with a number of harmless
Penguins. At school they used Basic English texts, and
Andrea deserved better than that.

' I'd forgotten that we live in a *situation*. Though, heaven
knows, it's an old, old story that those books tell ! '

It was an ancient *caracol*, bulging in all directions with
built-on rooms and precarious balconies, and so it provided
ample shelter from wind or sun. Scores of policemen stood
or sat around, chatting vivaciously with their families ;

there was much selling of baked maize and brewing of thick frothy coffee. Several of the *shawish* had removed their boots ; some were sleeping, while half-naked children tugged at their immense rifles. The women were squatting over bowls of greasy beans, their funereal robes at odds with their animated chatter and large emphatic gestures.

That all this was not incompatible with efficiency was proved by their reception. Armed figures suddenly converged from all sides upon the porch where a moment ago children had been playing a kind of hopscotch. It looked to Packet as if they would enter either under arrest or not at all. But Bacon spoke soothingly and proffered a suitably small gift, and the guards at once lost interest in them.

They walked along a wide corridor, where the whitewash had flaked away long before, picking a path between crouching groups of wailing women with mummified babies clutched to them, and naked youngsters dumped down on the dirty floor and quite unaffected by the wild grief around them. Bacon was worried. ' Not one of the better places, I'm afraid. Let's hope the officers are good-tempered.'

They entered a large hall crowded with moving figures. Packet came to a dead stop. Alarm and surprise he was ready for, but not this. Even Bacon paused for a moment : his good intentions wavered in front of this sight. Where could one begin one's explanations ? There seemed to be no foothold.

There was a long raised platform at the end of the hall which supported three tables. At each table sat a police officer in shabby uniform : one was intent on a newspaper, one was drinking coffee with a thoughtful expression, one was cleaning his ears rather proudly with a piece of pencil. Each was surrounded by a lively group of civilians who used the *caracol* as a kind of social club—relatives of the officer, who basked in his glory and at the same time contributed their mite to it, friends with a minute or an hour to spare, and

even sheer strangers (if indeed such there were) who happened
to be passing . . . Handcuffs, rifles, truncheons, wands and
ankle-irons festooned the walls, diversified here and there
with an official portrait of the monarch (the more sensitive
officials mitigated their patriotism by hanging early ones),
or an advertisement for some soft drink showing a very
Western young lady in the kind of bathing costume which
these policemen, had they encountered it on the public
beaches, would have been obliged shamefacedly to take into
custody. Remembering it later, Packet mused over the
innocence of it : it had been put up simply for its splash of
colour, it could as well have been a cow as the lush and
expansive blonde that it was, the schoolboy's dream of
woman. These people had no use for such excitations or
substitutes ; it really was the soft drink that they were
interested in.

But there was no time for such cogitations then. Part of
the wall to the left of the platform was taken up by a curious
machine which fascinated Packet : it resembled a witness
box, but was much larger, built out from the wall, with
a section of the front palings serving as a door. Inside this
wooden structure were packed between twenty-five and
thirty of the most frightening creatures that he had ever
seen—men of all ages, very ragged, some bleeding, and—
which upset him most of all—completely silent. Not a
sound came from them, they made not a movement, as they
stood crammed together, the heads of those nearest the rails
lolling apathetically over. A youngish woman in a *malaya*,
her head uncovered and hair falling over her face, stood in
the very centre of the hall, shrieking continuously at the top
of her voice and beating her breast and swaying from side to
side. No-one took much notice of her, she might have been
crying the evening papers on a busy corner in a city street ;
but from time to time a *shawish* shouted something to her
and an appreciative roar went up from those close enough to

hear. Along the long wall opposite the wooden cage was a row of boys squatting down, chained together wrist to wrist. A row of policemen stood behind them, roughly one *shawish* to three boys. At frequent intervals other boys were brought in and added to the collection, the policemen tapping the others sharply on their heads with clubs to make them move up. The *shawish* talked steadily among themselves, occasionally breaking off to administer a disinterested blow or twist an arm ; a boy would cry out in pain or fear, but no-one seemed irreparably damaged.

Packet pulled at Bacon's sleeve. ' But what chance have we got ? ' Above everything rose the yells of the madwoman. The two Englishmen had to pass between her and the squatting prisoners. Packet closed his eyes, making himself as small as possible, and hoping for everyone's sake that he looked not too outraged, not too clean and not too virtuous. Striving for some common ground on which he could meet this situation, and having nothing at all useful to say, he gesticulated excitedly to his companion, he screwed up his face in his determination to look villainous and thus to fit in somewhere, to become a part of this awfully foreign scene. ' O Christ ! ' Bacon swore to himself. ' O Allah ! ' he added thoughtfully, and slipped through the crowd maintaining a carefully neutral expression.

It was for the coffee-drinking officer that he was making. It seemed the most hopeful : newspaper readers are notoriously short-tempered, and the ear-cleaner too was preoccupied, and repulsive as well. He was received well, even with ceremony. He replied formally, with even more ceremony, for he remembered that the Prophet had said, ' If ye are greeted with a greeting, then greet ye with a better greeting, or at least return it ; God taketh count of all things.' And then he told his story in Arabic. There was a chorus of sympathetic murmurs from the bystanders, who were now drifting over from the other tables. Something was afoot :

foreigners often got themselves into particularly fascinating trouble.

'I do not understand well,' remarked the officer in English, 'what it is you wish.'

Helpful suggestions were noisily proposed by his friends and relatives ; he thumped the table angrily and shouted for silence. Bacon repeated the outline of the story, this time in English, partly to flatter the officer, partly to keep the ever-increasing audience out of the affair. If the captain could kindly tell them where the young Greek was, how he was, what charge was to be brought against him, where he would be taken. . . . Bacon hardly expected the man to know many of the answers, but he would enjoy being supposed to know them, and that would be something gained, that would be a beginning. The officer asked the name of the prisoner, looked in a large book rather like those in which careful housewives of the past used to compile recipes and household hints, asked the name again, and again searched painfully through the book. Then he put it down, threw up his eyes towards heaven, and apparently dismissed the matter. Bacon waited patiently ; Packet felt increasingly despondent.

After a few minutes of meditation the officer lowered his eyes, perceived that the troublesome Englishmen were still there, asked the name of the prisoner once again, his address and age, and then walked across to the desk of his neighbour. The latter put down his paper, greeted his colleague as if they had not met for several months, and they had a long talk. Eventually he returned with another book and thumbed slowly through it. It yielded no results, apparently, for he flung it down in annoyance and looked round for some legitimate victim for his wrath. Noticing the woman, still pirouetting in the centre of the hall, he shook his arm at her wildly. '*Bas, bas, yallah!* Ibrahim, take that she-idiot away !' A *shawish* hustled her out, but her wails were still audible in the distance.

Chapter 4

' *Fein el ketaab* ? Where is my book ? What fool has removed my book ? ' he yelled. Packet wondered whether they were both about to be bludgeoned and thrown into the cage : anything might happen, he felt. The wretches in the cage probably didn't know why they were there, and possibly the police themselves had forgotten by now, they had so much villainy to think about. Unconsciously he lolled his head apathetically, in preparation for that fate. Three or four *shawish* came running up, one of them with his club at the ready : the officer dispatched them in various directions and slumped back exhausted in his chair. After a few moments he remembered his foreign guests.

' They are fools. How much better was it in the time of Major Dawson Basha. They are. fools, these Egyptians ! '

Bacon shrugged his shoulders in a gesture that could have meant anything. In an agony of discomfort Packet suddenly broke out, ' Oh no ! ' The officer gave him a quick suspicious look.

After two refusals the officer took one of Bacon's offered cigarettes, with the utmost ceremony. He chatted casually with them. How many children had they . . . they were not married ? That was very strange . . . why were they not married ? . . . what was their work ? . . . *Ya salaam*, one of his sons was studying the English at the university— he hoped the reverend professors would be merciful to his son in the time of examinations . . . ' *Insh' Allah*,' responded Packet, ' If God wills,' hitting the right note this time and winning a smile.

He spoke English well himself, the officer confided, he had served under English commandants . . . everything had been much better then . . . if the English had stayed, he would have been a colonel by now . . . why, the Captain Jones many years ago loved him like a son, he would say to him " Mahmoud, you are the laziest, craftiest bugger in this bloody country ; if you weren't a *shawish* you would have been hanged long ago " . . . ah, a genteelman, the Captain Jones . . . The Egyptians, he confessed, were not genteelmen . . . he was sad today, he was unwell . . . he suffered much from diarrhœa.

'Gird up your strength, O Captain,' Bacon urged. The officer looked infinitely tragic but made the customary response. 'The girding up rests with Allah, O Teacher.' Packet was taken with a terrible desire to giggle : not, at any rate, with the English, he thought.

At last the book was found. The officer went slowly through it, following the entries with his finger. Clearing his throat, he spat delicately behind him, and began to write down Bacon's name, address, occupation and passport number, and then Packet's. As the question, it seemed, could not be delayed any longer, he asked Bacon what he would like the police to do ; he was, he insisted, a very sympathetic man, well known for his kindness, and ready to help everyone in their troubles. Bacon explained that the guilty books found in the Greek boy's possession were in fact his, and that therefore, if anyone ought to be in prison, it was he. The officer smiled broadly at the outrageous suggestion.

'But you are an Englishman. You can read anything you wish. In any case, this is a civilized land. We are compelled sometimes to put the students in prison when they make trouble. But never do we put the teachers there.'

This was too good to be missed, and so he repeated it all in Arabic for the benefit of the public. They were highly amused, with the exception of one little man who really thought that Bacon was expecting to be thrown into gaol therewith. He pushed his way through, clambered on to the platform, and clawed at Bacon's sleeve—'Neffer is the professor treated bad. They are the good wise man. We all love him.' So intense, Packet thought, so excited, like the humble admirer who springs on to the scaffold to plead for the condemned aristocrat : but he hoped that the little man would not create a crisis. The officer pushed and the others pulled and the little man disappeared from the platform ; below he was thumped and yelled at until regretfully he was forced to understand that no-one had threatened anyone, that everyone was friendly with everyone else, that the effendi had only been joking. He sidled out in a huff.

' But these books are not in the least wicked or harmful. These books in yellow covers,' Bacon went on soothingly, ' are very respectable—written by members of the English government.'

' Wait please.' The officer consulted the ledger. ' It is not the yellow books with the funny titles that are bad. It is the black book, the *Grigi* book—that is very bad book indeed.' No-one spoke up this time in defence : a general solemnity crept over the crowd.

' What black book ? '

' The *Grigi* book by the man whose name is Platon. A dangerous and wicked book. That is well known to all.'

' The *Republic* ! Oh dear no ! But that book was written over two thousand years ago. It is philosophy, it is not politics.'

Having a more subtle thought to express, the officer changed over to Arabic, and the discussion became general once again.

' What was bad two thousand years ago is no less bad today. It is more bad, like everything else. Philosophy is your clever word for politics. I am only a poor police captain, but you cannot deceive me. *Republic*—that is a political word, a bad word to speak. The *Grigi* themselves hate Platon—they will not allow his book in their country.'

' Books are evil things, O Captain,' interjected one of the hangers-on, a degenerate specimen who had obviously never opened one. ' An *Afrit* lives in them.'

' Except the Koran, except the Koran,' admonished the officer.

' The Koran is not a book, O Captain,' offered another, ' it is a Word.'

They all grunted assent and nodded in admiration of this wise saying. The officer called for another coffee. He invited the Englishmen to partake of it, but Bacon declined politely, not wishing to prolong the negotiations indefinitely. One of the company passed the officer a cigarette, another hastened to light it ; he stretched his legs luxuriously, murmuring, ' The Koran is not a book—very good, very good,' and nodded his head appreciatively.

' Then may I see the boy for a moment ? ' Bacon persisted. ' So that I can tell his mother that he is in good hands ? ' The temper of the assembly was verging on the aphoristic-metaphysical, he could see, and the question of poor Andrea was drifting out of sight. The officer contrived to convey a feeling of disappointment that the Englishman was something of a Philistine, with no taste for higher things.

' You love the *Grigi* boy,' he remarked in English, with the common omission of the interrogatory inflection. The spectators grinned uncomprehendingly.

' Certainly not. That is, I do not *love* him. He is simply my neighbour.'

They should have brought Sourayah with them, Packet was thinking, and let her loose ; or perhaps he himself ought to claim to love Andrea—they would appreciate that, a *grande passion* would enlist their sympathies. Disinterested action always looked a little suspicious.

' Then you love his mother.'

' No, not in the least. She is very old.'

' Perhaps you love his sister.' The officer leered incredibly, while the others waited agape for some tremendous if incomprehensible revelation.

' No, alas,' Bacon made a supreme effort. ' I regret to

say that he has no sister.' He achieved a gesture of intense regret and foiled lechery. The officer was greatly amused. He roared with mirth. 'I regret to say that he has no sister— good, very good . . .' The audience laughed in sympathy.

'. . . but I have nothing to do with this case, you understand. I have many important cases,' he pointed sternly to the wooden enclosure from which unsmiling faces peered in dull curiosity. 'Pickpockets and robbers—very bad men who have no education. I am their teacher. For the *Grigi* you must speak with the Captain Ahmed.'

They were conducted along the long mournful corridor, smelling more pungently of urine than ever, to a small room near the entrance, where Bacon again explained the nature of their errand. The young officer listened with great interest, asked them their names, addresses and occupations, passed some derogatory comments on the extra-mural activities of university students and commiserated with them on the same score.

'But you must see the Captain Ahmed. It is he who is in charge of political crimes. He has left the station just now.'

'How long will he be away?' Packet marvelled at his friend's patience.

'Not long, not long—three minutes, perhaps, or,—with a large and casual wave of the hand—'twelve. Please take a chair, sirs. Be at home.'

They sat down and waited. Three minutes passed. The young lieutenant manicured his nails, yawned gigantically, pored over some official instruction book. Bacon and Packet conversed in an undertone, but it sounded so ridiculously conspiratorial that they soon fell into silence. Packet tried to shake off this sick feeling of uselessness by thinking of Sylvie : so fresh, calmly independent, a little remote. But too remote from all this, there was no connection : he couldn't escape that way. Twelve minutes passed.

All the same, Packet was thankful that they had extricated themselves from the other place, the chamber of horrors—that apotheosis of Goya, Caligari and Kafka. Goya, Caligari and Kafka—yes, one could write up the incident and send it to one of the more serious weeklies at home. He composed a few sample sentences in his head, to get the feel of it. ' The suave officials, mounted on their high dais, scribbled importantly in large dog-eared ledgers. From time to time, they '—he looked hopefully at the young lieutenant—' they yawned, cleared their throats . . . hawked ? . . . While below them . . . in the pit ? . . . in the dreadful pit . . . the mad woman danced and shrieked, and the impassive policemen . . . impassive ? . . . rhythmically clubbed the filthy urchins . . . no, the miserable and half-naked children, chained together like . . . like . . . ' A shiver—of indignation, but also of æsthetic satisfaction—ran through him. He began to feel better, more at home almost. Yes, one of the left-wing periodicals. What should he call it ? In an Egyptian Prison ? Or something smarter, something to catch the eye. The Middle East, The Middle Ages ? Coca-Cola and After ? He felt for his pocket-book. The evening became much less painful.

Bacon was more vulnerable. He felt far from his best. Perhaps he was getting stale : he had been in this country a long time, and though its physical climate was comfortable enough, the same couldn't be said of its moral one. The awful discrepancy between the labour and the accomplishment, at any rate what one could glimpse of the accomplishment—wearing enough in any teaching of the arts—had seemed to weigh more heavily on him this year. Perhaps he ought to make it his last year here ? But by European standards he was a poor man : and what should he do instead ? Return to England's uncomfortable climate and its equable moral temperature ? His work here had unfitted him to teach English children in an English school, and at his age that was the only work he could expect to find. And, he went on to himself, what I am doing tonight is unfitting me for what I am supposed to do tomorrow night ; not that that matters . . .

'I'm on at the Cultural Centre tomorrow,' he remarked to Packet. 'They're having a sort of symposium on Education —yes, just like that—a Brains Trust—with a distinguished visitor, Professor Pitt, you know, the adult education man —who's on his way to lecture in India. And the Minister of Education from Cairo—who is it now ? Zaki Bey I believe. And old Still-Waters of course. They asked me to join in.'

'I should jolly well think so,' Packet emerged from his book. 'You know more about it than the rest put together.' He returned to his scribbling, looking up a moment later to say, 'I shall be there to cheer you.'

But why this invasion of bitterness, Bacon puzzled, why these assiduous attentions from the nasty little demon he had turned out years ago ? Old age perhaps : maybe idealism was to be his brand of senility, the little demon in his Sunday best. Ask for a lot, and ye shall receive nothing at all. Wasn't it enough to lose a wife and be poor and have no pension—wasn't that enough in the way of hostages—but must he be visited with boils as well ? Perhaps it was only the weather, together with this silly affair of Andrea. Andrea was a nice boy—rather shy, reserved, very clean—for an English boy of his age, he would be thought excessively tidy, but then, he had been born in Athens, and this spotless-ness of his was probably due to his consciousness of being a semi-exile in a city which became less Greek and more Arab every year. And perhaps a small unconscious protest against that fact. The neat suits, the fresh shirts, the im-peccably trimmed (but never oiled) hair, and the scrubbed sensitive face : these were harmless by-products of a historical process, a process which in Bacon's countrymen and contemporaries manifested itself in a crazy and inaccurate jingoism or in drunkenness or in other and rarer eccentricities.

There was old Lord Hubbard in his big house up on the hill, an ancient Anglo-Egyptian who gave the impression of having followed quickly on Napoleon's heels. He collected curious literature and young women. The latter he entertained *tête-à-tête* over tea and sweet cakes, grunting forbiddingly at them and yet steering the conversation away from indelicate topics with as much care as if they had been the innocent *débutantes* that none of them were. The erotic books he lent to their husbands—on the understanding, which was less than tacit, that they would thus be kept occupied and could therefore release their wives to take tea with Lord Hubbard. Occasionally it happened that a wife more ingenuous than the run of them would let drop the fact that her husband had shown her the borrowed literature. The host's red face would swell and purple and, once again incredulous, he would inveigh against the utterly impossible young people of today and their repellent marital customs. His chauffeur would be summoned to escort the trembling guest to her squalid home—and to collect the books—and Lord Hubbard would cast about him for another attractive young woman.

And then there was Ackers, previously director of some big bank, the owner of a large and handsome residence in the old foreign quarter ; closed to all but a chosen few who walked about it in their stockinged feet, it was given over entirely to lizards of all shapes and sizes. And Haytor, who by now had probably forgotten what he originally came to Egypt for, whose aged wife cooked cheap meals for them over an ancient charcoal stove, while ten skilled gardeners worked all day on his acre of land. The flowers were rumoured to make a breathtakingly beautiful show, and their perfumes could be smelt from afar. But he had built a twelve-foot wall around them, surmounted by cruel iron spikes and broken glass, and the door was unlocked only to let the gardeners in and out.

But Andrea was only a boy ; rather good at languages and fond of reading. Not philosophical in his tastes, nor political—if he had read Bacon's discarded books it was only to increase his vocabulary, and the *Republic* he probably hadn't read at all—it was in his room just as a symbol of the old Greece. He was concerned to keep himself out of other people's dirt, to give no offence nor to find himself in a situation where he could not but take offence : as if he were waiting, as politely as possible, for something to end, for a real life to begin, in a different house, a different street, a different land. There was no trace of superciliousness about the boy ; he was well liked by all the neighbourhood, a very mixed one, and a particular favourite with Sourayah. I suppose he really is a clean upstanding young man, Bacon mused, in the original and rare meaning of the phrase.

He recalled a story which Andrea's mother had told him once. It happened some ten years before, soon after they had come from Athens. She was sitting with Andrea on the verandah of a café facing the sea ; it was a birthday treat for him, and he was busy with a large and complex ice-cream. She had noticed three Egyptian army officers sitting at the next table in animated conversation, only vaguely noticing them, until she felt the elbow of one of them, the fattest and least prepossessing, determinedly rotating in her ribs. Moving her chair away did not help, as the officer's chair, protesting noisily, followed suit. It was not particularly surprising ; she was a rather handsome woman ten years ago. And so she merely changed to a seat at the other side of the table. Almost immediately a man who turned out to be the manager of the café came to her and whispered : ' *Mais, Madame, c'est le Roi !* You did not recognize him ? Why, you have won his favour—he is very agreeable to women, you have nothing to fear ! ' Securing no response he retreated, with a nervous glance towards the officers : he too was an alien.

She had not been long in Egypt, she did not see why Andrea's treat should be spoilt, and so she gripped her cake-fork and stared coldly back at her staring admirer. But then Andrea put his spoon down, he had turned slightly pale and his lips quivered. ' Let's go home, mama ! ' She refused to give in, to be driven away from her lawful tea. She was furious. But Andrea cried again, ' I don't like this place, mama, please let's go home, I don't like this ice-cream.' And so they left. ' He had not heard a word of what the manager said,' she told Bacon, ' he knew nothing, and yet he knew better than I. How foolish I was in those days ! '

The lad was most likely being transferred elsewhere while they were sitting there. ' The captain has not returned yet,' he remarked to the lieutenant, with only a hint of reproach in his voice. ' Perhaps he is very busy ? ' One couldn't be sure that this Captain Ahmed really existed.

' He will come at once, effendi, I swear it. Five minutes,' he jerked his thumbs, ' ten minutes . . .'

The fatal mistake would be to lose one's temper, to reveal oneself as the traditional Englishman, asserting authority, quoting laws, demanding action. No good would be done that way, and Andrea's cause might well be harmed. Egyptians could throw their weight about and no-one really minded : it was the accepted way of getting things done in an entertaining if roundabout fashion. Each little clerk yelled at the littler clerk below him ; and the process ran all along the line, like shunting, from the fat excitable basha at the board meeting down to the thin excitable doorkeeper at the warehouse.

But once let a European—and particularly an Englishman —throw his weight about, and things were very different. It simply wasn't the same kind of weight. And moreover it was like throwing your weight at a rubber dummy : the

status quo swayed serenely back into place. Cringing, begging
for favours, was equally dangerous. If they disliked foreigners
who behaved like foreigners, then they detested foreigners
who behaved like natives. There was a certain solidarity
about them, a communal and cheerful lack of respect, both
for themselves and for each other, which worked well enough
in practice, but was at once imperilled by the entrance of a
foreigner. A sense of disrespectful community, having
nothing to do with moral attitudes or attitudinizing, out of
which at times a truly glorious tolerance could spring.
Bacon had a good deal of admiration for this—what would
you call it?—system? It was by no means systematic. But
system or no system, it was sometimes more humane than
the systems of the serious-minded West. He thought of the
celebrated refugees who had found shelter in Egypt : those
who, guilty or innocent, would have been persecuted in
almost every other country, had found toleration here. But
Justice, for whom some representation altogether different
from the blindfold bearer of scales would have to be found,
was so frighteningly arbitrary. It was equally true that
many poor unfortunates had here met with horrors which
the more careful West would never have seen fit to inflict.
Poor unfortunates, the victims of sheer bad luck, like Andrea
perhaps.

Patience and humour were Bacon's best weapons, his only
weapons at the moment. The first he could simulate, he
had been well trained in that respect, but the other seemed
increasingly difficult to evoke. How powerful it could be,
a broad simple joke, rising out of circumstance ! Almost
powerful enough to bring Captain Ahmed running back
from the café where very probably he was lost in political
debate at this moment. Well, he was thankful that Packet
wasn't overwhelmingly British ; it was a comfort having
him here. Bacon turned to him.

' " The silence of a wise man is more wrong to mankind

than the slanderer's speech." ' A great thought, no doubt,
the kind of thing that students copy into their notebooks ;
but it seemed to mean nothing at all. Packet looked up
vaguely : the tone of his article was giving him trouble.

' What was that you said ? '

' I think it was Wycherley who said it.'

' Really ? Not about himself, I hope.'

' That's what I was wondering. You have to persuade
yourself that you *are* wise before persuading yourself out
of silence. And into print.' He managed not to cast a
glance in the direction of Packet's notes. ' It's so easy to
be a well-meaning slanderer. Intellectual political circles
are full of them—the international armchair experts. The
cream of the earth, no doubt—but in our political atmosphere
the cream is turning sour.'

' Slander ? ' Packet was only half-way out of his notebook, still busy taming reality, but he sensed Bacon's uneasiness. ' Of course, poor Plato—a wise old Communist !
That's what happens to philosophers when they give their
works comprehensible titles. Explains a lot. Er, that was
what you were saying ? '

' Roughly,' Bacon replied, ' very roughly.'

Yes, Packet was a comfort. But he'd got on well with
Egyptians right from the start. Perhaps because he was
interested in people's vices as well as their virtues—whereas
the Ascendancy representatives were careful to let it be known
that virtue was the only thing that interested them in the
least, and that only because it made for efficiency. The
favourite phrase of the Ascendancy—now so unmistakably
in the descendant—came into Bacon's head. ' This would
never happen in England ! ' He had certainly used it himself,
especially in those early years. But it was a stupid thing to
say. So many things hadn't happened in England simply
because they had happened, under English auspices, abroad.
And that thought, too, led to a similar bitterness. That salt

destroying sea beneath which nothing could grow, the sea which was eating away at our human coasts, all over the world. By association he thought of the great European reclaimer, that coastguard of humanity who, for once, had united energy with intelligence and intelligence with good will : and Goethe's words came into his head. ' How could man live at all if he did not give absolution every night to himself and all his brothers ? '

But he dreamt miserably, self-indulgingly, of Andrea in some English police station, drinking a cup of hot stewed tea, while the sergeant—who had attended W.E.A. classes in philosophy—read bits from the *Republic*. That was the thought of tomorrow's symposium again : Pitt would be sure to mention Plato, and very probably policemen as well.

Another half-hour passed by while Bacon's thoughts revolved in the same painful circle, all the events of his twenty-odd years in Egypt translating themselves into moral comment ; and while Packet bit his pencil, scribbled and crossed out, stared gloomily at the assiduously self-grooming lieutenant, or tried to recall Sylvie's features.

Then the Captain Ahmed arrived. A handsome young-looking man, in well kept uniform, with a brisk moustache and a pleasant smile—the two Englishmen felt their hopes rise again. The lieutenant began to explain the position to his superior in a pedantic manner, but the captain brushed him gently aside, came over to them and shook hands. He was sorry to have kept them waiting, he had been called to the Governorate (I was wrong about the café, Bacon gladly admitted to himself). Yes, the case of the young Greek : it was very unfortunate, and—between themselves of course —quite ridiculous, but he did not expect that any charge would be brought. It had been a mistake in the first case —he explained, in a whisper calculated not to reach his subordinate's ear—the police had been instructed to raid the house of an oldish Greek further down the same street, a retired printer suspected of organizing a Communist cell— but they missed their target.

'Greek names all sound rather alike to us Egyptians,' the captain remarked, not unpleasantly, 'just as all Egyptians look alike to you English, I believe.' The old man had vanished during the commotion set up by Andrea's protesting neighbours, leaving behind him quantities of leaflets containing scabrous anecdotes about His Majesty and embellished with appropriate cartoons, all unlikely to inspire loyalty to the Palace. The officer in charge of the raiding party, a more than usually susceptible patriot, had been so incensed by these leaflets that he insisted on holding Andrea ; it had also seemed preferable not to return empty-handed.

'A matter of circumstances,' the captain said deprecatingly. 'But, as for those silly books, I do not think that we need take them very seriously.' Stifling a blush, Bacon expressed grateful agreement.

The captain proposed that they should visit Andrea. 'You understand of course that I have no orders to release him, but we will take good care of him until they come. He has a little cell to himself, one of our better rooms.'

As they moved off Packet, feeling brighter, questioned the captain about the line of boys (miserable and half-naked children, he almost said) squatting in the hall. What had they done ? He was scrupulous to avoid any hint of censoriousness.

'Done ? Perhaps nothing. The policemen pick the boys up in the streets—begging, perhaps, or selling things without a licence, or in bad company—bring them here for a few hours, and then release them.'

Packet looked puzzled, so the captain continued, 'In the hope that they will continue to do nothing worse than beg or sell without a licence or frequent bad company.'

' So you do nothing to them ? '

' To them ? No, of course not. Nor for them . . . '

They walked back through the large hall, down another corridor, across a small courtyard, and thus came to a block of little cells. All was quiet here, in contrast to the hideous mixture of noises which poured from an outlying building. ' The big cells,' the captain explained, pointing in that direction, ' full with murderers and robbers and pimps. We have too little room for them.'

He peered into the first little cell, into the second and the third ; the next two were empty. They sensed a growing agitation as he walked quickly to the end of the row. ' He must be here, then.' But he was not. The three of them regarded each other with sickly smiles. Oh let there be some simple and tolerable explanation, Packet prayed. The captain's smile quickly faded, and Bacon's heart sank the rest of the way : there wasn't anything amusing about it, he thought he knew what had happened, and he suspected that the captain knew too. And the latter stated, with a painful lack of conviction, ' We must not jump to conclusions.' He yelled for the warder, and a fierce and ever fiercer discussion reverberated through the small building, drawing a couple of the less cynical political prisoners to the bars of their cells—' *Abou lissanen*—Father of two tongues ! ' —until the quivering subordinate almost grovelled in the dust. ' There has been a mistake,' the captain told them bleakly, and he strode off towards the centre of the uproar. Bacon gripped Packet by the arm and they hurried after him.

There had been a mistake. A mistake of category. But even so it took them a little time to locate Andrea. The warder was too terrified to be of any assistance, and the captain thrust his way into the crowded pen, flinging the contents this way and that, and shouting the boy's name. They would all be murdered, they would be trampled to death, the old warder screeched, as he rushed away to fetch reinforcements or at any rate to save himself. The prisoners, however, did no more than increase the volume of their cursing, making the captain's search as difficult as possible, elbowing each other and trying to trip him. Bacon pushed his head and shoulders through the open door of the pen, peering desperately about at the tangled indistinguishable limbs—an action which Packet admired but felt entirely unable to emulate : in any case it struck him that he wouldn't know Andrea if he saw him. A wall of stench rose around them. He plucked at his friend's sleeve. 'For God's sake be careful !' As if Bacon were leaning over the edge of a cliff. But he felt no fear, except the fear of being sick. A picture of Naples flashed through his mind : a hunchback dragged along the street by two policemen at night. That had been bad enough to see—but they had soon passed on, out of his sight.

The captain straightened himself, raising by an armpit a lean figure clothed in a *gallabieh* of shabby coarse grey material. Bacon knew that it must be Andrea : but the head had been shaved, the face was a nondescript yellowy-brown, sullen and glistening with sweat. It had to be Andrea —because the captain was hauling him out of the jammed cell, as gently as he could, swearing at the others and cuffing them to make them move over—but it could just as well have been a murderer or a thief or a pimp. Out of the goodness of his heart the captain was speaking to the boy in English, telling him that there had been a mistake, that he would spend the rest of the night by himself in pleasanter surroundings and his own clothes would be returned to him, that tomorrow no doubt he would be free. 'Yes,' Bacon put in, 'it's only till tomorrow morning, Andrea. Everything will be all right now.' But the blank head, the face that was raceless and even characterless, turned towards them for a moment, a tear or two ran to join the sweat, and Andrea turned away, pulling at the captain's sleeve. The captain led his prisoner past the gathering of armed policemen, speechless with curiosity, to the other block of cells.

Bacon had dashed away without a word to his companion. Just as he was about to catch him up, Packet was hailed by a sergeant. The latter had been instructed to hand over a number of books to the Englishmen. Would the effendi please sign a receipt for them? Four books in yellowish cloth covers. Packet snatched them up and ran out of the *caracol*, but there was no trace of Bacon. The fresh night air fell on his damp face like a shower. He began to walk to the nearest tram station: there would just be time to drop in at his flat and wash and change, and then he would call for Sylvie as arranged. There was nothing further they could do for Andrea. And it might be more tactful to leave Bacon to himself for a while: he would hardly be amused to see his books returning. He was not teaching at the university the next day, but Packet would be seeing him at the Cultural Centre in the evening.

There was a receptacle for rubbish at the station. Packet pushed into it the sheets on which he had scribbled the rough draft of his noble and indignant article. He had enough to carry, with the books.

Chapter 5

HAVE THEY A LADDER FOR HEARING
THE ANGELS?

' EDUCATION : Its Scope and Aims ' : it was an
ambitious project, this symposium, and the Cultural
Centre felt rather proud of themselves. Hundreds
of printed invitations had gone out, the event had received
great publicity in the local English, French and Greek press,
and the general public were quite free to attend.

There was a considerable amount of education in Egypt,
of one kind and another—English, French, Greek, Italian,
Jewish, Moslem, Armenian, Berlitz, Fax, Scottish, Swiss,
German, American, private, public, several kindergarten
establishments (one had been closed down recently when an
unannounced tax inspector had discovered a number of
rather old girls plying a different trade there), monastic,
conventual, and of course Egyptian. In addition there was
a considerable amount of plain illiteracy.

Yet there was next to no public *discussion* of all this. That
was to say, Greek headmasters rarely if ever got together
with their Jewish colleagues, to thrash things out; Moslem
instructors never seemed to sit down and compare notes
with the pedagogues from the Scottish Church School.
This latter, incidentally, was a somewhat paradoxical institution, in that it was sponsored by the Scottish Church's
Mission to the Jews and at the same time prevented by
Egyptian law from attempting proselytization. In the course

of time and adversity it had acquired teachers of every nationality or lack of nationality and of every faith or lack of faith. And, though in perpetual need of funds, it now offered a very reasonable approximation to British education for those who boggled at Egyptian schools but were unable to afford the inflated fees charged by the full-dress English ones. It is in such places that the true heroes of education are to be found.

On the whole, in fact, education featured as a secondary topic of café conversation—which school does your child attend? Oh? What kind of car have you?—and the question flamed up for a moment only when some influential parent in an access of bad temper removed his offspring from a school where it did nothing but play tennis and swim and develop unsightly leg muscles and sent it instead to a school where it thought clearly about a number of obscure subjects, took to wearing spectacles and lost weight. Or, as happened precisely half the time, the other way about.

The situation, it was felt, ought to be clarified. Of course, common tact—with which the Cultural Centre was perforce well equipped—forbade juxtapositions of too violent a nature. And language difficulties precluded the presence of some of the more distinguished educationalists, including the French —perhaps fortunately in the latter case, since it was known that they had strong feelings about the *programme scolaire* and were not above a sly dig at the conspicuous absence of intellectual strenuousness from English schooling. Indeed, when they sat down to planning the details, the event almost had to be abandoned, simply because of the paucity of mutually acceptable protagonists. In the end caution was not allowed to win the day entirely, and a programme was arrived at. The Minister of Education had been invited, as was proper, and had accepted, which was gratifying if rather alarming ; Professor Pitt, the adult education expert, was a natural choice on account of his presence in the city on the day fixed, and he could be trusted to introduce his special interest as a pertinacious red herring should the situation deteriorate ; then there was Still-Waters, a famous local character, a benign and exquisitely gentlemanly professor at one of the State Training Colleges who, in his seventieth year, had developed a burning enthusiasm for simplified Freud. When the question of making a fourth arose, it struck the Centre that it would be tactful to invite someone from the local university, and Bacon, though something of an oddity, was popularly rumoured to be concerned with the subject. The latter, after some reluctance, had consented to take part, it being agreed that no speaker was to hold the floor for more than fifteen minutes ('fifteen minutes or a lifetime,' Bacon had stipulated) and questions might be invited after each short address. Bacon gave as his title, 'The Usefulness of Education'.

It was one of the big events of the English-speaking season. As was only to be expected, no one of Robert El Hamama's circle had turned up, despite the hints dropped therein by Brett ; Said Mohamed Said expressed interest but regretted the necessity of attending a colleague's *vernissage*, where cocktails were to be served. Marcel Haggernetti had sent the director a very nice letter wishing the event all success and assuring him that only a preoccupation with something which 'if you will forgive me, is *bigger* than education' could have kept him away. However, most of the English community concerned with cotton, currency or culture— at that high level where the commodity is not actually handled—had rallied to the Centre. The consul himself was present, together with his lady and his eldest daughter (the other three were still at school, in England). The remainder of the invited guests consisted of several important Egyptian officials, some Greek business men with English affiliations, a few of the few Anglophile Jews who happened to be in favour at the time, and a considerable number of miscellaneous well-wishers who were sufficiently negative in character, politics and religion for their nationality or race never to have come under fire.

To reinforce the bidden guests, Brett had been dispatched on a sortie into the recreation rooms and along the corridors of the Centre, and a fair number of students engaged in table tennis or chess had been pressed, or rather jollied, into entering the lecture hall. Not that they minded very much, for in those parts a certain prestige still attached to lecture-going, and particularly when it was to hear some professor or man of letters sent out from England or France or Germany, even though France or England or Germany might not be aware of his absence or even of his previous presence. This was the great day of the prophet abroad. Brett also poked his head temerariously into the ladies' room, where he found several old faithfuls who had hung about the Centre for countless years without having learnt to speak ten words of English. He teased the ugly old dears until, glowing all over with pleasure, they picked up their knitting and trotted along to the lecture.

Meanwhile an unusual event was occurring, an event of some significance : a large, rather noisy and very proud deputation from the university had arrived. These were followers of Bacon, and they were present this evening only because Bacon, their Bacon, Bacon who had taught them and their elder brothers and perhaps even their fathers, was going to make a conference. All male, they sat in a solid block, huddled together, chattering, grinning and laughing, losing scarves, ostentatiously deploying handkerchiefs, and officiously preventing each other from lighting cigarettes, all much to the scandal of their well behaved neighbours. It was rather like a race meeting on bank holiday. From time to time the word ' Bacon ' or occasionally ' Pacon ' surged up out of the tumult, like the name of a favoured race-horse. No visiting celebrity could have brought them there—they were immune even to the charm of a Cocteau or a Raymond Mortimer—nor did they attend Bacon's classes at the university with assiduity. But this was different. Their beloved teacher (Arabic is an emotional language) was lecturing to the great world, in the grand (if extremely suspect) Cultural Centre, and they were there to support him, and to bask in the reflection of a glory which they alone were aware of. Their faces shone with exaggerated sweaty pride, awaiting Bacon's appearance, as if it were Prize Day and each one of them was the father of the immensely brilliant head boy.

The side door near the platform opened. Ten or twelve particularly favoured guests entered, some of the people who really counted in the life of the city, or had once really counted : they were ushered in by the director of the Centre, a pleasant man, thin, worried and smiling, who had long been exhausted by his successful struggle to be nice to nearly everyone without being too nice to anyone. This little procession of distinguished but shuffling personages was most impressive : it conveyed the sense of being after all more important than anything which might be done or said later.

Realizing that here, in the flesh, were some of the very people—native tyrants, foreign imperialists and capitalists— against whom they had spent the best years of their lives in protesting, the students exchanged their air of holiday enthusiasm for one of naïve curiosity, open envy and ill-concealed inferiority. For a while the hubbub died down, but soon the effect of the first impact faded, and the students were noisily cracking their huge jokes about the eminent newcomers. They did not mean to insult anyone, for they assumed that foreigners as dignified as these would never descend to learning Arabic ; as for their countrymen, they were members of the government and therefore fair game. Packet, who was sitting with them out of a sense of the professorial equivalent of *noblesse oblige*, felt acutely embarrassed. But he could do nothing to repair the situation since whatever he found to say was received by his avid neighbours with fresh roars of laughter and slapping of knees. To the shocked and withdrawn circles of Greeks and Jews and English around him it must have seemed that he was the obscene epicentre of the upheaval. As noise went in the Middle East, the students were not remarkably rowdy : it was partly that the rest of the gathering was so desperately, so deliberately quiet. Packet felt angry with everybody. 'The pox light on you all,' he murmured tactlessly, and another shriek of joy went up : they all knew a bit of Elizabethan.

At that point, luckily, the director re-entered, with the same non-commital smile, escorting the committee of lecturers, each of whom was nervously seeking to yield priority of place to all the others. In a silence broken only by their mumbled apologies and short coughs they mounted the platform and were forced into their seats. But then that distressingly localized hubbub broke out again, and Packet, his good feelings evaporating, looked round hurriedly for somewhere else to sit. Gradually the din became articulate, and once again it centred on the word 'Bacon'. '*Doctoor Bacoon fein ?*' And Packet then realized that in fact Bacon was not present. Groans of extreme dismay and anguished disappointment surged from the student body. Strong objection was being taken, their professor had been suppressed, the university had been spat upon, they themselves had been contempted. Not one of them honestly believed that, but it made a good story, worth living up to.

Experiencing a more genuine dismay, Packet edged between the chairs, placating the students as best he could, and hurried down into the street. There he bumped into Brett, much exasperated. The latter had asked an organ-grinder politely to remove himself, had been grinned at stupidly, and had then made the man—a crafty fellow who knew his profession inside out—a present of twice as much money as he made in a day.

'What's happened to your friend Bacon?' he asked.
'The chief's frightfully put out.'

'Ill, perhaps,' Packet replied. 'I'm going to see—doesn't matter too much if he's a bit late.' He stopped a taxi and gave Bacon's address.

Sourayah opened the door, welcomed him briefly but warmly, and hauled him in. 'He is sick and talking too much,' she said, and went through a pantomime of emptying glasses, 'all night and today too. No sleep.' She shrugged her strong shoulders vehemently and shook her head sorrowfully. 'The demoon drink,' she added, pleased with the foreign phrase. 'Go in—he will be glad to see you.'

Bacon's voice, in the intonations of an unctuous preacher, was raised from time to time in the next room.

'The blessings of education, dearly beloved brethren, are manifold . . . I shall remember them in a moment . . . Ah, the pleasures of browsing, let us say, among the rich and divers volumes of the Left Luggage Club. Where should we be, without the gift of literacy? Not, at any rate, in prison.' There was the sound of a glass breaking. Sourayah moaned softly.

'Where should I be now, dear brethren, had I not been vouchsafed the joys and privileges of education in the three degrees, primary, secondary and a third? Sitting in the Plough and Harrow in Birmingham, calculating my profits; sitting in a Humber Snipe, calculating my mileage; sitting in an obsequious and well-appointed office, calculating. *Mush*, as the Prophet puts it in his primitive way, *kwyass* . . . Where, we may well ask ourselves, would be the Book of the Bunch, without its educated readers? And, with equal truth, where would its readers be without the educated Muck of the Munch? In the beginning was the Word, in the end shall be a Public Library . . . ' There came the creaking and soughing of a congregation getting down on its knees.

'And now let us pray for the soul of one, Professor Packet,
who has fallen among students, whom sinful curiosity has
led to desert the common room and to consort with harlots
and thieves and disorderly policemen and other unlawful
cods . . .' He broke off as Packet peered timidly in. 'Am
I my keeper's brother?'

'Oh Bacon! How wrong of you! The Education business at the Centre—it's already started!'

'Oh Montessori! I knew there was something of that
sort in the air,' he offered in accents of shame, 'but I just
couldn't put my finger on it. Is this a blackboard that I see
before me?' He kicked at an empty whisky bottle. 'I've
been making a fool of myself, dear boy. You'll have to
have me put away.' He offered a few apologetic words in
Arabic to Sourayah. 'It was seeing that young lad with
his poor face dirty and his head denuded that knocked me
over . . . Do not, indeed, let me hear of the wisdom of
old men.'

What was to be done now? Should he present his abject
apologies tomorrow or himself, such as he was, today?
Packet had felt that at last the Cultural Centre, and therefore
in a way official Britain, was recognizing his friend's ability
by inviting him to lecture, and he could not help but be
vexed at this miserable, unprincipled *débâcle*. He did so want
Bacon to make good. But how he put it was, 'Well, there's
still time, and you had better put in an appearance if you
can manage it, if only to pacify your noisy fans. They
were on the point of tearing the house down when I left.
And you don't seem to be in *too* bad a state, if I may say
so.' He squinted surreptitiously under the chairs for other
empties.

'No-oo,' the culprit acquiesced with a mournful expression. 'I think I can still talk . . . Well, on with the show,
then.'

The lecture notes were lying under the desk; Packet

thrust them into a brief-case while Bacon straightened his tie and fastened his shoe-laces. Then Sourayah threw a coat over him and patted his hair into place, and the two of them rushed down the stairs and into the waiting taxi.

Bacon appeared to be in full possession of his senses ; indeed it was his excessive sense of humour which alone worried his friend. The journey was passed in the highest of spirits—except for the puzzled Packet—with Bacon telling the taxi-driver what seemed to be extremely indecent jokes in Arabic. The car shot along at a considerable speed, klaxon full on, while the two of them heaved about mirthfully. Packet, who had planned to spend the time in steadying his friend's nerves and increasing his morale, felt like a maiden lady abducted by foreign brigands.

On arrival at the Centre, Bacon tipped the driver with an eccentric extravagance, and they sped up the stairs. As they passed between the policemen leaning on their fantastic musketry at the entrance, Bacon sang out, ' The armed guard at the door makes me love culture more ! ' Hesitating in the deserted and hushed corridor outside the lecture hall, Packet was shocked to see Bacon fling the large door open with a crash and rush headlong through it.

After a short speech of welcome and introduction from the director, the Minister had commenced proceedings with an elegant and meaningless little discourse on the world-famous British educational system and Egypt's progressive action in employing British teachers in her schools and universities. He embellished his address with descriptions of the Oxford colleges (he had received his education at Magdalen and the Sorbonne) and brought it to a neat con-clusion with a quotation involving young barbarians and lost causes. It was very tasteful, and in good though slightly faded English.

Chapter 5

After the applause the director announced that the Minister
had graciously agreed to answer any questions put to him.
The usual few minutes of ghastly silence ensued, and then a
tall youngish Egyptian with American-style spectacles rose
to his feet. The director bit his lip : he had suffered much
from this person, who described himself on every possible
occasion as the editor of an Arabic journal and threatened
to become editor of an English one just as soon as he managed
to pass the Cambridge Junior Certificate in English Language.
Aware of a general lack of appreciation, the young man was
in no way discouraged : he intended to make his mark in
life. And so, having secured universal attention by clearing
his throat as if about to eject his tonsils, he announced :
' I have met many well-known English teachers who have
studied the studies at well-known schools as Cambridge
College and Oxford College and Liverpool College, and
have many letters after their name.' He paused a moment.
' But not one of them knows why it is that the moon changes.'

He took his seat, quite satisfied with himself. The poor
Minister stared blankly at the audience, hoping that someone
would rush into the breach. There was a low mutter of
disapproval from the university bloc : who, they wanted to
know, was this rude and ignorant fellow ? He was no
university student, that was certain. No public comment was
made, however, and as the interrogator was seen to be rising
to his feet again, though perhaps only to explain why it was
that the moon changed, the director quickly announced that
since there were no further questions, he would now ask
Professor Pitt to address them.

The next speech, like the first, was impressive, but in a
different way. Professor Pitt was soft-spoken, and so only
the distinguished few at the front were able to catch the
larger part of what he said, and even they failed to make very
much of it. A mysterious entity called the Doubleyoueeay
kept recurring, and a personage, apparently very famous, by

the name of Mansbridge was cited with inaudible reverence several times. Great play was made with some rare and apparently coveted phenomenon referred to as a Shift Tutorial, an expression completely new to ninety-eight per cent of the audience, as was also the Mechanical Institute, a phrase which those few who caught it supposed to signify some sort of modern instructional device. Vast numbers of bakers, postmen and policemen were adduced, along with miners and railway workers bearing such strange names as Spinoza, Hegel, Fabian and The Webbs. The speaker closed with some general remarks on man's native zeal for self-improvement and the necessity of education for democracy. 'We must still,' he wound up with unwonted clarity, 'educate our masters.'

The Minister raised an eyebrow slightly but, together with everyone else, applauded respectfully. It was indeed another world that the Professor had been dimly revealing to them, and there is nothing untoward about worlds so utterly *other*, however strong the language used in describing them. It is this world, the Bey was probably thinking, that requires such circumspection.

Questions were hardly to be looked for on this exotic topic, but much advising and encouraging and pushing and dragging was in progress among the university delegates, and eventually one of the youths was up, blushing and simpering horribly, to ask the reverend professor whether it was really true that in England every policeman, even those of low class, could read and write. The Professor was on his feet at once, very gratified, sportily cupping his ear in the direction of the questioner and apologizing humorously for his hardness of hearing. After further exhortation the question was repeated, but the Professor had not mastered the local accent. He appealed to the director for assistance, the director tried to brush the question aside, the Professor insisted with a laugh that he was there to answer questions, if he could. Very unwillingly the director repeated the question aloud, in a weary voice—and it was in the subsequent moment of silence and suspense that Bacon made his abrupt entry.

By the time that the large door had swung to behind him, in front of the petrified Packet, Bacon was already half-way up the central aisle ; he vaulted on to the platform, landing in a squatting position at the feet of the tongue-tied professor of adult education, and nimbly seated himself on the vacant chair. Having arrived there in what he felt to be good order, and misunderstanding the protracted silence, he supposed that by happy chance he had reached the hall just in time to perform. He rose carefully and walked with deliberation to the edge of the dais. The bewildered Professor sat down quickly ; and a burst of wholehearted cheering came from the danger area. Their leader, against great odds, had won through.

'No, no ! Your notes ! ' Packet hissed from the side door to which he had hastened on recovering his faculties. 'You left your notes in the taxi ! '

Bacon smiled benevolently at him and beckoned him invitingly to enter and take a seat : Packet shook his head frantically : Bacon shrugged pityingly.

He then coughed portentously and searched through his pockets. Finding nothing, he walked solemnly back to his chair and peered hopefully beneath it, and then retraced his steps. The audience waited in dumb horror ; and Packet felt himself again involved in nightmare, a nightmarish farce that followed on the previous night's melodrama. Only the university students, regarding the earlier proceedings as no more than boring curtain-raisers to the main act of the show, were unaware that things were not running according to plan. They were as good as gold now—only too good, only too quiet—all ears, like a herd of gazelles examining some unusual but pleasurable sound in the distance, sitting upright with large gleams of proleptic intelligence on their faces, waiting for their master's voice.

' Necessity is the mother of intoxication,' Bacon at last proclaimed regretfully, ' and also of invention, if I may coin a phrase.' He pulled an old envelope out of his breast pocket and slowly unfolded it.

Packet, transfixed in the doorway, cursing his own officiousness, looked round at the frozen faces, row on row. To his surprise he noticed Sylvie sitting there, calm and relaxed : she caught his agonized glance and returned a smile of encouragement.

' It may happen to any one of us,' the speaker went on in the same tone of immense forbearance, ' his body naked, his skull cropped, lost his passport and lecture notes, to face his fate, alone on a bleak scaffold.' The director, half in his seat and half out, sank slowly back, torn between acute alarm and good manners. The student body grinned broadly, knowingly, and alone.

' A series of curiously inapposite misadventures has, it appears, deprived me of my thoughts on the utility of education . . . However, I shall instead recite a short poem to you. Pope did the same—he wrote poetry on the backs of old envelopes, I mean of course. This piece is entitled " Children, Beggars and Schoolteachers ", so in one way or another it should be of interest to most of you here this evening.'

Then, in a horribly clear voice that there could be no getting away from, he delivered his poem :

> ' *Careless of the future, tolerant of today,*
> *Gay in their frozen moment, and so warm :*
> *Flat feet buffet the pavement :*
> > *things fear them,*
> *They have no fear. And these are children,*
> *For whom, they say, all is intimidating, mysterious,*
> > *unknown.*

Bent in ugly balls against the wall,
The past forgotten, a dim and distant present,
            the reckoned future unresented :
Only a stump of arm, a withered leg—
            that is
Their sedentary occupation.   The quiet beggars
Sleeping with their hands held out.
All mysteries solved for them, no possible fears.

In nervous transit from tram to tram,
A present past, a dubious present, and a future
            full of fears.
Feet that mistrust the slithering earth : we,
The teachers, bearers of diplomas
            and mysteries still unsolved,
We who should guide the children,
            lest they
Should later come to begging.'

Turning the envelope he began in the same tone of voice
to read his name and address, but thought better of it, and
descended the platform in a dignified manner and walked
slowly to the side door.   Packet was waiting for him, together
with Brett.   The latter had a pale, thin-lipped, suffering look
about him : he had sat through the performance with a
mounting sense of the necessity of repudiating this awful man,
on behalf of himself, the director, the Centre and England
itself.   But what made such an act imperatively necessary
—the presence of foreigners—also made it quite impossible.
And so, his righteous feelings thwarted, he was now in a
thoroughly bad temper.

As Bacon reached the open door, Brett snatched at his
lapel.   'Tut, tut, dear boy, no violence, remember where
you are,' Bacon rebuked him mildly and, turning towards
the gaping audience, addressed a last word : 'If anyone

wishes to ask a question, I am sure that my respected colleagues will always be ready with an answer.' Thereupon he sped down the stairs chanting ' the local is focal ', with Packet in hot pursuit. A great and sustained burst of applause followed them, but Packet knew who was responsible for that.

Reaching the street, he could see nothing of his disgraceful friend : for the second time in two days the fellow had disappeared without a trace. Packet looked into three or four of Bacon's favourite resorts in the neighbourhood but without success. He hastened back to the Centre but everything was over, and Sylvie had disappeared, too. In some annoyance he boarded a tram for home. Really, nothing could be done for Bacon.

Chapter 6

IT IS THE POETS WHOM THE
ERRING FOLLOW

THE demand—Packet pontificated to himself, in the course of one of those splendid impromptu lectures which nobody ever invited him to deliver—the demand that poetry should convey philosophies, that literature should be mythology, used to be considered a characteristic of the more primitive peoples. And the demand was supposed to grow less pronounced as the people grew more ' civilized '. Of course, ' civilization ' had more or less declined into a term of abuse these days, but Packet didn't consider it sound policy to cut off your nose to spite your face—a curious self-disfigurement to which he had been prone in his earlier years. On the whole his students were unsophisticated ; and he felt little inclination to use the adjective as a term of unqualified approval.

There were exceptions, however, rather violent ones : a small minority of senior students who read Proust and Gide when they should have been studying the set texts from Shakespeare and Milton, and indulged over-strenuously in alcohol and women when they might have been reading Proust and Gide. They were invariably polite and often amusing, and they kept clear of the interminable political or pseudo-political activities—he assumed that they corresponded to the arties in English universities, while their hard-working and harder-shouting contemporaries were the nearest Egypt could offer to the hearties ; there was, however, no sign of ill feeling between the two.

This little minority were shockingly irregular in their attendance at lectures ; they knew too well that they could not fail to get good degrees (good for what, in any case ?). They were ' europeanized ' in advance, most of them having been to English or French schools. Packet had given up trying to teach them sustainedly, and instead they enjoyed informal and energetic discussions on such topics as drug-running, the secret police, French films, suicide, prostitution, modern metaphors and the like. Packet consoled himself with the thought that it was good practice for them in colloquial English—and he at least learnt a lot.

They were a rather jaded and cynical set, like most young Egyptians blest with a fair amount of money and some intelligence, and Packet's usual role in these debates was that of the idealistic uncle, his most frequent contribution being ' It's not really as bad as that, you know.' It had alarmed him at first to find out that they were all apparently on the brink of self-destruction : their money enabled them to look squarely at the corruptness of society, for they would not need to curry favour or hunt for a place, while their adolescent eighteen-nineties' imagination led them to exaggerate it. And he had feared that a conscientious determination on his part to persevere with (say) Seventeenth Century English Prose might drive them over the brink. It did not. It merely resulted in their absence, which out of regard for his feelings they would later ascribe to urgent family business, a trip up-country to the estates or the divorce of a sister. They soon got to know him better, and then, should he show any tenacity in keeping to the syllabus, they would say gently, ' Oh no, sir, don't bother with that now : we can do it at home by ourselves. We're all friends here, just let's talk.' And after all, they did hand in written work, good if infrequent—partly to satisfy the regulations, but

chiefly to protect him from the evils of self-reproach. They
had gathered that for some obscure European reason he
would like to feel that he was earning his salary. Several
of them had become good friends of his : if somewhat lacking in finesse on certain points, they were generous, high-
spirited in practice however gloomy in theory, and as tolerant
of his lapses as they were of their own. With them it was
possible to talk about style—or, rather, to let style make
itself heard above the din of ideas. They were prepared to
look at literature as something more, or less, than great
thoughts.

With the great majority of students it was far otherwise.
Comprehensibly enough, since their knowledge of English
was far from intimate, and ideas it seems are common
property, entities so pure and impeccable that they do not
require to be clothed in words. But Packet still felt depressed
that Wordsworth should mean quite simply ' love of nature,
nature the best teacher ', especially in a country so deficient
in that commodity—and that, however many poems of this
author you should study, their total apprehension of him
remained the same. Similarly, Shelley signified ' love of
liberty, hatred of tyranny ', terms which in their case could
not even be described as pre-defined. And Keats was ' beauty
is truth, truth beauty ' : that, they felt, was certainly all
they needed to know. And judging from their written
work it would be impossible to gather whether these gentle-
men were prose-writers, poets, painters or lecturers.

That, Packet considered, was typical of a primitive people
—the narrow utilitarian attitude to art as either magic or
instruction. And yet, as Bacon had pointed out, this was
pre-eminently a Western intellectual way of looking at
literature, and the Arabs simply had more reason than anyone
else to adopt it. True enough, the periodicals from home
told the same story, though of course in a cleverer way.
There, too, people went to poetry looking for a portable

Weltanschauung, something to provide them with uplift,
a brassière for the weary spirit. If poetry hadn't ideas,
they couldn't bring themselves to take it seriously ; if it
had, then the ideas were the only part of it they took seriously.
And yet—Packet gibbered silently as he paced the floor—
could one say even that ? For they didn't bother to 'live
by' those ideas, as far as one could tell, in spite of the fuss
they had made. They were just exerting a general intellectual curiosity, quite disinterested. Though if you dared
to protest against this awful idea-sucking, you would be
accused of flippancy, of æstheticism, of lack of pity for this
bleeding old world : you would be shelled from Right,
Left and Centre.

More and more openly people were going to poetry to
find what they apparently couldn't get from religion. But
from the way they talked about it later, it was difficult to see
why what they found couldn't have been obtained in a better
condition from religion. Firstly the secular reader goes to
poetry for consolation, with the comfortable assurance that
he can reap the benefits of religion without paying the price
of belief—and then the religious reader sets off on the same
tack because he thinks he can reap the benefits of poetry
without paying the price of effort and understanding. 'If
I had one,' Bacon concluded when they had been discussing
the matter, 'I should like to have my religion straight. I
shouldn't go squinting round the poets for it.'

So it wasn't only characteristic of a primitive people—it
was also typical of a comparatively sophisticated one. A
queer situation—primitive and sophisticated up to the same
tricks ! And so, having lost track of both Bacon and Sylvie,
Packet spent the rest of the evening preparing a lecture on
D. H. Lawrence. Nothing would be said of the dark
gods—who had festered in the imaginations of several genera-
tions of university students—the words ' Messiah ', ' prophet '
and ' teacher ' would be employed not at all, and ' sex ' as

infrequently as possible. He would read them the opening of the short story called *Tickets, Please*, which was probably the liveliest and possibly the funniest piece of prose written in the twentieth century. And no doubt they would be sadly disappointed in him.

But he began again to worry over Bacon when it was time for bed. Bacon was a sociable creature in his own way, not given to sudden disappearances or solitary drinking, and altogether averse to melodramatic behaviour. He must have been in a bad way, in spite of appearances. And he might be in a worse way now. Lost weekenders who wandered into the sidestreets were an unfair temptation to the permanently lost who lived there : they were sometimes found with a knife-hole in them.

Packet had once got caught up with an oafish middle-aged boilermaker, out from England on a year's contract to build boilers for a new rayon factory outside the city. He earned good money, and spent it all, firstly on drink and then on beggars, passers-by, children of the gutters and revolting old witches, tottering about the small native alleys all through the night till the sirens called him back to work. One experience of this had been enough for Packet, to whom Bill had taken a violent and demonstrative liking. Why was it, he asked a seedy Egyptian hanger-on, that old Bill hadn't been knifed long before ? The man had answered, 'Everybody here knows Beel. And they know that he is worth more to them alive than dead.' And Bill was therefore treated like a king : the hard-bitten little goblins of the night picked him up and brushed his clothes when he fell into the gutter, the most desperate of ageing whores would lead him back to his bleak lodgings unmolested, as careful as goose-girls. Intellectuals such as Bacon couldn't expect the same privileges ; but surely Bacon would have enough sense to take a taxi back from wherever he had gone to—and his command of idiomatic Arabic was certainly enough to discourage any thoughts of sudden wealth that might enter the driver's head.

In spite of these assurances Packet passed an uncomfortable night, dreaming of his wayward friend, with his head shaved bare, clothed in a filthy *gallabieh*, standing on an immense scaffold in the middle of Ramleh Station. At the edge of the platform sat several rows of ancient Anglo-Egyptians, male and female, knitting away intently ; while the hangman, who bore a close resemblance to the King, hung the noose about Bacon's neck, nudging him violently in the ribs and roaring with laughter.

Consequently he over-slept in the morning. After a quick cup of coffee he hurried to Bacon's flat. The indeterminate unnerving wind had dropped and it was a beautiful spring day, warm and fresh. It seemed another city. The streets were pleased with themselves ; the fruit glowed in the little shops ; the newspaper-sellers ran exultantly through their polyglot catalogues. The tram purred along, every other window open, while the conductor cracked jokes with the driver or with great politeness collected the fares. Nonetheless it was with much misgiving that Packet rang the bell of the flat, and the sight of Sourayah was not reassuring.

' He is out,' she announced coldly.

' He is still out ? ' Packet enquired fearfully.

' He is out again,' she said cryptically. And then, a little less coldly, she invited him to wait in the study. Muttering something of an ominous nature in her own language, she disappeared. Oh dear, Packet wondered, did that mean he hadn't been back since last night ? Certainly Sourayah was furious with him, she must be blaming him for not bringing Bacon back safely. Suddenly she reappeared in a clean apron and flung her arms in the air.

' He is here, he is there. In and out. And finds trouble

everywhere '—her inadequate English was cramping her style, but she made the best of a bad job—' He has too many friends, and that is a bad danger. He can catch a disease in a dirty prison ; he can catch a sickness, coming home in the night without a coat. Ha ! And for what good ? To help his friends, who laugh at him ! He is becoming old, and '—the great climax came—' he needs much sleep ! ' On the way out she turned with a last word.

' And you will be as bad, if you drink the whisky ! ' She tilted her head back, opened her mouth wide and poured down it a pint of imaginary alcohol, ending the performance with a brilliant roar of inane and drunken laughter.

Happily Bacon himself arrived a moment or two later. He looked weary and worn but not unhappy ; Packet noticed that he was carrying the brief-case left in the taxi the previous night and also his coat, which had apparently been mislaid at some other stage. He had just been along to the *caracol*, he explained, unnecessarily as it happened. Andrea's uncle had flown in from Cairo on an early plane and called on the Commandant ; some money changed hands, and the warder took the boy hot water and soap and a new cloth cap for his head. Simultaneously the Patriarch was conversing over the telephone with the Governor of the city, and some elevated sentiments changed hands. When Bacon came away, the commandant was waiting for a written order of release. Andrea would be home in time for lunch. ' Allah be praised ! ' Sourayah put in ardently, and they concurred.

' And what about some coffee for us ? ' Bacon hinted. But Sourayah glowered at him. For one thing, she wasn't ready to give up the pleasures of indignation so soon ; for another, she was really worried about him.

' *I* am going out now. To the market. To buy food. Someone has to think of that.' In that case, he said resignedly, he and his fellow-liberator would go out too and find coffee elsewhere. The two of them crept away.

Bacon was perking up. 'No harm done. I've made a double fool of myself, that's all. We fools are useful citizens, you know, so long as we don't get too self-conscious about being fools—or useful citizens. We involve ourselves in the seemingly tragic, and lo! it turns comical—so altogether ridiculous that the grand protagonists have to abandon their roles for the day. As the noble hero is led to the scaffold '—the dream came back to Packet and with relief he glanced at the speaker's rich and agitated locks—' we slip up on a banana skin, the executioner gets hiccups and the ceremony has to be cancelled. We are the great reconcilers, and it costs us very little—a certain loss of dignity, and sometimes a bruise on the backside . . .'

He skipped down the street, with his young friend following less agilely. Packet had been going to console Bacon for yesterday's fiasco : really, the man ought to feel just a little guilty.

' You didn't amuse Brett, anyhow,' he said, as accusingly as their rate of progress would allow. Bacon halted suddenly.

' Did I say anything utterly unforgivable ? Unmistakably derogatory, I mean ? No ? Well then.' He hurried on, shouting something over his shoulder which Packet could not completely catch.

' The Minister . . . very gratified . . . a letter by special messenger this morning . . . his homages . . . a moving poem . . . to the very heart . . . shows the great need for education in our country . . .'

They bustled into the dark coolness of the café. Packet surreptitiously removed his tie : Bacon was not wearing one. ' So you'll get a rise, you shameless rascal !' he said with what could be mustered by way of a snarl.

'Alas, no ! All I shall get is, once again, rightly or wrongly, not the sack.'

The grim and rather new word set them talking. Their colleagues were increasingly anxious on this score. Every two or three years a bright pupil emerged ; after graduating he would be sent to England to take a further degree, followed by a Ph.D. Some of these accomplished young men and women had already returned, with considerably better academic qualifications than their old teachers, to take up miserably paid assistantships in the department ; others would be returning in due course, to stand uneasily about the common room, the young brown gods who after all could hardly be expected not to want to take over from the old white ones, fond though each party was of the other.

'And one of these days, when the political situation gets just a little more hectic than usual,' Bacon remarked, 'that is what will happen. We have worked well enough to make ourselves redundant.'

'Yet the students always prefer to go to one of us. I told a student of mine that he'd have to transfer to an Egyptian colleague and he refused downright. " You are my teacher for English, sir," he said, " So-and-so is only an Egyptian, like me." I told him not to be a snob.'

'How long do you think that attitude would last, under political stress ? In any case the government these days is taking students less seriously than of old. Ever since they demonstrated outside the Ministry of War—" We want to go to Palestine ! We want to go to Palestine ! "—and the Minister came out and told them that there was a recruiting office round the corner.' They both smiled reminiscently : there had been no work for a clear week on that occasion.

'Where else,' Bacon continued, 'will you find a State university employing Englishmen to teach English, Frenchmen to teach French and Germans to teach philosophy ? Certainly something will be lost—apart from our livelihoods

—when the day comes : but it won't be on the academic side.   Once westernization gets going in the East, it takes a few Westerners of good will to put the brake on it.   By *being* the background to their own ideas—unfortunately backgrounds don't travel as quickly as ideas—they can give their Egyptian colleagues some notion of what adaptations are advisable.'

' Some of us are a dreadful warning, aren't we ? ' Packet agreed.   ' It will be a sad day when the East sees nothing of us but our business men and the odd celebrity, here today and gone tomorrow.   A sad day for the likes of us, too, when we can only get about as tourists.'   A week in the Channel Islands every third year, he thought sadly, pretending it was Paris.

What would Bacon do, he asked seriously, if his services should be dispensed with ?   Bacon would take Egyptian nationality for a start.   What chance had he of that, not being a displaced weight-lifter or a lawn tennis champion who had crept under the iron net ?   As he was saying, he would acquire Egyptian nationality, with the help of his admirer, the Minister of Education ; he would retire to the country and live on Sourayah's altogether moral earnings, on her property in the village ; he would write nature poetry and achieve a reputation for holiness among the peasantry.   And what would the young Packet do in those circumstances ?   He would go back to Europe (or to Syria, he made the mental reservation) and teach the same things to different faces.

' Or you could write a novel,' Bacon suggested, ' about our Alexandrian revels.   Why not make some intelligent use of those crammed notebooks ?   But promise me to leave out the usual high-minded chatter about liberty and justice and the human condition—and keep fornication within the limits of feasibility.   This coffee is making me sweat— let's have a bottle of beer apiece . . . '

'I think we'd be justified, seeing how warm it is for the time of year.' Packet had managed to rid himself of the persistent feeling that drinking—in spite of the silly prejudice against it—was obscurely sinful, but he wasn't yet entirely happy about drinking before six o'clock in the evening. He hurried on in a more cheerful tone, 'and it would also be rather pleasant.'

'As should be your novel, too. I was reading a novel by one of the more intellectual practitioners recently—a tough, sophisticated, cultured and ironical author who sells well on both sides of the Atlantic, as the advertisements say—when I came across this purple patch of *avantgardisme*, which I jotted down for your information and admonition, Packet. Ah, here it is. The chief character, who obviously speaks for the author, is thinking to himself, thus : " Women, simple animals like ourselves, produced upon a similar model, monotonous and banal, to which only the recurrent brimming over of accumulated spermatozoa imparts a recurrent attraction . . . " The character, who is no chicken, is then reported as feeling " dismay rather than cynicism " . . . '

'I suppose twenty years ago he would have felt cynicism rather than dismay.'

'There has been a slight change in the *Zeitgeist*, and he feels dismay. Precisely. The dismay of a sentimentalist. Having discovered from other modern novels that women have—to use the good old metaphor—back passages, he assumes that they are, in fact as in fiction, back passages incarnate, simply—as he says—if not purely. Our grandfathers produced the art of the front, and our brothers and sisters are producing the art of the back. Sentimentalists both '—he brought his empty glass down sharply on the table—' and it's hard to know which brand is the more harmful. In the end they become indistinguishable. The only image that Sartre (suitably Mephisthophelean name isn't it ?) uses to evoke the act of sexual love is the squelching noise that breasts make on separating from chests ! He's so upset by the fact that men and women perspire that he forgets everything else. That's the way to make a reputation and a bank balance, my boy—by the sweat of other people's arm-pits.'

Packet nodded gravely. It was just as well, he felt, that the café was practically empty.

'You know, Packet, there's only one living novelist who seems to be aware that a front necessitates a back and a back implies a front—and that's Thomas Mann. Unfashionable writer—he hasn't got a line, he doesn't prove anything, he doesn't make a judgment (what are novelists supposed to be ? A Board of Magistrates ?), he sits on the fence—instead of falling on his face in the mud like the others, presumably. No doubt someone has accused him of intellectual dishonesty—of not letting his front know what his back is doing. The same charge has been brought against poor old Goethe . . .' Bacon brought his glass down again, more in sorrow than anger, but it broke all the same. Two waiters rushed up apologetically to remove the debris, Bacon in some shame bent down to help, bumped his head against the table, and Packet's glass followed. When a general extrication had been effected, he continued.

'Mann and Goethe—you see ? Eminently enjoyable and improving writers, both of them—the two virtues the intelligentsia can't abide. They go for Kafka—the back passages of the soul—nothing like them—very handy for sticking politics up, too . . .'

'I must read them,' Packet answered in the hopes of mollifying. As he had suspected : beer in the morning was bad for the temper. 'But, you see, I think I know what my imaginary novel ought *not* to be about—the trouble is that I don't know what it *ought* to be about. What on earth —it would have to be on earth, for you know I haven't much imagination—could the subject be ? At this moment, for instance, I feel really quite happy—especially on account of Andrea, and the Minister of Education. And Sylvie too, come to that,' he added shyly, ' but if I were to start on a novel I'm sure it would turn out to be quite gloomy. Writing seems to be like playing the fool, but the other way about.' He too had become excited. ' The clown's heart is breaking, but he stands on his head and wiggles his ears—the writer, full of iced beer and the joy of living, lays his beloved heroine out with a Mickey Finn and has her seduced by a schizophrenic curate who has temporarily mislaid his faith. People ought to be warned that literature isn't life, just like that, and isn't meant to be.' Packet called to mind the unfortunate who was translating Thomas Hardy into Arabic : he committed suicide before he had finished : he made the mistake of confusing literature with life.

' Yes, it's unfortunate that our sweetest songs are those that tell of saddest thought. Modern earnestness grabs at the saddest thought but despises the sweetness of the song ! As for these novels we're talking about, though—the salt has lost its savour and the songs never had any sweetness. Supply and demand. One doesn't know whether to laugh or cry at the sight of the public paying out good money to have pots of their own excrement thrown in their faces ! *La pudeur* of the fathers is visited on the children in terms of *la merde*—it's about time for the next reaction to set in.'

' If I should ever have any offspring,' Packet's thoughts were on his early years at home : he must have been one reaction behind, he supposed, ' I expect they would be thin-lipped and delicate-minded, and always lecturing me on my loose thinking. I'd probably be forced to run away from home.'

' Ten shillings and sixpence to hear your bodies squelch ! Oh dear me ! As for you, Packet—I'm all for novels being down to earth, as you say, but earth—as Henry James suggested—is not dirt. However, you don't suffer from too complete a lack of self-respect, and so you're bound to respect others. If I carry on like this much longer I'll have to have some more beer ! But I mean—you might well write a very decent novel of a certain kind. Not a best-seller, and not a great work of art—but never mind : what thou seest, write in a book, and send it to the seventy-seven publishers.'

He rose to his feet, rather like a distinguished visitor giving away the prizes, and bowed slightly.

' You may not have any work, Packet, but I have a lecture to get in before lunch. But not, thank God, a lecture on Education.'

Chapter 7

APOSTLES CHARGED TO ANNOUNCE
AND TO WARN

IT was a warm day in early March ; and so, having no
lecture until ten o'clock, Packet had decided to walk to
the faculty. Along the Corniche a steady breeze blew
off the sea, and the little waves were showing their claws.

He had been absorbed with Sylvie during the last month
or so ; more accurately, with the thought of Sylvie—she
herself had been away for some time, visiting her little girl.
It was really very worrying ; and as he had given up the
local newspapers and possessed no wireless, he was rather
vague as to the current political situation and its concomitants.
There was, he had gathered in the common room, trouble
of some sort, but nothing out of the ordinary—about the
Canal Zone, or the Israelis, or possibly a trade agreement
with Britain that some other Arab state had been disloyal
enough to sign.

These bothers went on more or less continuously—and
if it wasn't actually a bother then it was the anniversary of a
bother, which was sometimes rather worse—and one only
began to take it seriously when all the shop shutters went
down all the way together, or one's servant gave one the
tip. Sometimes, in the midst of a bout of excitement, assum-
ing that Britain was in disgrace again and therefore prepared
for a hard word or worse from street loungers, one would be
surprised to discover that this time it was America or the

Argentine or the whole of the United Nations who for some reason was the object of contumely. Not that this made any practical difference, for an agitated patriot, particularly if he is hungry, is in no fit state to appreciate the fine distinction between an American and an Englishman or even between an Englishman and an Argentinian. Oddly enough, Packet mused, people got hurt for the wrong reasons more often than not, out of their season as it were. A Greek grocer would be torn to pieces in the course of an anti-British riot, a French tourist might have his camera broken over his head because the Bolivian press had said something wounding about Egyptian diplomatic techniques, or a non-conformist Welsh engineer would be stoned at a time when feelings ran high against the Jews.

Still, the wonder was that, with so much turbulence, so few people should be damaged at all severely. How different from Europe ! There people lived in security and peace, for comparatively longish periods, and the streets were quiet, apart from transport and commerce, and only the odd and the drunken yelled out in the night. Then suddenly an organized cataclysm arrived, and thousands of them were killed off, not perhaps painlessly but quite efficiently. Later on the cataclysm was legally terminated, and everyone went back to security and peace, for a longish while, and got worried and bored, waiting for the next time. But here the situation was altogether different. Here they cared so little for peace that they couldn't be bothered to wage a war to defend it : 'as Allah wills,' they would say, and since Allah wasn't particularly interested in either peace or war, his protégés saw little of either. They were born guerillas, of a primitive kind. Life was made up of short violences and short calms, brief sorrows and brief joys. And the majority could see no point in discriminating in favour of one or the other, they felt there was nothing to be gained by concentrating their forces on one or the other, in a single and sustained effort. Deliberateness was a western conception which so far had not taken root.

Marriage, now : that was a single choice and a sustained effort to live up to it. And it was this problem that had been weighing on Packet's spirits for some time past.

When they met for their first private and arranged meeting, a few days after El Hamama's party, Packet had felt extremely ill at ease. Packet drunk was no different from Packet sober—he reflected with some pride—only rather bolder. But Sylvie in the bright light of afternoon—they were taking tea in the garden of a very expensive hotel—might easily be different from Sylvie on a dusky dance floor. And the former Sylvie, he surmised, would be less favourably disposed towards an English teacher with neither money nor looks to recommend him. Presumably a young lady selected a marriage partner less casually than she picked a dancing partner.

For Packet, who was just a little of a sentimentalist, was still incapable of experiencing tender feelings towards a woman without at once entertaining thoughts of matrimony. This tendency to premature planning often added a sombre tinge to his behaviour. So that, while he was earnestly reckoning up his financial prospects and wondering whether she would be likely to want children at once, the current lady was apt to be feeling that this rather nice young man didn't seem very interested in her company after all. In his student days this habit had positively alarmed the few shop-girls or typists whom somehow he had plucked up courage to address—detecting in him a seriousness to which they were unaccustomed, they promptly misconstrued it.

And so, that first afternoon with Sylvie, he had been extremely formal and even cold. Cursing himself for his presumptuousness, he looked up blindly at the magnificent trees surrounding them, grimly resolved to betray no feeling of any kind, muttering only some idiotic commonplace from

time to time. Sylvie glanced at him in some astonishment.
Could this be her new friend, the young man *si sympathique*
whom she had met at that rather boring party ? But she
could not well do other than emulate, as best she was able,
his apathetic absent-mindedness. And to that motion he
reacted very swiftly : it confirmed his fears. She had had
time to think things over, no doubt—or perhaps there had
been nothing to think over ? But surely, after all that had
passed between them that night ! They had rattled on like
a couple of children, they had shared vast if obscure emotions,
and afterwards she had turned down several offers of a lift
in comfortable big cars and walked along by the sea with
him, and on separating they had kissed (they had kissed,
hadn't they ? He began to doubt his memory). And did
all that mean nothing ? As a manifestation of the party
spirit, a way of merely passing the time, it struck him as
unduly strenuous. It had taken him a day or two to recover
from the physical energy expended on the occasion, let alone
the rest of it. On the other hand he remembered the monkey-
faced man's outrageous suggestion and the strange lack of
resentment which she had shown. No real feeling, he
decided miserably, glancing at her covertly as she poured
out tea : at least, no special feeling for him. She looked all
the more desirable, in a charming frock (which normally he
wouldn't have noticed), her movements so graceful, her
hair so silkily black : and his cognizance of this made him
all the more certain that his wretched conclusions were
correct. There was an awful emptiness in his stomach.
Unseeingly he reached out for a luscious-looking cake, bit
it savagely, and the cream spurted over his face.

Cogitations of this sort took up a considerable time, for
Packet would have considered making polite conversation
merely a cowardly sparing of himself. Reflections of a
similar nature passed through Sylvie's mind, but she was
less of an intellectual and more of a stoic, and so she had time

for a spasmodic gentle monologue, concerning the trees or the majestic Sudanese waiter or the other people in the garden. Unfeeling, that was what it was, this chatter, Packet felt ; and he squelched his way stolidly through a second over-sweet confection. The woman had to do the talking, Sylvie maintained to herself, since the man did the paying : but she found it uphill work.

Until, that was, a small black kitten suddenly bounded from under the table and leapt on to Sylvie's lap. They were both fond of cats, and the ice began to thaw slightly. And then the kitten, a half-savage stray, slashed a claw across Sylvie's hand and shot with a ferocious hiss into the bushes. Fortunately Packet was provided with a clean handkerchief. His wits returned to him : he swore energetically at the little monster, he examined the pretty hand, he called so imperiously for disinfectant—cats were dirty animals, it might be mad, and so forth—that the magnificent waiter fetched it at the double. And altogether he fell a prey to his feelings.

By the time that this little crisis was over, the ice was bubbling merrily ; and they both began to talk about the party at the same time. It struck Packet that he would have to go over the evidence once more and reinterpret it. But he left that pleasurable occupation till later, for they were chattering and laughing away, while their tea grew cold and the garden faded.

That seemed a very long time ago, now. And now Packet did perhaps have some justification for worrying about ultimates. How much did Sylvie and he owe to the peculiar atmosphere of the city, a city in which they were both foreigners ? They started off with something in common, a common excitation perhaps : the sense of being, to some extent and not too painfully, exiles. But in England —and Packet couldn't at the moment see any future for himself elsewhere—only one of them would be a foreigner.

And perhaps more than that, an exile. And that would not be fair at all, nor auspicious. There was also the child to take into account (was it a boy or a girl, he could never remember) : and with the best will in the world Packet could not visualize with much conviction the three of them safely and solidly established in some cold and crowded English provincial town. To relieve the consequent feeling of depression, he tried at intervals to visualize the three of them settling down in Syria : perhaps it was only ignorance of that country which prevented him from succeeding very clearly, and so he plied Sylvie with repetitious questions about the educational system in Syria and other matters concerning which she knew very little. She had left the country as a child, and really had no desire to return to it, but all the same she was moved by his sudden interest in her motherland.

In this anxious state of mind he turned inland, and reached the faculty to find its gates surrounded by small ominous groups of unfamiliar faces. They were students from other faculties ; and that meant trouble. The Arts Faculty ranked low in the university hierarchy. In fact it came immediately above the Faculty of Agriculture, and Agriculture was at the very bottom. This implied that its students, apart from a very small few (women, for example) who actually wanted to do an Arts subject, were made up of a huge number who humbly knew themselves unfitted for anything more elevated and a considerable number who had failed repeatedly in other faculties, had slipped desperately from Medicine to Engineering perhaps, and then out of Engineering, and had found in Arts a safe footing and a last or penultimate resort. These latter youths were awkward to handle, their hearts full of resentment and their heads crowded with glamorous and ambitious dreams.

Very probably connected with its low status was the reputation which the Arts Faculty bore for pusillanimity in the matter of strikes and demonstrations ; though of course it would be pleasanter to attribute their comparative mildness to the civilizing influence of their studies. Be that as it might, the rest of the student body regarded their colleagues in Arts with a good deal of mistrust and a little contempt. When Science burnt down a lecture hall, Arts at the best would have broken a window ; when Medicine was throwing its professors into the street and breaking policemen's heads, Arts might be gossiping in its refectory over coffee while its grateful teachers caught trams home or strolled into town to look round the bookshops. There had even been occasions when Arts was absent-mindedly at work in spite of the fact that the more reputable faculties were sweating away at a really spectacular holocaust. And therefore it had become the custom for the responsible faculties to send round representatives to stiffen Arts, to bring it to a sense of its obligations and make sure that it toed the line. Arts was conscious of the humiliation, presumably, but had no thought of offering resistance : it wasn't really disloyal, and it soon fell victim to the manly eloquence of the delegates, who were generally from Law. Law was famous for producing reasons for strikes and also first-class orators to make the reasons cogent and known. Just as Science with equal appropriateness specialized in the manufacture of bombs for the graver occasions. Not that there had been any very grave occasions here in Packet's time : the university as a whole, it had to be confessed, was unmistakably decadent in comparison with its elder brother in Cairo. Mediterranean and Mariut, those encircling waters, cooled the city's courage perhaps : the damp *ambiance* of the bathing beaches crept over the political and ethical battlefields and befogged the issues involved. Then too, Cairo was the seat of government, or of misgovernment, and contained many large official buildings with provocatively large windows, such as the Ministry of Education.

There was certainly an air of half-heartedness about this morning's activity. One of the bystanders shouted at Packet, ' *On ne travaille pas aujourd'hui, Monsieur* ' : presumably a student of Law since he spoke the language of Napoleon. But no attempt was made to prevent him from entering the building. This, as ever, evoked a smile from him. It was eccentric both in its original structure and in its present adaptation, for it was in the first case the summer palace of some royal prince, who had sold it to the country in a state of picturesque disrepair and at a high price. Signs of royalty had all disappeared, but the disrepair flourished.

' Are we working this morning ? ' he asked on reaching the common room.

' Can't say yet. We've had classes—but small ones—for the last hour. They don't seem to know whether they're striking or not.'

It was going to be one of those irritating days, then, when work might be off for an hour and then on again, so that the staff had to hang about all morning and perhaps return in the afternoon, to find three students or thirty or none at all waiting for them. In the intervals they would sit gloomily on the dusty leather settees from which horsehairs and some-times springs were emerging, very conscious of their humiliat-ing position. They were not supposed to absent themselves until the strike became officially recognized, whereupon Abdou, the faculty messenger but one of the most intelligent and trustworthy souls about the premises, would come round from common room to common room proclaiming the welcome news in Arabic and English and French. " Offici-ally recognized " meant that a ministerial order had been issued, or that violence had taken place, or merely that strike-noise was clearly predominant over work-noise. None of the staff—servants, resident police or teachers—had the slightest desire for martyrdom.

Outside the unkempt room allotted to him for his ten

o'clock lectures six or seven of his students were wrangling moodily with several from another ten o'clock class.

'Well,' Packet asked one of them in a bored voice with— he hoped—a tinge of menace, '*Fee shogl?* Do we work?' The others stopped arguing to look at him incuriously for a moment and then resumed. The youth turned down the corners of his mouth and opened his palms. 'Some of us want to work, sir, some do not. Myself,' he added magnanimously, 'I think it is better to work.' He and some of the others followed Packet into the room. Once again the latter was overcome with inarticulate rage at the sight of chalk dust over seats and tables, the absence of chalk from its proper place, the ever-broken window and the cigarette stubs and scraps of torn newspaper on the floor. Only a week previously he had addressed a formal but mordant letter to the dean, drawing this gentleman's attention at the same time to the pervasive smell of the urinal just along the corridor. Not that he minded the smell very much himself, one soon got into the habit of freezing one's nostrils at the right moment, but he thought it must be extremely unpleasant if not embarrassing for the girls. Some of the girls were very shy and refined-looking and fragile.

His girls were already seated demurely in the front row, waiting for him. He beamed at them, his temper improving at once : they were quiet creatures, some of them colossally stupid but of good cow-like disposition, while a few were very bright. All of them were loyal : always, indeed, on their best behaviour, because the female student was still an innovation, and they were careful not to shame their sex in any way. Nor did the male students wish to shame them, though they did not think twice about voicing obscene Arabic innuendoes in the publicity of a lecture. But in private it was otherwise : male and female were but brother and sister, and no-one showed too much interest in anyone else—or if they did, a scandal quickly blew up, authority intervened, and it was generally felt that they got what they deserved.

In point of sexual behaviour—Packet had been quite intrigued by this—the university was probably the most respectable in the world, for it was practically non-existent. The students were too busy fighting for abstract liberties to have time for this one. And teachers fresh from Europe were warned by their colleagues that this was no place for pedagogic sheep's eyes or for the sentimental education which provided the English press with some of its gayest moments.

There had been, however, an odd case earlier in the year. An Egyptian lecturer had reported a woman student for permitting a man student to kiss her behind a tree in the faculty garden. The boy was left to whatever shame he might summon up, but the unfortunate girl was summarily expelled. A kiss, they all agreed privately, was a little thing in itself, but they all knew that the girl's name had been soiled and her matrimonial prospects ruined. By chance this had happened at a time when relations between the student body and the faculty board were seriously strained —cuts had been imposed on the sports fund—and the students were very willing to impugn the good faith of authority whenever and wherever possible. A loophole was soon discovered : first of all, the girl had not paid her fees for the preceding year—and the faculty was displeased with her on these grounds. Further, the lecturer who had witnessed the crime—an unpopular man—came under suspicion : his eyesight was poor : how could he be sure of what was happening since on his own testimony he was never nearer than fifteen yards from the couple ? So it was argued and debated. And when was a kiss not a kiss ? When, for example, it was a fly being removed from an eye, a brotherly act. A suggestion was even launched to the effect that the lecturer was himself an unsuccessful suitor to the lady : it was in all likelihood purely fictitious, and it did not seem to prove anything to the advantage of the cause, but it gained ground. The outcome of it all was the firm belief on the part of the students that the alleged kissing was a foul pretext for getting rid of one of the many of them who were too poor to pay the exorbitant fees charged by a reactionary university. Unanimously they went on strike.

The strike was the first the European staff knew of the affair, for the authorities had hoped to wash their dirty linen in private : or perhaps they feared that the Christians would fail to realize the gravity of the issues involved—and it was true that the Christians were great users of the consular divorce courts. Admittedly the French Department at once decided that since so slight a thing as a kiss could not conceivably warrant expulsion, therefore there was indeed dirty work afoot. The English Department, however, debated more seriously the rights and wrongs of kissing in Moslem faculty gardens, and, on the whole, agreed to respect the moral attitude adopted by the authorities, while at the same time deploring the severity and onesidedness of the punishment inflicted. The girl was a good student, and she had a pretty face. Moreover, they too were ready to believe the worst of the authorities (the same authorities had held back the salaries of several of them who had been delayed for three weeks in Venice by a maritime strike as they were on their way back from home leave). And thus both the French Department and the English were highly gratified when the authorities decided that in view of the ugly fog which now obscured the affair it would be wiser to beat a retreat. The girl's matrimonial value had sadly depreciated, all the same, but she would be able to take a degree and earn her living as a teacher.

Packet smiled protectively at his girls as they took out pens and opened notebooks. How much braver they were than their noisy males ! A scattering of youths fidgeted behind them, glancing nervously at the door and, to be on the safe side, trying over-hard to look as if the last thing they were doing in that room was attending a lecture. To this end they perched sideways on the seats, or stared out of the windows, or crouched down to tie their shoe laces. Packet sniffed loudly at them : let them not think that he did not know !

The class had arrived at that great moment in *Silas Marner* when the old man dimly sees the golden-haired child on his hearth. It was a gift to teach, Packet thought—the gold coins gone and the golden hair come : love of money replaced by love of a human creature. Simple and strong. Carried away by a gush of emotion, he enacted the scene —not so much for the benefit of the men, who plainly indicated that in their opinion Silas had lost both on the swings and on the roundabouts, as for the girls, one of whom was already deep in her handkerchief.

He stood stiffly at the door—that was old Silas in his cataleptic trance—with a puzzled look on his face he slowly relaxed ; he moved little by little into the centre of the room, ' when to his blurred vision it seemed as if there were gold on the floor in front of the hearth '. Packet sprang back in what was obviously amazement. ' Gold—his own gold— brought back to him as mysteriously as it had been taken away ! ' The class, male and female, gazed at their teacher in stupefaction. Painfully he bent down, stretching out his hand to his brief-case on the floor near the desk. But instead of the brief-case with the familiar swollen outline, ' his fingers encountered soft warm curls '. At this juncture Silas fell on his knees to see better, but Packet, with all his enthusiasm for the Direct Method, had no intention of grovelling on that filthy floor. Instead he bent over a little more acutely and reinforced the look of bewilderment on his face.

At this tense moment the door was flung open to the accompaniment of a short-lived knock, and a young man unknown to Packet stood on the threshold. Before Packet had even straightened up, the intruder had commenced his address : it was in Arabic, and it was fiery and stern, a clarion call to duty. Packet folded his arms and stared contemptuously at the orator : this had not the slightest effect.

' What the devil do you mean by interrupting my lecture ! ' he yelled, taking advantage of the speaker's pause to draw breath. But somehow the English tongue simply wasn't capable of the primitively thrilling overtones and lowering undertones of Arabic, and the ineptitude of his protest infuriated him further.

' If you don't get out this moment, I shall throw you out ! ' No sooner was this threat uttered than he realized how rash it was. The youth looked an awful tough, he had the shoulders of a wrestler, and at the best a scrimmage was undignified. But there could be no retreat : he must not betray the local legend that an Englishman's deed was as good as his word : and so, with a determined expression on his face and a mind entirely blank, Packet strode towards the intruder. The suspense was too much for his pupils, and happily one of them sprang from his seat with arm outstretched as if to bless and cried, ' We all honour you sir, you are our teacher. But we cannot work today—it is Down with Britain day—if you will excuse it, sir.'

And thereupon all the young men slunk out under the censorious eye of the agitator. Love of mankind ! Packet snarled inwardly. He slammed the door behind them and walked masterfully back to the remains of his class.

' Now we can get on with some real work.' He sounded as if he had ejected the lazy young men. ' We shall get along much more quickly without them.' Two or three of the girls smiled with faint gratification, and Packet went on to demonstrate the strange quiverings of tenderness which,

after so many years of petrifaction, Silas experienced anew
on finding the sleeping child.

'What, after all, is life ?   Not the big words—Liberty and
Equality and so forth,' he exclaimed with a scornful wave
in the direction of the door, behind which a number of
disgruntled voices could be heard.   'But simply this—what
George Eliot, a woman like you, calls " pure natural human
relations ".'   The girls nodded uncertainly and glanced at
each other.   They never fidgeted, but they were very near
it at the moment, he felt.

'At any rate, that is the end at which to begin.   You
cannot *create* Liberty or Peace, just like that, by passing a
resolution—or going on strike,' he sneered largely.   'These
things begin where they end—in human relations, in your
relationship to yourself and to other people.'   Rather impressive, he told himself.   But, good heavens, they were not
listening to him !   In fact they were whispering to each
other.   He adopted the air and posture of a resigned martyr,
waiting for them to realize the enormity of their offence.
One expected such behaviour from the men—but the young
ladies !   What were they coming to ?

All this whispering, it transpired, had been to appoint a
spokeswoman.   They had picked his favourite, a thin brown
girl, demure but firm.   She spoke.   'We would like to
work, sir.   That is what we come here to do.   But the boys
will be angry with us if we do not follow them.'

'But this is none of your business,' he stuttered angrily.
So that was it.   He felt betrayed.   'Let *them* get on with
it . . .'

'But it will not be fair,' she continued patiently, 'because
we shall do better in the examinations than the boys.'

So what ? he roared.   Had he spent his time at the university, when he was a student, chanting political slogans at
the top of his voice ? he asked them.   No, he had not, he
told them.   He had worked.   (In one way or another, he

assured himself.) If he hadn't worked—a note of pathos crept in—they would have taken his scholarships away. But England is a democratic country, one of the girls objected bashfully, and there is no need to chant at the top of the voice. He was about to contradict her, on principle, when the first girl spoke again.

'If we stay here they will say bad things about us. They might'—she too resorted to pathos—'they might even beat us.' There was some gentle tut-tutting at this : a lack of unanimity among them as to whether the boys would really go that far. But Packet had cooled down by now. Either way it would be unpleasant for the girls ; and the lesson was ruined beyond repair. Better to give them permission to go before they went without it.

'Very well,' he announced frigidly, 'you may go. And perhaps you can spend the time in writing an essay for me —if that won't give you an unfair advantage over the poor young men.' A docile hum of agreement came from them, they collected their belongings together, and left the room in a quiet and dignified manner.

And quiet everything was, and the old palace wearing an almost dignified air, as Packet made his way to the common room. Male and female, they had all vanished. He peered through a harem window on the stairway—no mob whipping itself into a fury, no young men beating up unpatriotic young women, but only an ugly-looking mule which had strayed from the scavengers' compound nearby.

The convention was that during an emergency students should take time off from burning desks and bruising police-men to rescue their own particular teachers from other students who, free from such ties, might otherwise bruise or even burn them. On rare occasions, however, they would all be so carried away, so completely dehumanized by their collective chanting, that they lost their memories entirely and failed to recognize their beloved mentors. That could be unfortunate. During the last serious incident of this nature, Packet had been met by a Coptic follower of his who warned him fervently, ' Better to go away from this place, sir, it is dangerous this time. I can tell—because their eyes have turned red.' But really, Packet reflected, they wouldn't actually attack anyone, not wantonly—not unless he tried to intervene or to address them or happened to be standing in their way. The faculty was riddled with passages, luckily—it had been constructed to accommodate palace intrigues, he supposed—and they probably wouldn't break formation to bring down a professor as he sped in the direction of the tram. One suppressed one's western or perhaps pedagogic inclinations to yell back, and one disappeared.

Just as they, apparently, had disappeared now. Rather odd : exactly as if they had left a time-bomb on the premises : but they wouldn't do a thing like that—not foul their own nest, at least not without being in the vicinity to enjoy the spectacle.

As he mounted the stairs, however, he heard somewhere above him a faint squeaking noise which quickly grew louder and shriller. This didn't fit into the programme at all : it was as if an army of agitated mice was on the move. As he reached the landing an orderly mass of very small boys, most of them in shabby black tunics, swept rapidly towards him. In the forefront a worn Egyptian flag was being manœuvred energetically. The childish trebles of their chanting sounded quite ridiculous, but their facial expressions were serious and purposeful and their movements surprisingly disciplined. Like a tribe of ferocious pygmies embarking on some enigmatical but momentous war.

Packet gaped for a moment, then recalled stories of primary school headmasters gladly breaking their ankles as they leapt out of study windows to escape their enraged pupils. The door of the common room was directly opposite, and the flag was no more than a foot away when he skipped towards it. Someone jostled him roughly as he turned the door-knob, and the utter and shocking grotesqueness of the whole thing—a university lecturer sent sprawling on his own thres-hold by a gang of little schoolboys—got the better of his discretion. Standing in the doorway, he pushed a foot out stiffly behind him, felt an impact, shot into the room, slammed the door with a triumphant war-cry and turned the key.

'An impressive entrance,' Bacon commented.

There was the pleasing noise of small bodies falling on top of each other, and a brief outburst as of expostulation, but no attempt was made to open the door. Ranks were quickly restored and the procession passed on at the double, down the stairs and out into the street.

'What on earth was that in aid of?' Packet demanded. 'It's like the Pied Piper, but less useful.'

'The Children's Crusade?—that's the one to beware of! The younger they are, the wilder they come—thank God there are no State nursery schools. They arrived a little time ago, from a school down the road. And that's why our people vanished so abruptly—the sight of schoolboys demonstrating on faculty ground was too humiliating for them to bear. A dreadful reproach.'

They strolled down to the tram station, where Bacon gave a piastre to his regular beggar, a filthy and savage little girl with a monstrous vocabulary.

'A funny business, today,' he remarked in the middle of a yawn. 'How tiring it is, not to work! Yes, a queer do. Less than half-hearted. Wonder whether it wasn't a put-up job.'

'Put up by whom?'

'Who knows? By the government perhaps.'

'What for?'

'How do I know what for? In the hopes of giving the police a little gentle exercise maybe.'

'Coo!'

It would make a good story to tell Sylvie, Packet thought.

Chapter 8

FACES ON THAT DAY WITH
DUST UPON THEM

IT would have been nice, they felt, to have the next day off, properly off. But, arriving reluctantly at the faculty, the staff found their students awaiting them, and in unusually large numbers. Some of the more sensitive wore a sheepish air, but nothing was said about the previous day's *débâcle*—except by Packet, who was still feeling piqued.

'Yesterday, as some of you may possibly recall, I was endeavouring to communicate to you the sterility of a life devoid of human affection'—when in a bad temper he tended to use big words—'but a gang of small boys assaulted me.' The class winced. 'Or very nearly,' he added out of respect for the dignity of an Englishman.

'So today we shall continue with *Julius Cæsar*. Let me see.'—Why was it that no one else in the class was capable of keeping the place? 'Oh yes, Act One, Scene Three, Line twenty-six—

> *And yesterday the bird of night did sit,*
> *Even at noon-day, upon the market place,*
> *Hooting and shrieking—*

Ah, " hooting and shrieking "—the owl wasn't the only one to be doing that yesterday.' The class gave a pathetic sort of titter.

'Now this behaviour on the part of the owl was regarded as an evil omen. Can anyone tell me what an evil omen is?'

'It is an evil omen,' responded Ibrahim Metwalli, the class jester, to whom they looked to turn aside wrath, 'if our teacher is angry with us when he marks the examination papers.'

Later, as they walked to the tram together, Packet remarked to Bacon, 'It's a bit too near to the exams to have a really good strike, that's the trouble.'

'There's something fishy about it, all the same.' Bacon seemed gloomy this morning. 'I've a feeling that there's more to come yet.'

And the next morning, Packet's servant arrived half an hour late and in a state of great excitement. There was trouble in the streets, Packet gathered : Hassan would prepare lunch and clean up the flat quickly and then hasten back to his family—his wife was expecting another baby, she was very nervous. What was it about this time, Packet wanted to know. But Hassan's explanations were very confused ; he came out with some sensational story about the police struggling with the army. The army had risen, then? That was really exciting : a *coup d'état*, at last ! Packet had a vision of slim intellectual lieutenants occupying the palace at Montazah, while in the capital the monstrous king was hauled before a firing squad of cannons.

At that moment there came the sound of firing in the road outside. Who was that, Packet demanded as he handed Hassan a soothing cigarette. Was it the police or the army ? Hassan rolled his eyes up : no, it was the mob. He had seen nothing but the mob in the streets. The army was said to be coming from Cairo in lorries and tanks, the police had vanished. There was a distant baying, and the noise of people running quite near the house. Packet's excitement

evaporated. It might be a serious outbreak—and Sylvie
would be alone in her flat, in the very centre of town.

After a quick cup of coffee he went downstairs to see
whether his Greek neighbour had any further information.
He tapped at the door : there was a scuffling noise, but
no one appeared. He rapped again and hummed en-
couragingly, then asked gently, ' Mr. Papadopoulo, are
you in ? '

' *Min da ?* ' came a voice. ' *Qui est là ?* '

' It's me—Packet—from upstairs.'

The door was opened a couple of inches and then a foot
or so.

' Come inside quickly,' whispered Mr. Papadopoulo.
Locking the door again, he said, ' Excuse me for not opening
to you at once, but oh my dear young Mr. Packet, they
are shooting in the streets ! There is a Greek factory owner
lives behind us—he is very unpopular with his employees,
and they are seizing the opportunity to attack his house.
Oh dear, there is no-one to help us, we are at their mercy.
Why do I bother to lock my door, I ask myself ? Even
my servant has not come today . . .'

His plump cheeks wobbled pathetically. Silently he
pointed to his treasures—some finely bound books, a few
handsome pieces of heavy furniture which his father had
brought back from China, some classical pieces in plaster, a
pianoforte and a large ornate mirror. He regarded his
reflection in the latter, twitched despairingly and shrugged
his shoulders. Then he delivered himself of something
which Packet took to be verse. Turning to his visitor he
added in English, sombrely, ' Cavafy, our own poet—
waiting for the Barbarians—he complains that they do not
come, that there are no Barbarians any more ! Poetry,
poetry ! '

Remembering his manners, he invited Packet to take
coffee with him. Over this he passed on all the information

he had anxiously gathered—from neighbours, over the phone before the exchange had ceased to operate, and from the servants of neighbours. It appeared that Packet's bright vision of an indignant and risen army was wholly inaccurate. What had happened was more mundane : the Alexandrian police, men and officers alike, had decided that their rates of pay were ridiculously insufficient—in which they were justified, considering the extent and strenuousness of their duties—and that their best course was to strike. They knew very well what that would mean : the hungry, the unhappy, the bored and the evil would rise, there would be burning and looting and killing, and the just demands of the police would be met without delay. As it happened, however, rumours of their intention had reached the government a little in advance, and martial law had been proclaimed at once. Local troops were already in the city, a few minor clashes with the police—those who hadn't preferred to sit quietly in their homes—had occurred, and fresh military detachments were said to be on their way. The rioting in town, all accounts agreed, was extremely serious.

' Is there any public transport at all ? ' Packet asked.

' None. A few taxis and *garrys* are out, doing fine business—fifty piastres for a five-piastre ride. But my dear Mr. Packet, you cannot possibly be thinking of going out, I trust ! Please spend the day with me—I have some tinned meat from America. . . . Though even here we shall not be safe ! They will seek out the Europeans—especially the English and the Greeks. . . . '

Packet thanked him warmly, but he had to seek out a friend in town. Even the Syrians, whether European or not, would be in danger, he feared—particularly if female. It would be a long walk to Sylvie's flat, and the sooner he set out the better. Grieving sorely, Mr. Papadopoulo saw him to the door.

' You English are foolhardy—your history has not taught

145

you to fear situations like this. But I cannot prevail upon you, I know that. You will go—like Odysseus in quest of his Penelope.' He smiled wryly and quoted some more Greek. 'Cavafy's poem, *Ithaka*—

" *Ithaka has given you your lovely journey.*
Without Ithaka you would not have set out.
Ithaka has no more to give you now . . ." '

The door was opened just sufficently, the bolts were shot behind Packet and, as he ran upstairs, a series of bumpings and draggings indicated that the Greek was barricading his door. I ought to stay with the poor old boy, he thought, but one can't be in two places at the same time. Or was he merely doing what he wanted to do ? Luckily going to Sylvie was the proper and accepted thing : she was a woman, and in the middle of it.

Sporadic shots were ringing out as he put on his shoes, and he felt further qualms about leaving Mr. Papadopoulo to his plaster casts and his poems, his memories and fears. It still seemed to him safer, morally speaking, not to be doing what he really wanted to do, when there was a choice to be made.

'You are not going out *today*.' With a triumphant gesture she handed him a cup of coffee. There had been much coming and going of naked feet, much yelling and some shooting, during the past hour, and Sourayah had picked up the full story in the porter's lodge, where all the servants of the block congregated.

'Tell me exactly what is happening,' Bacon requested her in Arabic.

'The police force has struck and the army is occupying the centre of the city. In the poor quarters the mob has burnt down cinemas and cafés. Some of the police are fighting the army. And your students '—she became more

triumphant still : she had always distrusted Bacon's charges
—' your students are helping the police, out of kindness ! '

That was comic indeed. The students fighting side by
side with their traditional enemies. But they wouldn't fight
for long—not against the tommy-guns of the army. Comic
was hardly the word, though—one knew that the affair
would follow the usual pattern. Its origins were obscure
and they would never be brought to light. Were the police
genuinely striking for better conditions ? No doubt the
wretched illiterates on the beat, the bemused peasants who
were pushed in masses against the sticks and stones of the
students, no doubt they believed that. But did the officers ?
Was it inspired by one of the opposition parties ? Was it
engineered by the government, to strengthen their hand ?
Was it for, or against, the Palace ? That one couldn't tell.
But one could foresee the pattern.

The poor and dishonest made for the nearest shop windows.
A little later, when nothing much was left to make off with
and the police or the soldiers were closing in, the poor and
honest would throw overboard their honesty and join in.
A few Jews or Greeks or other non-Egyptians would have
to die, because they were unlucky or careless, and because
their deaths would give the affair a veneer of respectability.
And one killing usually led to another, since not more than
a dozen or so could be in on a killing, and the others hated
to be left out. There would be no rape, since unlike
Europeans these Moslems put first things first and they
seemed to prefer their own women. And then, after the
looting, the burning would go on all night, wantonly.

Apparently that stage had already been reached. And
characteristically the mob had destroyed its own little cinemas
—the dirty, bare wood-and-plaster shacks in which for a
few pence they could watch five or six instalments of
American serials, comic or cowboy or superman, enjoying
them vociferously as they buried themselves in the shells of

melon seeds. Or gloat over their own unsophisticated products, in which honest upstanding peasants were unjustly accused of theft or city husbands discovered the infidelity of their plump wives and shot them together with their oily lovers, in between long and emotional vocal sessions provided by the people's favourite singers. And these dilapidated little places the people destroyed in its fury, the places of entertainment into which no European would dream of entering. If only they would stream into the local West End, Bacon thought, and burn down the palatial picture-houses where the latest American and English and French and Italian films were shown—that would at least be logical ! But they left such places alone : they were not at home there : the luxuriousness cast a shyness over them, the chromium, the meaningless murals, the candelabra and the air-conditioning sobered and even intimidated them. And so they turned their madness against themselves, or against some small local tradesman, some old Greek who had lived all his life there, in a little room over a little shop, who religiously displayed a portrait of the King, never cheated his customers of more than they could afford, and was in fact really well-liked by them.

The army would arrive, probably in the form of raw recruits so terrified by the sudden obloquy into which their uniforms had somehow brought them that they fired at everything that moved, cars or cats or men. Until enough blood had been spilt, until the last dregs of energy had been poured out in an orgy of looting, of looting what had already been looted, or in playing football with the blank insignificant head of some convenient scapegoat, under the silent shuttered windows of the grand hotels.

And then a week of hangover : detachments of troops at every corner, sullen faces in the streets, half-empty cafés and cinemas, the European schools closed, arrests of ' ringleaders' announced in the press, recriminations passing between the political parties, a resignation or two, rumours of the movements of foreign destroyers, claims from business firms for damages to property—and eventually the affair would expire some two years later in the law courts, when the busy breath of the lawyers could no longer keep the sparks alive.

'So you are not going out today!' Sourayah repeated emphatically. 'If you do, then you will be torn to pieces —by the soldiers or by the criminals or by your students.' Which would teach you a lesson, her tone of voice implied, but would not suit my book at all. 'Allah be praised, we have plenty of food in the house, and it will do you good to rest for a few days.'

He pulled out an untidy pile of manuscripts. Of course it was a chance to get on with his work. The book was not really about Education. It was meant to treat of the practicality of teaching English in countries which, like Egypt, had next to no living literature of their own. And, for once, from the student's point of view rather than the teacher's. Certainly he had no wish to engage in a technical treatise. No-one, as far as he knew, had worked seriously on the subject : and it needed doing. There was no call for every educationalist to write books about books about Intelligence Testing. The trouble was that the people who were in a position to say something useful were generally too busy with the job itself to have time for the book about the job.

From a little way off came the long high roar of falling glass. The trouble lay in the imponderable nature of what he was trying to discuss—though that didn't seem to worry the Intelligence Testers—and here there was so much to discourage one, as soon as one ventured out of the school into the street, out of literature into life. It was like embarking on a sentence that one couldn't bring to an end : there was always a conditional clause to insert somewhere, or a parenthesis, or else the person you were talking to went away abruptly, or you were interrupted by a doubt, a hiatus of knowledge, or a revolver shot.

The art-writers wrote for posterity, according to the general public—who often thought of themselves as posterity, but rarely as contemporaneity—and sometimes according to the writers themselves. That was a consolation ; and, sometimes, an alibi. But Bacon couldn't take advantage of it ; he was no art-writer, nor a research worker. Come to that, what kind of writer was he ? (It had always been the same, ever since he came to this country—mob violence produced in him a quite uncharacteristic consciousness of self.) He wasn't even a political writer. It wasn't the time for politics: that was a luxury trade (a phrase which Packet, he recalled, had once used of teaching literature). There had been too much politics over the last twenty years : one had almost forgotten what it was to be merely human. For humanity was always the first casualty in political schematizing—it was reduced to a series of highly coloured dolls, a Russian Peasant or a Japanese Lady or a Prussian Officer, with explanatory statistics attached, a label like those in Botanical Gardens.

This wasn't the Age of Anxiety (that flattering slogan !) so much as the Age of Definition. The plague of clever-cleverness afflicted the world in all its members ; you could see it in literary jargon and philosophical jargon, as well as political jargon. The Age of Conceit would be another way of describing it—for we really seemed to believe in our definitions. They were arrived at by the aid of reason, and with the assistance of the newspaper to which we subscribed. Of course when we let our hair down, it transpired that we weren't so sure, after all—but we didn't let our hair down on public platforms or in committee or in print. And it wasn't merely a question of academic misconception or harmless self-delusion. No, people were apt to become the bad names you called them, in time : in time you were left with a world of monsters, monsters created by political man out of humanity—with only a thin sheet of newspaper between you and them, an apt protection against their atomic warfare.

It would be ridiculous of course to suppose that ignoble sophisticates could be turned into noble savages, hey presto ! —it was too late in the day for that. The lone wolf was a romantic exception : most of us would go on living in tribes, and tribes have to be organized. Yet, he knew it in his mind as well as in his heart, the great inhuman political combines must be broken down : the idea of the individual would have to be salvaged from the mud, and soon—before it sank entirely out of sight. Who could do it ? Or who could try to start to do it ? By its very nature, only an individual here and an individual there, or else it would turn into a Society for the Preservation of Individuals, something like those non-party parties which cropped up so frequently those days (and were always either extreme Right or extreme Left).

No, the best hope lay in the teachers, after all. Especially, he smiled to himself, the teachers of literature—those despised creatures, rejected for their irresponsibility, who could never organize themselves effectively, who were generally reckoned to be a decadent lot, politically speaking—simply because they couldn't resort to the glib hypnotic slogan or produce the ready, virile and confidence-inspiring answer. Their fitness for the task lay in what had caused them to distrust their own age, the Age of Abstractions.

No, he certainly wasn't a political writer. Nor had he anything to confide to posterity—except the hope that posterity would exist. If he wasn't useful, he wasn't any-thing—that was what it came to—and, in spite of what he had said about its being a long job, he wanted to be useful here and now.

Two voices were screaming at each other below his

window, the noise rising above the clatter of a handcart. The cart was being propelled by a ragged youngish fellow : it was stacked with flat round native bread, and perched uneasily on top of the bread was what seemed to be a complete tea service. In very cheap china, with a dark brown flower design so large that even the teapot could not quite accommodate its pair of roses or whatever they were. It was new, fresh from the shop, for wood shavings were sticking to the cups and the lid of the teapot was still secured by a rubber band. Cups and saucers and plates were jangling together as the handcart sped along, while an old woman, clutching her *malaya* about her with one hand, made frantic grabs at them. The man stopped every five or six yards to pick up a disc of bread that had jolted off into the road, taking the opportunity to hit out at the woman. She fell back, but returned to the attack as soon as he took up the shafts again, screaming and spitting at him, ' *Klefti, klefti*— thief, thief ! ' The man yelled back at her, ' *Klefti, klefti !* ' And the equipage passed out of Bacon's sight, the withered old woman still struggling to clamber on the cart, the bread falling off into the dust, and the crockery dancing and clashing wildly.

Back at his desk, the manuscripts, the notes, the data, awaited him dispassionately. Perhaps it would be better all round if I stayed inarticulate, he questioned himself—we intellectuals *must* formulate, and the easiest things to formulate are our doubts and fears—to tell of saddest thought—especially as doubts and fears are so fashionable. If all I can articulate is doubt and fear, what's the use ? Better get on with the job, since it has to be done, it has to be do-able, if life is to be worth anything. After all, it's not as if I were pursuing a Ph.D. And I don't suffer from verbal diarrhœa (except after alcohol, anyway). And I'm not the kind of chap to talk himself into suicide.

He sighed lightly, looked at his watch, and decided that

it was time for some more coffee—or perhaps even a bottle of beer, if that wouldn't strain Sourayah's forbearance.

The people at the hotel, a shockingly craven lot, had warned him not to go out, but Brett insisted that a little to-do in the streets would not prevent him from turning up for work. In any case, it was no more than two minutes' walk to the Centre.

Once out of the hotel he could not return without looking extremely foolish, though what he met—ragamuffins clubbing each other, a lake of splintered glass, an overturned car, a woman with a bleeding face huddled in the gutter—changed his notion of what a to-do could be. However, he had speedily got through the groups of disorderly troops, all wrangling among themselves in acute nervousness, and reached the Centre without being molested.

There he found himself alone—except for a Maltese clerk who felt that the stout doors of the Centre offered better protection than his own ground floor flatlet—and two of the Egyptian servants. These two were loyal old employees of the Centre ; they valued the prestige which it afforded them in the world of *suffragis*, and they intended to see that it came to no great harm. Brett did not realize that, should the building be stormed, only the servants could save him, that they could save him only at considerable risk to themselves, and that they would take the risk without a second thought. He only granted that they were, as *suffragis*, polite and efficient and more than usually clean—which indeed was all he would think of asking of them. He had not yet gathered how much more than servants they were, that in fact they were in a small but perhaps not unimportant way diplomats—ambassadors who were actually trusted by both sides. And this morning they were at their posts ; they had even thought to bring in extra bread, in case any of the staff should appear, and a pot of jam and some eggs—for which

Brett was to feel thankful, as lunch time approached and the tempo of the rioting increased. He had no thought of insisting on returning to his hotel for that meal.

The Maltese, with an immensely sad look on his face, was typing out an official report on the recent Education symposium, destined for the London office. 'I wish I were in London,' he lamented aloud, and bent again to the typewriter :

'. . . Professor Pitt then delivered an extremely informative and interesting account of the aims, history and organization of adult education in Britain. This was followed by a somewhat original form of address by Mr. Bacon, which was received well by the younger Egyptians in the audience. To end with, Professor Still-Waters gave a suggestive talk on free expression in children and the dangers consequent upon frustrating their natural impulses . . .'

Brett had exhausted his powers of sympathy, and of patience, on the Maltese. The latter could talk of nothing but past bloodshed—the massacres of the past twenty years, the dreadful things that were done to and sometimes by Australian troops during the war—and their present chances of escaping through the skylights should the mob find out that two hated Britishers ('he and I?' Brett asked himself) were trapped in their midst. In the end Brett had directed the clerk's attention to the paper work waiting to be done, and then retired to the reading room to look over the latest batch of English periodicals. They were three weeks old and, he felt, they might have been thirty years old, for all their power to grip. One of them carried a scholarly article contending that no serious and honest art had been produced since the end of the sixteenth century, another printed a heated attack on the sadistic violence and unbridled sexual passion which characterised children's films. Fascinating ! The most recent issue of *The Times* reported that some obscure M.P. had asked a question in the House about the possibility or otherwise of drawing up a pension scheme for English teachers in the service of foreign governments. That didn't concern him, either.

He walked across to a window overlooking the main thoroughfare, though the servants had warned him to keep well inside the room. Advice ! People were always giving him helpful advice in this country, people of all kinds, as if he were a complete idiot. But he could stay away from the window no longer, he had to see what he certainly did not wish to see.

Uproar had been continuous for some time past, as a miscellaneous gang of men and women, old and young, were smashing the windows of the shops opposite the Centre and quarrelling over the contents. Some fifty yards away a group of soldiers with rifles and a machine-gun was stationed outside the National Bank : they ignored the looting, it was nothing to do with them, they were not there to protect the tradespeople. Probably they were wishing that they could join in. But they merely looked on, dispassionately, leaning on their heavy old rifles.

They were supposed to be preserving law and order, Brett thought angrily ; they were armed, the looters were not—yet they just stood there and let all this go on. An English cadet corps equipped with air-guns could have cleared the vicinity in five minutes ! He felt so shocked, so outraged, that the blood was beating in his temples : the dirty impudence, the foul inefficiency of it all ! Jabber, jabber went the excited robbers, a woman was yelling in ecstatic anguish because she had cut her hand on the broken glass, a one-legged beggar pushed his crutch through a tailor's window and snatched up a pair of fawn-coloured slacks, another woman was squatting down on the kerb and suckling her child (who must have been four years old or more) while the husband scuffled busily in the burnt-out shell of a Jewish watch-mender's cabin.

The thought crossed his mind that he had been here no longer than six months. But that was enough, he raged, that was more than enough. The country was hopeless, utterly beyond redemption. He and his colleagues were *allowed* to stay here, to talk about Shelley, T. S. Eliot, Charles Morgan, as the case might be, or to play recordings of Vaughan Williams and Benjamin Britten. The leading daily papers, the weeklies from *The New Statesman* to *Punch*, the more respectable monthlies, technical magazines devoted to photography and model railways and bee-keeping (why, they were sufficiently broad-minded, broad in their appeal, to take both *Blackwood's Magazine* and *Scrutiny*)—all these were neatly set out on the shelves for anyone to read, anyone who cared to walk in. Then an upheaval like this came along—six or seven toy soldiers were sent to lounge against the marble walls of the National Bank—and that was all. The mob was left at leisure to cut its fingers or other people's throats. One day there was a government, there were laws, the consuls gave their cocktail parties—the next day there was no government, there were no laws, one dared not walk in the streets.

He was living a lie. How could he solemnly stand up in this very room next week and recite ' It is a beauteous evening, calm and free ' in front of those mongrelly old local females who doted on him, as if this simply had not happened ? He was living a lie—not such a gross lie as Packet from the university and his friend and senior, that Egyptianized *pagliaccio*, Bacon. For they even pretended that it wasn't actually a lie. But his anger was directed against those who had forced him into the lie—that sudden eruption of a world he should have had nothing to do with, those animals cavorting and howling outside : they couldn't be considered human beings, they weren't human.

Yet the city was in their hands. *No-one did anything to stop this monstrosity.* He could hardly draw breath, thinking of the British troops in the canal zone, so near—frozen into uselessness by some fantastic so-called agreement concocted by a gang of fat cynical demagogues. Where politics were concerned, he himself was by no means a reactionary, at home—certainly no Colonel Blimp. Communism was already *passé* when he went up to the university ; but all the same he was, he would say, quite liberal in his opinions, if anything. It was all very well to be liberal in England : *there* one could afford such feelings. But here—if only he had a bomb large enough to destroy them all ! A moral fury blinded him to his own danger and, close up to the window, he glared down at the industrious rabble. He would throw it there, into the middle of them.

The city itself was a colossal lie. Its very name was an empty pretension—and the palatial dollar-studded head-quarters of the World Health Organization, the King's yacht in the harbour, the scores of chromium-plated travel agencies, the Greco-Roman Museum (a give-away at the best of times since an insecure roof had kept it closed to the public for the past two years), the multiple stores, the fine *cuisine* of *Le Petit Coin de France*, and Bacon's farcical university . . . What had held the whole thing together so long ? A tacit conspiracy of appeasement on the part of people like Bacon, a conspiracy of pretence, of turning a blind eye and nodding and winking. And what possible compromise could there be between Bacon's taste for poetry (he even wrote it, apparently) and this bestiality in the street ? Only shiftiness, quibbling, at the best, a long-term dishonesty.

The plundering of the tailor's shop, a fashionable establish-ment, was well under way. A bony little boy of five or six crawled over the broken glass and re-emerged with a thick roll of cloth. He staggered under its weight a few steps along the street and round the corner, where his mother waited with what had once been a pram. She took the cloth from him, patted him approvingly on the shoulder, and he returned for another roll, this time in a grey herring-bone pattern. Meanwhile, Brett perceived, a sergeant of fierce appearance had joined the group of soldiers outside the bank, on the other corner : he waved towards the looters and shouted something imperiously. The soldiers straightened up reluctantly and reached for their rifles ; then they all shouted at the busy civilians. One or two of the latter slunk away, but the others paid no attention, apart from a conciliatory gesture and a perfunctory chorus of ' *Maalish !* ' By this time the little Egyptian had deposited his second load and was back in the shop front tugging at a roll of navy blue pin-stripe. He was lifting it on to his shoulder just as the small party of soldiers, urged on by the fiery sergeant, advanced towards the shop. They were outnumbered, they were frightened, and since the looters showed no signs of dispersing, they began to fire—at first over the heads of their countrymen, but very soon they were merely firing, in a panic, neither deliberately at nor deliberately away from any-one. The little boy, preoccupied with his mission, oblivious of the changing situation, was hit ; his burden rolled into the gutter and he fell without a sound. That was enough for them all : the mob vanished silently in all directions, and the soldiers, terror-stricken by the thought of what reprisals might follow, ran back into the grandiose portico of the Bank where, between huge columns veined with red, they huddled behind the protecting machine-gun.

It was enough for Brett, too. The bomb he had wished for had exploded, but after its own fashion, and he could not face the results. A skinny little body, in a sudden awful silence, lying face down on the deserted pavement, bleeding sluggishly into the debris. His anger turned to a feeling of imminent sickness, and he drew back from the window.

The old servant had entered noiselessly to tell Brett that his lunch was ready. As he began to speak, Brett backed away from him in a kind of horror : ' Keep away from

me ! Go away ! ' The servant shrugged his shoulders very
slightly and left the room without another word. Brett
slumped into a chair and sat bunched there for ten minutes,
waiting for the sickness to pass. It seemed ages later that,
hearing a voice outside, he went slowly back to the window.
Was the body still lying there ? Perhaps the child had been
shamming dead, or was only wounded, perhaps it would
have crawled away ? But the voice was the mother's, wailing
as she rocked the corpse.

The fact that again there was movement, there was noise,
there was life outside, served to restore Brett to his earlier
indignation. He was put in the right once more, he felt
justified : after all, nothing had happened that wasn't to be
expected of these people.

She's shrieking about the death of her son, he told himself,
whom she sent to his death. She claws at the brave soldiers
shivering behind their machine-gun ; the sergeant says something sad and placatory to her ; she curses him lengthily ;
she kisses her son's face—probably he had nothing but kicks
from her when he was alive, he and his seven or eight brothers
and sisters. How typical it all is ! The dirty dishonest game
that they call life, this degenerate race of cheap actors ! She,
she should have been shot, as well. Give them more efficient
arms and training in how to use them—he prayed—help
them to destroy themselves, all of them, once and for all.
In a moment, he said to himself, she will load the body on
top of the stolen cloth and wheel the pram home : no-one
will molest her, no-one will dare stop her, like that. But
somehow or other an ambulance had been called, and, still
nursing the body and still lamenting wildly, the woman was
coaxed and pushed into it by the two harassed orderlies.
The soldiers stared dully at it as it moved away, the sergeant
lifted his hands and let them drop in a movement of regret
and resignation. There was no-one else in sight.

He had better eat some lunch now ; his stomach felt

dreadfully weak and empty. He would explain to the old
servant that he had been upset for the moment by what he
had seen from the window.

Marcel was upset. 'Frightful! Frightful!' he squeaked,
as he bounced to and fro across his room. It was fortunate,
he admitted, that he happened to be paying one of his
periodical and uneasy visits to his father when the shocking
business broke out.

'Barbarians, savages, idiots!' he complained. 'I abhor
violence of any kind. A quiet life—that's all I have ever
wanted.' A generous tear suffused the large eyeball. 'And
it's the one thing I have never been granted.'

He shivered at the thought that he might have been trapped
in his lonely house out on the edge of the desert. He was
rather well thought of thereabouts, but all the same he
doubted whether the Bedouins would have gone out of their
way to defend him against the arabs of the town. However,
here he was: for once virtue had been rewarded. His
old father was a popular hero with the downtrodden and
oppressed: so clever, so cunning a man, they argued,
deserved to be so rich. That, in a sense, was virtue rewarded.
And even if they changed their minds on that score, the
paternal house had been built to keep out an army—under
no matter which flag it might march.

But the rioting had prevented Marcel from making a
rather important call. He had planned a serious talk with
his old acquaintance, the sub-editor of the *Journal d'Egypte*—
to ask, as a special favour, that the special favour which in
the past he had often requested might not this time be
granted. In short, that the social columnist should not
mention either directly or otherwise his presence at that silly
party given by Said Mohamed Said a few days previously.
Needless to say, his own behaviour during the short time he
was present (one needed to keep in with judges, he had

always felt) was altogether impeccable. But that unhappy little jest of the host's—producing two of his native models out of the kitchen, at the height of the party, one of them male and the other female, both professionally unclothed, and then inviting his guests to take their pick ! The story had spread about the city. And Marcel had to preserve a perfect decorum during his present delicate negotiations with the priesthood. It was already difficult enough, having to smooth over this ridiculous tiff about the origins of the Holy Ghost.

' A lot of old women,' he snarled. Then added unctuously, ' The salt of the earth.'

Still, there was the consolation that the newspaper couldn't appear as long as this hullabaloo continued. He cast a happy, ambitious eye on the sheaf of papers decorating his desk. Names, names, titles, titles. *Le Révérend Père*, the Venerable, the Right Reverend, the Most Reverend, His Superiority the Archimandrite, His Eminence the Cardinal, His Sublimity the Patriarch, the wholly holy His Archness the Marcel. All things were possible—he twirled heavily on his toe—simply a question of the right man finding his way to the right place.

' Marcel ! ' roared the voice of another patriarch, upstairs. ' Marcel, *viens ici* ! ' His expression changed ; he went, very quickly. The Father, too, gave trouble at times.

' And what is this, pray ? ' The old man was seated at a huge desk covered with a mountain of papers that quite put Marcel's to shame. He was holding out a bill. ' Repairs to your house, eh ! ' A coarse guffaw exploded from the leathery cheeks. He reminded Marcel of a bull-frog leering over a pond of water-lilies.

' I must live as befits my station,' Marcel rejoined with dignity. ' Is it a very large bill ? ' he asked nervously. ' You know how much importance these ecclesiastics attach to such evidences,' he added pathetically.

'Very large indeed,' growled the patriarch, bristling up his bushy eyebrows. 'Your new friends cost me more than your old.' Then he laughed scornfully. 'But I made enough on the market last week to pay it ten times over.'

'Clever papa,' murmured Marcel, who had been expecting the interview to end in this way.

'How much does it cost to be made Pope?' the old terror joked, holding out his cheque book. Marcel giggled in admiration and backed out of the room.

All the same, on regaining his cloister, he gave vent to indignation. The old man didn't realize how much it *was* costing his son—how much of some commodity which couldn't be drawn from a bank. Nor did the old man even begin to realize how significant it all was, how momentous —for humanity. For humanity.

He gazed out of the window. Smoke was rising in the distance ; the noise of some bloody fun-fair seeped in through the brick and the iron. What did they know of it, those zealous destroyers, what did they care ? Well, he wasn't working himself to the bone for *them.* The wall-eyed who would never see who their real friends were, the poverty-stricken, too poor in spirit ever to turn on their real enemies— better let them alone to cut each other's throats. Humanity ? —well, one drew the line somewhere. But at the moment, between his father upstairs and the mob outside, he wasn't quite sure where.

Idle speculation, he chided himself, the Devil's temptation for an intellectual. Back to work again. Like Saint Antony. And that reminded him : there was another unknown saint he had his eye on—quite acceptable to all parties, he had checked tactfully on that, and with a timely message for the modern world—Saint . . . Saint Who-was-it ? He sat contentedly at the desk, the fleshy face cupped in the plump hands. A glass or two of his father's excellent port would refresh his memory. He rang the bell for a servant.

It was no time to quibble about legal fares, and so Packet took the first *garry* he came across : there were very few of them about and he had walked almost a third of the way into town by then. The *garry* took him another third of the way, along the Corniche, threading its way stiltedly through crowds of *gallabiehs* that swirled and shook while their wearers cast about for something exciting to do or watch. And then the driver refused to go any further. ' I cannot,' he declaimed indignantly, reaching out for the ten shillings and pointing to his broken-down old horse, ' risk the life of this valuable beast '—or so Packet guessed. Changing his tone suddenly, he whined, ' Give *baksheesh*, effendi— food for this poor horse ! ' Aware of the English sentimentality on the subject of dumb animals, the cabmen generally expressed their desire for a tip through the horse's mouth—who, after all, had done most of the work. Packet retorted forcibly in the common tongue, and the *garry* trundled away in search of other Europeans mad enough to go out in the midday rioting.

He decided to turn inland and follow the Route d'Aboukir for the rest of the way : it would probably be quieter and, if the worst came to the worst, the road offered more in the way of shelter—big houses, stout trees and hedges, and a straight run through the rear of the Sporting Club. Also there was no sea to be thrown into.

To his alarm, however, he found that the army had had the same idea. Lorry after lorry was speeding along the Route d'Aboukir. He could not help but gape at them, while remembering to look as respectful as possible, for it was a strange sight. Each driver, tense of face, had his left hand on the steering wheel while his right hand, poised outside the door of the cabin, gripped a revolver. Attack, to judge by appearances, was expected from right, left, in front, behind, above and below. On the platform of every lorry was mounted a machine-gun, at the ready, worshipped by two motionless crouching soldiers. Except for the speed at which they were moving, it reminded Packet of an Armistice Day procession, or better still, the bas-relief on a cenotaph, with its statuesque vigilant figures in ideal postures, which had come alive.

What a splendid sense of the dramatic they had, these people ! For there was certainly nothing in the neighbourhood to cause alarm or provide suspense. Where was the enemy ? *Who* was the enemy ? In fact there was absolutely no-one to be seen apart from Packet and a handful of Egyptian children who also were staring open-mouthed at this enthralling and mysterious spectacle. Lorry after lorry surged past : with so few to admire, the military must have felt like Antony ' enthron'd i' the market-place, whistling to the air.'

Where indeed was the enemy ? All at once it struck Packet that this mighty display of armed force was proceeding in the wrong direction—at any rate in an unexpected direction—out of the city. The portentous poses of the city's saviours seemed all the more comic, and Packet stopped himself only just in time from laughing aloud ; that would have been most tactless. But perhaps they had quelled the city ? Perhaps they were racing out to win the old European suburbs from which he had so laboriously come ? Perhaps they had been summoned to Cairo, which would surely be in a shocking state ? He must remember to buy a newspaper tomorrow.

To have been striding along in the same direction as this seemingly endless cavalcade of military would have inspired feelings of alarm but also of a kind of nobility : but to be plodding along in the opposite direction made Packet feel rather ludicrous—like some cold sober person arriving at a public house five minutes after closing time. Ludicrous, and puzzled, and still rather disturbed.

No doubt Sylvie would be safe : he didn't feel that she was the sort of person to perish in the sacking of a city. But of course he had to *know* that she was safe. He couldn't possibly have stayed at home in the knowledge that he didn't *know* that she was safe. And probably he wouldn't come to any great harm himself. He could imagine himself being killed in a road accident or, more romantically, struck down by lightning ; but he simply couldn't visualize an enraged mob kicking his head round the square. He would die because he looked to the right instead of the left when crossing the road, or because he ate toadstools instead of mushrooms ; but not, surely, because he was white instead of brown or nominally Christian instead of nominally Moslem. Packet was convinced that God would

> *give everyone his own death,*
> *the dying which follows from his living,*

as the German poet had asked—in his case at any rate.

Which was not to deny that many might die today, and die horribly. In spite of himself, his imagination began to work. First there would come a denunciatory scream from some half-mad and probably half-starved individual ; and the tearing grip of a filthy claw ; then the slip-slap of running feet and an onrush of shabby *gallabiehs* ; blows from bony fists from every direction everywhere, then sticks and knives ; the smell, the saliva and the panting, the pain, the inhuman eyes and the barely human cries. One would be glad to die, at last.

The imagined experience had been so vivid, so present, had come to him so readily, with an awful irresistible ease, that he felt his bowels softening. His firm convictions as to feasible ways of dying melted away as well. What could be imagined with so little effort could easily happen, and what happened to other people could easily happen to him —how could it be otherwise ? Or to Sylvie. In a sudden panic he quickened his pace, keeping his head down as the last trucks of the convoy passed him. His imagination ground on like a machine out of control—the brakes would shriek as the lorry came to a stop, with a clatter the soldiers would jump to the ground . . .

He bit his lip and with a deliberate effort slowed up. The imagination was a traitor : this was not the first time it had unnerved him, or led him into trouble. During his adolescence, in despair, he had ignored it deliberately, distrusted its every motion, hoping that eventually it would die away and leave him to his common sense. But the only result was that he lost himself entirely and his links with other people, while common sense, thumbing desperately through basic assumptions and old precedents, was soon reduced to impotence. He must be really backward, he reflected once again, seeing how other people went gaily on, completely master of their own situation (and other people's), laying down the law, so thoroughly assured. Or were they merely cheering themselves up ? Well, that was all right too. As long as one didn't cheer oneself up at the expense of other people.

Some ten minutes later he noticed smoke rising from a grocer's shop in a small side-street. The old proprietor, a Greek or perhaps an Armenian, held his head and moaned, while a small crowd—neighbours and passers-by and, quite likely, the original incendiaries—rescued what they could. A burly Egyptian in shirt-sleeves staggered out of the smoke carrying a barrel of olives ; he dumped it beside the old man, slapped him cheerfully on the back and disappeared into the shop again. A nearby ironmonger was rolling stacks of new buckets out to children, who ran to fill them with water. From their merriment it was clear that they found extinguishing a fire quite as exciting as starting one.

A little further on Packet was alarmed to hear diabolic yells of joy close at hand, the voice of the Maenads. But it was only some very young children, some of them carrying younger children on their backs, who were savagely smashing Coca-Cola bottles in a little riot of their own. 'Don't cut yourselves!' he warned them absent-mindedly in English as he hurried past, half-expecting to receive a bottle ignominiously in his rear. But, like the salvagers, they were wholly given up to their task.

Soon it was time to turn towards the sea again. A narrow side-street would take him into the main square, his next objective. The square, he could see as he approached, was deserted, except for a few armoured cars and several trams, one of which lay on its side. Judging by the broken glass, the scattered stones and the abandoned skull-caps and unrolled turbans, there had been a considerable scrimmage earlier on. This was the nerve centre of the city, hectic by day and with a certain dark life of its own by night. Packet had never seen it silent and empty before. It was as if the English Sunday had descended upon the Middle East.

As he reached it, however, his way was barred by three soldiers of sullen demeanour. He wished them good day politely, to begin with, then pointed out the street he wished to gain and said something about a friend living there. But the apparition of a suave blue-eyed Englishman at this stage in a wearying day—the sun was overhead—an Englishman who seemed on the point of discussing the weather with them—an Englishman apparently oblivious of the fact that there had been grave trouble and the centre of the city was closed by high military order—no, even granting that foreigners were prone to eccentric behaviour, this was too suspicious. They waved him back threateningly.

Packet retraced his way to the road he had come by. It would be a long walk back to the flat, he reflected glumly, and no chivalrous intention would speed his steps. Better try again to break through the cordon, a little further on. Three minutes' walking brought him to another side-street parallel with the first. Adopting a business-like bearing he launched himself down it, at a dignified pace, not too fast, but without a hint of loitering. As if one were a distinguished foreigner, one whose services to the country were valued highly—an eminent surgeon, say, whose car had broken down on the way to an urgent operation. Yes !— what was the word for sick ? *Magnoun ?* No, that meant mad, that was going too far, it might be misunderstood. Ah, *ayyan*, that was it !

The guards at this corner were bored to death, half-asleep. He coughed gently to attract their attention ; decided quickly that a military-style salute would be unsuitable ; wished instead that Allah might be with them ; and rushed on to explain in atrocious Arabic that he was on his way to visit a sick friend, a very sick friend, over there—he waved his arm vaguely in Sylvie's direction. Complete silence ensued. He repeated his little speech, at half the speed and with some attention to accent. The guards showed themselves non-committal rather than hostile. In reality they were very ready to let the gentleman go wherever he desired : he was a well-spoken gentleman, if practically incomprehensible— and apparently he was sick, which made it better that he should go quickly. On the other hand, they were wearing uniforms, which meant that they ought to be forceful, brutal and suspicious. They were scared of their officers and doubtful as to how that unfathomable institution called military discipline would have them behave in this business. Accordingly they behaved as if the gentleman had said nothing at all, as if indeed there were no gentleman agitating there in front of them.

But Packet instinctively seized the advantage : he implored them with eyes and lips, with shoulders and arms. And finally, without actually looking him in the face—still keeping up the pretence that no-one was there—they waved him on brusquely, as if brushing aside some irritating little insect. Better get rid of him before an officer turned up to make a scene. Packet thanked them heartily, found that he had no cigarettes to offer them, and walked quickly into the square wiping the sweat away from his eyes. One of the soldiers shouted after him, ' Make hurry, effendi ! ' He did, as far as he could without breaking into a run. Running looked queer, especially at noon, not to mention the humiliation of it.

Chapter 9

THE BEAUTEOUS ONES, WITH LARGE DARK EYEBALLS, KEPT CLOSE IN THEIR PAVILIONS

SYLVIE occupied one of the 'furnished' flats in which this city of transit abounded. A small apartment, containing the minimum of rather cheap and quite unco-ordinated furniture, it had the air of a first-class waiting-room. But she would not hear a word against it. Comfortable homes complete with elegant furniture, tasteful curtains and fine china were associated in her mind with uncomfortable husbands, forced entertainment of boring business contacts and the oppressive attentions of a horde of loquacious relatives.

Yet she was only playing for time. She could not go on living apart from her child indefinitely, even if she could from her husband. The child had the right to a family—perhaps *she* would enjoy family life—or at least something in the way of a homely home. Bedroom-lounge-kitchenette : this was an interlude only, time for Sylvie to get her breath. But she needed it, and it was precious to her. She had few illusions—and certainly not the illusion of permanence —and so she was very willing to enjoy what she found to enjoy. It may have been this trait that had intrigued Packet ; for his own weakness, as he was increasingly aware, had lain in an obstinate tendency to postpone all possible happiness until the arrival of ideal circumstances. But never, alas, the time and the place and the loved one and world peace and a small capital in the bank, together. No, he was finding out, *aut Cæsar, aut nullus* was a stirring piece of literature, but as a rule of life it seemed unduly restrictive.

Packet's ring at the door was followed by a subdued shriek or squeak and a rustling noise. The door was then thrown vigorously open.

'You !' Sylvie exclaimed incredulously. Packet was more conscious of the surprise in her voice than of any pleasure. 'You ! But what are you doing out of your house at such a time !'

He tried to explain the anxiety he had felt for her, and how he couldn't stay safely—more or less—in the suburbs when she was in the thick of it. But he soon stuttered into an embarrassed silence, a little dismayed lest his feelings should embarrass her.

She took his hand. 'You must never do such a thing for my sake again.' She seemed even angry. 'They might refrain from spilling my blood—Arab, like theirs—but yours, never. You should not tempt anyone to become your murderer. Least of all me . . .'

They walked into the lounge. Sylvie added, 'In any case, I am not alone—Simone Nader, a relative, is with me . . . But you know, it was very sweet of you to come. And all that way. I do appreciate it—I could never have expected it.' She was feeling deeply ashamed of herself for her clumsy reception of him ; and irritated that he should have put her in the wrong.

Packet remembered then that a relative of Sylvie's, a cousin or second cousin or aunt, a widow in her mid-forties, occupied another small flat in the same block. Of course they would be together ; the circumstance had never entered his head. And now his role of protector had been doubled —or rather, he felt, halved.

Before Sylvie could mention her visitor's name, Madame Nader had rushed upon him.

'Ah, a man ! At last ! To watch over us poor girls !
Monsieur, we have sat here all morning, shivering in terror,
alone, waiting . . .' Sylvie coughed cynically. '. . . Sylvie
and I, with no-one to preserve us. I swear to you, *Monsieur*
——' She turned to Sylvie : '*Il est anglais, n'est-ce-pas ?
Tiens, j'espère que personne ne l'a vu entrer !*' Then back to
Packet, 'I swear before you, *Monsieur*, that this dark day has
aged me. My hairs must be quite white, is it not ? And
is that to be surprised at ? Ah, at times like this it is I miss
my dear husband. He would say to me—but why should
I sorrow you with my troubles ? I must be looking almost
middle-aged . . .'

'Not at all, *Madame*,' Packet was obliged to interject.
'Oh no, far from it, I assure you.' He hoped that his voice
carried conviction. What Sylvie found to amuse her in his
embarrassment he could not imagine.

'*Mais comment s'appelle-t-il*, Sylvie ? Ah, Monsieur Packette
—*quel joli nom !*—you are indeed a true English, a perfectly
pleasant knight as your poet says, so full of thoughts of the
women, so full of *courtoisie* . . .' How desperately frenchified
the woman was ! Or was she pulling his leg ? '. . . You
have come from far ? *Oh là là ! Incroyable !* And you
have not been brutally attacked ? The roads are passable ?
Ah, but you are a brave sir.' Turning to Sylvie again, she
asked, '*Mais pourquoi est-ce qu'il est venu ?*' And then
swivelling back on Packet, who was frantically trying to
think of an acceptable reason, 'But tell us of what is passing.
Have they burned down the *Lycée Français* ? Or *Saint
Marc* ? No ? Is Baudrot unharmed ? Yes ? Indeed, where
should we take tea if they destroy Baudrot ? But surely they
have attacked the *Consulat Britannique* ! No ? But there
is still time for that, oh yes, there is still time, huh !'

Taking advantage of the momentary silence in which the
woman was relishing her grim prognostications, Packet gave
himself to a sober and even tedious matter-of-fact account

of the little children breaking Coca-Cola bottles on the Route d'Aboukir. 'Hah!' she cried out, jumping in her chair, 'I knew it, I knew it!' As if the bottles had been friends and relatives of hers. Her plump breasts wobbled self-righteously.

Sylvie returned from the kitchen with a plate of sardines, bread and butter and a pot of coffee. 'Not quite a Baudrot tea, but the best I can manage . . . . He must be worn out and hungry, Simone. Let him rest a while.' Madame Nader gazed avidly at him as he settled self-consciously into a chair. Obviously his arrival had been the making of her day.

'*Il est gentil, tu sais, ton chevalier!*' she hissed at Sylvie.

'*Oui—et il comprend le français,*' Sylvie replied in a normal voice.

Madame Nader put her hand to her mouth in mock dismay, failed to summon up a blush, and instead giggled exaggeratedly at him. If only he had ridden up at the head of a crack British regiment, preferably in full-dress uniform, her happiness would have been complete. But even as it was, he must be made the most of.

'Ah you English,' she set off, 'so noble, so idealistic . . .'. At this moment, as if impelled by curiosity, a large fat and wet dog, of more than middle age by any system of computation, emerged cautiously from beneath the table.

'Ah, my little Alexandre!' Madame Nader exploded, 'is he frightened by the big nasty Egyptian men? There, there—a big strong Briton has come all this way just to protect you, *mon petit*!' She heaved the animal up—in his decrepitude he resembled something that had been run over by a heavy vehicle and left in the rain for several days —and presented him drooping and dripping to the Briton, who, in the confusion caused by this unexpected introduction, let fall an oily sardine on the carpet. Sylvie giggled, and whispered to him, 'Aren't you sorry now that you set out to save me from a fate worse than death?'

Well, at all events he was glad to sit down after that long and uncomfortable walk. Relieved, as well, to be inside a solid-looking house : the empty square had demoralized him rather, he had felt like the solitary tree on a hill in a thunder-storm. It was a pity about that disgusting grunting old dog, of course—and he wouldn't walk far to save Madame Nader's life, even though she was Sylvie's cousin or second cousin or aunt. And why was Sylvie so prickly ?

' But what was I saying ? ' demanded Madame Nader as she suddenly dropped Alexandre on the carpet, where he landed with a sort of squelch, at once snuffling round the sardine in senile excitement. ' I *know* that it was something of importance.'

' We English,' Packet prompted reluctantly, against his own interests he feared, ' so noble, so idealistic.'

' *C'est ça !* So idealistic—you invent democracy, you extenuate liberty and equality and—ah no, that is the French of course—and you make a *Déclaration d'Indépendance*—or was that the Americans ? I am *so* unknowing in history, poor little me ! And then—' she changed from cooing to thundering, as she pointed a finger menacingly at the brave protector of the weak—' then you insist to share this with all the savages of the world ! Like the base Hindu in the play, who threw away pearls to swine, you lavish freedom to the Egyptians ! ' She paused to take breath and Packet, hastily swallowing down a piece of crust, could not refrain from a mild protest.

' We didn't exactly *give* it to them, as I remember . . .'

' —you give them freedom. Freedom to do what, may I ask ? To rob and destroy, to slaughter poor helpless girls such as Sylvie and me . . .'

' Speak for yourself, Simone—I refuse to be described as a poor helpless girl. If there are any such in Alexandria— and I have never met one myself—then I am not of their company. And I am sure that you would quickly frighten away any Egyptian who should be so ill-advised as to try to slaughter you.' Sylvie really went a little too far, Packet felt. She added placatingly, ' But perhaps the fact is that you miss your husband and I do not miss mine, and that is the difference between us.'

' *I* am not joking, Sylvie.' Madame Nader drew up her podgy body and assumed a stern and serious expression. ' The barbarians are running wild in the roads, all is given into their hands, while the great and celebrated army of *Grande Bretagne* sleeps behind the canal.' Her voice attained new heights. ' Come back, I say to those good and gallant soldiers——'

' Asleep on the canal bank,' Sylvie suggested idly.

' —come back——'

' To Erin, mavourneen, mavourneen,' Packet joined in, getting into the spirit of the thing. At least Madame Nader could take a joke without offence ; she took it in her stride, it collapsed into dust beneath her tread.

' —to Egypt, and save this miserable land from anarchy and ruin.' She dropped the denunciatory finger with a fine effect, and pierced the enfeebled representative of Great Britain with a fiery, questioning and expectant gaze.

' They don't want to come back,' was all he could think of to say. ' I don't think they liked it much here.'

' *Do not want*——'

' If you bothered less about world affairs and more about your dog,' Sylvie came to the rescue, ' it would be better for all concerned, Simone. Alexandre is choking to death— I think that a sardine tail must be stuck in his throat.'

And in fact Alexandre was coughing and crowing and shaking all over : only the intensity of his mistress's indignation could have drowned the hideous racket he was making. It was more alarming than anything else in his morning, Packet thought, the sight and sound of this heaving bundle of rags.

'But what monster gave him a sardine?' Madame Nader dived at the unhappy creature. 'Oh, *le pauvre petit* ! What naughty person gave him a wicked sardine?' With a nimble twist of the fingers she extracted the cause of the trouble and Alexandre relapsed into somnolence forthwith. Well, she was good with animals, Packet admitted, and his heart warmed very slightly towards her.

'Perhaps it was a naughty British counterplot?' suggested Sylvie.

By tea-time Madame Nader had swept aside the last vestiges of opposition ; she reigned supreme. From British statesmanship she had turned her attention to education. With a large number of well-chosen words she had put Packet in his place, as a purveyor of that commodity.

'In teaching these young Egyptians you are betraying your trust. Why, it is as if a doctor should break the Hypocritic oath. The more they learn, the worse they will become ! Drunk with knowledge they enrage the harmless peasants to revulsion. I have read in a play called *La Tempête* —what is that in English? Ah, *The Storm*—about a dirty man called Cannibal, who told to his professor : "You taught me how to speak, and so I spit in your eye !" That Cannibal was an Egyptian student, I well believe.'

'As you see, Simone knows an awful lot about English literature. She used to attend courses at the Cultural Centre . . .'

'Ah yes. That was when my dear husband was lively. I have always been devoted to the arts. And a lecture in the cool quiet rooms of the Centre was such a relaxation for me . . .'

'Do you still go there?' Packet enquired. Brett must be earning his salary.

'No, I have not been there since the death of my poor

husband.' Her body slipped into the lines of a Mater Dolorosa.

'Life is one long relaxation for Simone these days, you see. And she has so many friends and relatives to visit.'

'And who would look after poor little Alexandre when I should assist at a lecture?' For once, Packet meditated, that linguistic *faux-ami* had told the truth.

'Well now,' said Sylvie sweetly, 'you two can have a little chat about books while I prepare some tea.' What had he done to her, Packet asked himself miserably, to deserve such treatment?

It transpired that Madame Nader, to speak frankly—'and you have understood that I always speak frankly'—really preferred American literature—'perhaps because I am just a little *vulgaire*—you see, I can be frank about myself, too.'

For instance, she was fascinated by Poe (who, as she remarked, was really a French writer), and she liked Hemingway (so easy to follow, even though one's English was limited!) and Paul Bowles, who wrote about the desert and was just half-way between Camus and E. M. Hull. Modern English poetry? No, she could not honestly say that she enjoyed it—though she had read T. S. Eliot (or was he American, too?): she preferred orthodox writers, like Francis Thompson and T. S. Eliot, because one always knew what they meant even though one could not understand what they said, and that was a great help . . .

At long last Sylvie returned with a tray of tea things— she grimaced at her *chevalier* in a way that was only partly pitying—and proposed that Simone should pour out. But the latter suddenly shot to her feet—Packet nearly dropped the plates he was grappling with—and shrieked out the news that in her flat were some delicious little sweetmeats, they would adore them she was sure; just a little minute and she would be back with them. She raced away in a whirl of skirts, like a victim of snake-bite in search of an antidote.

'Poor dear.' Sylvie stroked his hair. 'You are the one who needs protection now. I think she has taken a liking to you.'

In spite of his low estimate of the lady, Packet felt perceptibly flattered. 'Well,' he conceded, 'I do seem to be rather redundant.'

'Oh no. You have paid me a great compliment. So great that it troubles me. And so I am being a little wicked.'

'But why? Why should it trouble you? Any more than flowers or a box of chocolates? And surely those are permitted me?'

'I have nothing against flowers, nor against chocolates, except that they are fattening. But your gift is—how shall I say?—too expensive. And I don't like to be overwhelmed.'

'But don't be silly!' It was a relief to display a little anger. 'I haven't given you anything, Sylvie. If only I had more money . . .'

But Simone reappeared at this point, bearing aloft her confections, and they commenced tea. Packet was left horribly in the dark; with something so crucial at stake, he could hardly manage to be civil to Madame Nader. Couldn't she sense the fact that she was *de trop*? Wouldn't Sylvie drop her a gentle hint to that effect? No, in both cases. She had now assumed the role of hostess—the cakes, which she conveyed as if to a starving garrison, gave her the right to that—and she seemed less likely than ever to depart.

Only a fresh outburst of yelling and firing in the vicinity deterred Packet from abruptly making his adieus. But Madame Nader did not appear to notice the accelerated tempo of the rioting, she was gloating so vivaciously over her offerings. They were *beklawa*, Syrian cakes, impregnated with honey, dripping with fat and studded with diverse nuts—minute triangles but solid throughout and capable of breaking a plate if dropped from a height. Packet was well acquainted with them : on his arrival in the country, happy to have put the sawdusty buns of post-war England behind him, he had given himself up to a mild orgy of middle-eastern sweetmeats. He had not touched them since. But now, with his teeth aching savagely and his stomach curdling, he fought his way through a couple of them. Rather martyrdom of this sort than to have Madame Nader discoursing on the insularity of the British, their bad teeth, their ineptitude in *gastronomie* and so on. While the ladies were engrossed in questions of clothes and hair, he slipped half of his second cake to Alexandre—there was nowhere to conceal unwanted articles in this bare flat—but the old dog snarled nastily and Packet had to pretend that he had dropped it accidentally.

'Oh my poor little cake ! Is it truly too dirty to eat ? You know, Sylvie, this carpet is in a scandalous condition. We may very well need all the food we have before this terror is ended. Who knows how many days we may be trapped here ?' Packet winced : that thought hurt him more than his teeth. Penitently he bent down to rescue the carpet from the cake, and in so doing caught Alexandre in the act of lifting a leg against his chair. Better report it now, he thought fearfully, or else it would be blamed on him. Shyness drove him into French. '*Madame—votre chien—er—il a besoin de—er—d'une toilette.*'

'Oh the poor dear, he is only human after all,' she cried. '*Alexandre—ça suffit* !' She bent her brows and fixed the dog with a stern reproachful stare : at once Alexandre dropped his leg and his tail, and retreated under the table in utter confusion. Yes, how good she was with animals.

And indeed Madame Nader continued to expand. As time went on, she sloughed off her French and her English became increasingly fluent. After all, Packet had to concede, she was good with riots and disorders, too, in her way. Himself, he would prefer a game of cards or, if circumstances allowed, a game of bowls, or some gramophone records—and an upper lip not stiff but reasonably still. Nonetheless it could hardly be said that Madame Nader was going to pieces.

She thrived in fact. As the cakes disappeared, it seemed to Packet that she grew visibly plumper, the oil of the *beklawa* re-emerged on her skin, she glistened with a strange light, her hair outshone her black silks, she ran with milk and honey. And she talked and talked, in such a smooth paste of languages that what she said began to sound quite witty.

At half-past eight they consumed a light supper, of cucumbers and salami and cognac. Madame Nader was softening in spirit as the evening wore on; she turned to discussing family matters with Sylvie; it seemed to be a large family and it had many matters. Scores of names were cited: from *Grand'tante* Josephine who lived in Suez whence she controlled a large cotton estate in Upper Egypt —she had married an otherwise inconsiderable White Russian who thereupon passed the remainder of his days writing feeble verses in four languages and quoting the many apposite things that Tolstoy had said to him as a boy on their one momentous meeting—down to little Gaston who had been born two months ago in Beirut. Husbands, wives and children, their health, their finances, their domestic fortunes, their schooling, they appeared to have no secrets. . . . And the talk took them all over the world; there were representatives in Mexico, Brazil, Ceylon, Jamaica, Madrid, Marseilles, Naples, Istanbul, New Orleans . . . Packet sat there in a state of peaceful semi-consciousness, while the names and the places swept about him, a saw-mill in the Cameroons or a shipping office in Buenos Aires, and the mild evening light softened the bleakness of the room. Behind their talk the rioting went on, but it seemed remote and trivial, now, shadowy and not altogether real. The richness of the woman, after all! The two of them, chattering away in perfect understanding, gently fluttering their hands or their heads : they were like ears of wheat in a vast wheat-field. He was almost asleep : I ought to be listening more closely, he told himself, I must learn about Syrians.

Towards ten o'clock the gallant Simone began to show signs of succumbing. It had been an exciting day, she remarked in stifling a yawn, and the noisiness of other people was really very fatiguing—never did she sleep so well as after a day of disturbances. Alexandre was snoring beneath her chair.

Outside, soldiers were marching languidly up and down. It had been a fatiguing day for them, too ; the guard was relieved, and doubled for the night. The military, it appeared, were in full control of the situation. They were, however, a nervy lot, alarmingly quick on the trigger—the flash of sun on spectacles in an upper window, as if someone were firing down on them, had brought about the death of a Czech medical professor earlier in the day. And these simple men had a horror of darkness and what the night might bring—they shot to kill, then, they shot the corpse to make sure, and afterwards they investigated. The terror of lawlessness had been succeeded by the terrorism of law. And the latter was more dangerous in a way, because it was more organized and better armed and it had less of a sense of humour. Such thoughts were passing through Packet's mind, though he had twice brought up the question of his departure and had once even risen to his feet.

'Oh no, dear boy,' Simone was now much less formal in her address. 'It is certain that you cannot sleep *chez vous* this night. It is much too far away, and you will never find a taxi. *Alors, qu'est-ce qu'on peut faire*, Sylvie ? Hum, yes. Now there is a young Lebanese with whom I am acquainted, and he inhabits an apartment above this . . .'

'But what are you thinking of, Simone !'

'But surely, Sylvie, at a time like this, an emergency, a crisis? Do you not think?' She turned to Packet. 'He is a young man, of an excellent family—his connections are without reproach, *vraiment*——'

'No, Simone, not even during an emergency.' Sylvie turned to the object of their planning. 'The young man comes of an excellent family, as they say. But his connections are another matter. I don't think you would feel at home with him.' She added in a whisper, 'I shall return the compliment—and save *you* from a fate . . .'

Packet learnt nothing further about this unsuitable young man, except that he was related to the Queen in some way, for Simone conceded the point without contest : it had been a purely academic contribution.

A pleasantly cool breeze was blowing in through the window : the city seemed silent at last, but for a vague and subdued humming, as if from a distant happy fairground. 'I believe that it is almost over,' Simone murmured, 'and we are still alive. There will be another day for us.' With her foot she nudged Alexandre, a dim throbbing heap of old fur. '*Est-il heureux!*'

It was half-past ten. 'I shall go to bed,' she announced, 'and in my own bed. I am much too sleepy to be afraid of anything, and if I stay with you chattering boxes I shall have no sleep at all.' Having collected her handbag, some books, embroidery and other sundries, she added, 'I shall leave you to work out your problem.'

Packet offered to carry something for her, preferably not Alexandre, and the two of them accompanied her to the lift. That was still in working order. And Packet felt sorry, in a way, to see her rise up, with a richly benign smile and a '*dormez bien!*', over their heads and out of sight.

'Will she be all right?' he asked.

'As safe there as anywhere else, you know.'

'But won't she feel nervous?' He had a guilty feeling

that she would have spent the night with Sylvie if it hadn't been for him.

'She is a very brave woman.'

'Really?'

'You don't believe that, do you?' She was almost jeering at him. 'You think that she is vain, frivolous, stupid and noisy. Yes, she is something of all that, but she is courageous, too. But courage is not a very enjoyable virtue to exercise—one cannot make much out of it—except in a crisis. Oh, you English are fine in a crisis—there you are in your element. But life is not all a series of emergencies.'

'Here, here,' he put in, 'you're going too fast. I admit that she got on my nerves at first—and my nerves aren't particularly sensitive—but as a matter of fact I was beginning to like her—I could see that there was something very admirable about her, a kind of vitality . . .'

'You began to admire her vitality when she began to get sleepy.'

'Well——'

'She got on your nerves—oh, I don't blame you for that. Your nerves are English, your nerves are Anglo-Saxon . . .'

'Here, I say, there's no need to be rude!' It was his turn to show a little fire. She knew very well that he had Celtic blood in his veins.

'And Simone is Syrian.'

'You are making too much of it. Ridiculous!' They were on familiar ground.

'But it needs to be made something of,' she answered, more gently. 'Can't you see, my dear? Simone is what I shall be, at her age. I might well be much worse, indeed, for your nerves.'

'Nonsense. You are entirely different from Simone. All Syrians are not alike, any more than all Englishmen are. Look at Brett, for instance—you remember meeting him at the great party?—isn't there any difference between Brett and me—well, between Brett and Bacon, say?'

'Of course we are different—but at the same time we are all Syrians. And you and Brett and Bacon are all Englishmen, however you may differ one from the other. And I assure you that you do differ from Brett.'

They walked back into her flat in silence. Then she continued urgently, 'Yes, Simone is pretentious, empty-headed, vulgar and excitable. And in another fifteen or twenty years your nerves would find me equally unbearable.'

'But, good lord, she's not that bad! Why, I believe I have a higher opinion of her than you have.' He made a great effort and said masterfully, 'And if you marry me, you won't come to that, in any case.'

'Really? For your sake I shouldn't wish to risk it. Nor for my own sake. We Syrians do not stay young for ever, like you Englishmen . . . But, thank you . . . How rude I am always! How can you tolerate me? But I do mean thank you. That makes twice you have risked your life today.' She smiled. And they gave up arguing.

A little later Sylvie said, 'But to be practical for a moment. It is only a single bed, I warn you. Because I have come to think of myself as a single woman.'

'Well, er . . . I could sleep on the sofa, very well, you know.'

'Not very well—the springs are bursting through . . . And in any case, you are not being very chivalrous, are you, my dear?'

They inspected the bed solemnly, and Packet pronounced it satisfactory. Sylvie turned to him with a slight smile, hardly a smile.

'Don't be angry, or hurt, if I say something?'

'Of course not. What right should I have? And this is exactly the time to say it.'

'That's what I mean.' She smiled again, less shyly. 'I

ought to warn you now, Monsieur Packette, that this does not bind me to marry you. Even if you should ask me again . . . And I *think* that you will,' she added after a pause. 'Oh I shall,' he responded fervently, 'more than ever.'

When Packet returned to his flat the next day the city was reasonably quiet. The army had settled in, the mob had melted away, to lick their wounds and take stock and compare notes, the police kept tactfully out of sight. Although the trams were not running, most of the taxis and *garrys* were on the streets and not charging much more than twice the normal fares.

And the day after, the army had returned to its camps and the police were back at their posts, as good-natured as ever and not in the least sheepish, nor bearing any malice, in spite of the fact that their rates of pay remained precisely the same as before.

Packet stood at his local tram station, on his way to work. The shop-keepers who had not suffered damage were leaning smugly against their doors, condoling with the less fortunate. There was animated talk of insurance and claims and new panes of glass and stolen stock, of ancient examples and new hopes. Gradually all the victims were warming to life again. Their disasters secured them a certain status— nothing at all had happened in Cairo and so for once, it was felt, their city deserved a grander title than '*notre deuxième capitale*'—strangers came up to them with sympathetic enquiries, they elaborated their losses, they began to enjoy themselves. All of them except the dead.

A blind old Egyptian shuffled along in the centre of the tracks, until a Greek schoolboy led him into safety; two newspaper sellers cuffed each other vigorously in mock anger; a couple of pale but reddening English ladies, tall and thin and upright, discussed the comparative prices of nylon stockings; a large Buick containing an elegant chauffeur and a portly Egyptian gentleman scattered a mixed covey of jay-walkers ; and a seedy individual tried half-heartedly to sell Packet some mildly indecent photographs.

The troubles were over. Not for ever, of course, but until the next time.

Chapter 10

WRETCHED THE DRINK !
AND AN UNHAPPY COUCH !

IT was early in May, and the academic year showed its
first signs of ending.   For examinations were approaching.
A month or so previously a great though annual change
had swept across the dusty face of the faculty.   The facetious
or boisterous had turned soft and respectful—as for the
downright offensive, it seemed that one must have misunderstood them—and perhaps for the first time in the year
they were to be observed in class, pencil in hand, assiduously
taking notes.

Classes, in fact, were once again as large as they had been
in the first week of term, when registration took place.
It might well happen that a lecturer would be startled to note
among his own particular flock faces which he had never
encountered before—the first time this happened to Packet
he had really thought himself to be in the wrong room, or
even the wrong faculty—large ageing men, with white hairs,
who shyly explained that as they were the Assistant Station-
master of some or other minute village they had never been
able to attend a lecture.   But they had worked every night
by themselves, of course.   And what of the lectures they
had missed ?—the lecturer would ask the question with
heavy sarcasm.   ' Oh sir, I have borrowed the notes of my
friend Mohamed El Din who is in your class, sir.'   And
Mohamed El Din stood up and solemnly swore that such

was indeed the case ; and everyone was satisfied and happy, for they knew that it was notes that mattered, stiffened a little maybe with relevant bits from Legouis or Elton. Everyone except possibly the lecturer, who often believed himself to be a much better teacher than his students' notes would suggest.

There existed a regulation to the effect that no-one should be admitted to examinations who had not achieved an attendance of seventy-five per cent at lectures. Every year at this time the staff were peremptorily reminded of the regulation. And every year attempted application of it merely brought a flood of medical certificates and tearful explanations into the secretary's office. By the time these had been sorted out, the examinations were over, the results published, and the foreign teachers on vacation in Europe. Or in the case of the less well-to-do—the unsubsidized English, that is—hiding out rather nervously in the shady suburbs of Ramleh.

And as Bacon pointed out to his disgruntled colleagues, was there any sense in debarring some unfortunate student who was obliged to work for his three or four children, while the class jester who made a nuisance of himself during three lectures out of every four was allowed to sit ? Nor, he went on, was it *only* the malcontents who disappeared into prison for a few months in every year.

The weather was oppressively hot and damp. From time to time a neurotic wind whirled through the corridors, carrying with it dust, scraps of paper, cigarette ends too small to interest the servants, and the year's work in chalk-dust. Tempers were a little on the ragged side all round, for the staff knew that the real work of their year was about to begin and that they would have neither time nor official permission to do it well. Moreover, the tension with which the students bristled had communicated itself to the staff. Stoicism was a virtue quite foreign to the students, and at times like this even the Englishmen were surprised to find themselves less gifted with that virtue than they had supposed.

In the mornings they met to discuss the question papers under Bacon's leadership. The first and second years, pre-specialization and huge in numbers, presented the greatest difficulties. The questions had to be, firstly, at once comprehensible and entirely unambiguous. This precluded the use of a number of conventional expressions such as 'relevant' and 'contextual' which the student mind had steadfastly refused to absorb. And secondly, they had to be of a kind which did not immediately invite a cascade of parrot-learnt notes. Thanks to Bacon's long experience of the student mind's capacity for misunderstanding, the first of these conditions was usually achieved. Though in this sticky weather, and further harassed by loitering pupils with their leading questions, it was easy to forget that 'Julius Cæsar' was the name of a play and the name of a character in a play as well as the name of a historical personage—and that italics meant little or nothing to a shattered examinee.

In the grounds of the faculty workmen were erecting a gigantic marquee, in which most of the examinations would be held. It consisted of rough wooden poles and masts hung with large and worn carpets, and it turned out to be amazingly cool. Here and there the sun poured through a hole, in a beam so hard and precise that one bent the head to pass under it. Meanwhile, on the other side of the faculty, in a blaze of blue, the slow sea sighed and slapped along the hot sand, and children ran squealing into the water, fully clothed, as fully clothed as they ever were, or stood a moment in the sun for their frocks to dry. *Julius Cæsar* and *Silas Marner*—Packet mused torpidly—they might well mean something to these people—surely they did—but to *examine* them in the books ? Were examinations feasible in this country ? The *genius loci* really had nothing in common with the Spirit of Competition.

After these meetings the teachers pushed their way mercilessly through the groups of agitated students and, drowsing uneasily in the tram, went into town for iced beer. In the afternoons the more sensible invariably slept for a couple of hours. But Packet, who could not rid himself of the feeling that there was something slightly degenerate about the siesta, sat stupid and sweating over a book until a pervasive sense of ill-being drove him out to the beach. Sometimes he would meet Sylvie there, but not often, as she objected that in this weather the sands were covered with her relatives, and their reunions were so strenuous that it was cooler to stay at home in a shuttered room.

Then came the day allotted to the department for the printing of their examination papers. In the past there had been scandals connected with these papers. On one occasion more notorious than the others every single question in a number of subjects had been published in an Arabic newspaper the day before the examination. And so the process of printing—more exactly, of duplicating—was carried on under conditions of extreme secrecy. And of extreme discomfort.

Carrying their painful concoctions, the whole staff crowded into a small unlighted and unventilated room—it was used as a lavatory during the rest of the academic year—dominated by a large electrified duplicating machine. This machine was surrounded by a huddle of unsteady desks, stacks of paper, stencils, sealing-wax, a dirty old bucket, a metal seal, a glass of water, and a servant. The latter played the eunuch's part in this establishment. He oiled and polished the delicate machine, he fed it with the best paper, he informed it of his masters' desires and those desires were met. One might have supposed that his tongue had been cut out, too, in the interests of security, for he rarely spoke. He was indeed very competent in handling the machine, over which he

hovered lovingly, looking up with savage suspicion each
time the door opened. The teachers were not allowed to
meddle with it—much to the disappointment of Packet,
who had always wanted to operate an electric model. They
handed over their stencils to the expert and then stood
respectfully back.

All went well for the time being. Shuff, shuff, shuff, the
sheets flew out, white and innocent. But soon a pile of
bad copies and used stencils had accumulated, and the operator
—whose livelihood was at stake—declared a state of emergency. All the odd scraps of paper were collected and flung
into the bucket and set on fire. A stencil flared up and Bacon
recoiled with an oath, his eyebrows singed. Carried away
by excitement—he had always liked a good blaze—Packet
flung in a load of oddments, including some stubs of sealing-
wax set out for them by parsimonious authority : the
bucket gave out a dull roar, and for a few moments it looked
as if the ceiling would catch fire. The slave of the machine
clutched his darling and yelled out in anguish ; an inferior
servant then rushed in from the outside world with a Coca-
Cola bottle full of water, which he tossed dramatically into
the conflagration. Semi-burnt fragments hovered on the
air—what was left of it—and Wiggins, a teacher who suffered
from asthma, flung open the door, to reveal three students
laboriously crouching down as if to tie their shoe laces. He
rushed out upon them, wheezing and gasping and coughing,
and waving his arms like a maddened windmill—he had been
in Egypt for a long time—drove them away in terror. ' *Mush
kwyass*,' the servant moaned out the understatement : it
was not good at all : he slammed the door, in awful fear
lest some decipherable cinder should escape on the breeze.

' But why don't they have the things printed properly ? '
Packet complained, very conscious of having been the chief
cause of this crisis.

' Printed ! ' someone yelled. ' What printer in Egypt

could be trusted with the job ?   Do you want to be hauled out of bed at two in the morning to think up some fresh questions ! '

' This is the most perfect security possible,' Bacon added, ' the result of years of trial and error.   Don't you see ?   There's practically no human element in it—only a highly specialized engineer, too besotted with his precious engine to think of being dishonest.   Of course, the whole faculty may get burnt to the ground—but that's no concern of Examination Control.'

Being junior, Packet had been assigned to the job of sealing the copies in their envelopes : the envelopes would then be handed into Examination Control and locked in massive safes until the appropriate day arrived.   Black sticks of some inferior wax, smelling and generally behaving exactly like tar, had been provided—and had to be employed —together with an ancient candle-end from which the wick had vanished.   The official seal of the university was lying in the bottom of a glass of water : the seal had to be dripping wet if it were to be withdrawn from the molten tar at all.

Packet burnt his fingers several times with matches.   He tried his lighter, but this was soon obliterated by a fall of tar. He then trotted along to Examination Control, a highly-strung organization living behind locked doors, guarded by faculty policemen.

There he found the *élite* of the Egyptian staff, pacing neurotically between ash-trays and coffee cups, and debating newer and further ways of safeguarding their secrets.   Normally they were decent fellows, easy to get along with, but as members of the Control they were changed men— haunted by the most perverse suspicions, deaf to reason and blind to impossibilities, and overflowing with a devilish ingenuity.

They all stared at him, with fearful enquiry.   The English

sometimes had strange ideas. They did not feel that they could stand a strange English idea at the moment.

' Can anyone give me . . . ' It was only a box of matches that he was after, and if possible a candle.

' It is known,' broke in one of them feverishly, ' that the sealed envelopes must be signed——'

' Oh yes, but I want——'

' Across the flaps,' the man demonstrated in detail on an empty envelope.

' Oh yes,' and with some pride in his efficiency Packet added, ' by *two* people.' He held up two fingers.

' Not by two *people*,' came the gentle reproach, ' by two responsible members of your department.' Packet wondered who the irresponsible members were, but he merely nodded his head.

' What I want, please, is——'

' In red pencil provided by the faculty ? ' The juggernaut of a question at last rolled to its end. And Packet could not return the looked-for answer. Most of the signing had already been done, he explained, in blue-black ink with fountain-pens provided by responsible members of the department.

' As was the rule last year,' he added in righteous indignation, exaggerating the indignation in defence against the impending wrath. He was not going to be put down too easily.

A general gasp arose, and the clicking of tongues against teeth. That was the trouble with foreign staff : they were not dishonest, they would not think of selling examination questions—but worse, they simply failed to carry out the precautions which were carefully calculated to render honesty unnecessary. Were they being offensive ? Was it political ill-wishing ? Not in the case of the French, who were friends with Egypt, and by nature inclined to be scatterbrained. But when the English, a race renowned for efficiency and regularity, suddenly turned inefficient and irregular . . . Certainly there was something offensive in not bothering to study the current regulations which were posted to their private addresses in registered envelopes a week or more in advance.

The current regulations, Packet was thinking, they must have been those two pages of Arabic which he forgot to ask the servant to translate.

'The regulations have been improved this year,' the current director of examinations told him. 'You must therefore put the papers into new envelopes and sign them with the red pencil provided by Abdul Aziz Effendi.'

Packet hurried downstairs to the office of Abdul Aziz, Examination Control Stationery, and requested an official red pencil. What did he want a red pencil for? To sign the envelopes containing the examination questions. Abdul Aziz, a pleasant old man with a cunning smile, regarded him in silence. He explained that the Control had refused to accept envelopes signed in ink. Abdul Aziz threw up his hands.

'But why? It is stupid. Blue, red, green, yellow! If it is signed, it is signed. You can use your own pen. You have your own pen?'

He relapsed into his chair and began to count sheets of blotting-paper. Packet had gathered from his earlier dealings with the administration that in officials a scrupulous concern for their own regulations often co-existed with an utter and most reasonable contempt for those obtaining in the office next door. He agreed heartily with Abdul Aziz Effendi, he was ready, nay eager, to use his own pen—but this year the rule had changed, and it had to be a red pencil. Abdul Aziz lost count, threw up his hands again and explained, as if to an imbecile, that he had not one single red pencil in stock. There was only one coloured pencil—he held up one finger —and that was green in colour, green.

Upstairs again, Packet informed Examination Control with a certain pleasure that Abdul Aziz possessed no red pencil. They were staggered for a moment.

'Perhaps one of the professors has a red pencil?'

No professor had a red pencil, Packet stated dogmatically. Probably there was a propelling pencil fitted with red lead somewhere in that stokehole, but he had no intention of saving the Control from their dilemma.

The Egyptians went through their pockets, but no red pencil emerged. The nearest likely shop was a couple of kilometres away. An agitated silence ensued—broken only by Packet softly humming a rousing tango—until the director announced, as if it were the lightest thing in the world, 'Then we will make a new rule. Envelopes shall be signed by two professors, across the flaps, in green pencil.' They all relaxed. The honour of Examination Control had been saved.

'You have a green pencil?' the director queried. 'No? Then,' in considerable scorn, 'you must obtain one from Abdul Aziz Effendi.' They all turned away from him, he held no further interest for them, the question was closed.

An attack of gigantic irritation set the sweat trickling down his chest. They were impregnable; they could not lose. He was speechless. He could do nothing but fly out of the room, slamming the door behind him.

Some twenty minutes after he had set out for a box of matches, Packet got back to the printing closet, with a stub of green pencil for which he had signed—'it is a rule'—and a primus stove which he had abstracted from the kitchen without signing for to melt the sealing-wax. He was received badly. Finished papers had piled up during his absence, first and second session questions were lying about on the floor in close proximity, and there was the dreadful possibility that a second session paper might be distributed along with the first, in which case an entirely fresh set of questions would have to be fabricated by such professors as were available at the time. The room was dark with smoke. Bacon's red face was spotted with smuts, and someone's fountain-pen had fallen into the flaming bucket. In fact everything was going wrong, except the inexorable machine.

Packet broke the news about the green pencil. 'Oh Christ ! Another —— new rule !' screamed Wiggins. He threw down the envelope he had been signing and pounded out of the room.

'Dear me,' Bacon remarked. 'We're getting to be quite like the French Department.'

Bacon suggested to Packet that they should meet for a drink in the evening, to celebrate the *début* of the examination papers—he was expecting a visit from an old student, one who had graduated four or five years previously. They arranged to meet at Athinoudis.

It was a place of some tone, Packet mused, as he waited for the others. The chairs and tables were solid and handsome, and between them the distinguished-looking Mr. Athinoudis steered himself precariously, more and more precariously as the evening grew, with a vinous and benign smile for each of his guests. There was of course nothing in the way of *bouzoukia* to be heard here : only the incessant tinkling of plates and forks, ice cubes and glasses, a music which cost appreciably more. A pleasant place, though : he must take Sylvie there some time : unfortunately she was going to the ballet tonight with Simone.

Bacon came in with his old pupil, Salama, and they ordered beer. Salama was a teacher in Zaga-Zig, and they would have to contrive that he didn't pay for a round. He explained to Packet that he was now working in a girls' school.

'And that is a pleasant change. They are really very nice, and so quiet and obedient. Ah, I think there is hope for Egypt yet.' Salama was an agreeable creature, of dreamy appearance, tall and thin, with large and dark and rather moist eyes, and a sizeable moustache. He suddenly clapped his hand to his heart, looked burningly up to heaven, and then bent forward towards Bacon.

' Ah, how good it is to see you again, sir ! ' By means of a brief and cogent pantomime he gave them to understand that his feelings had got the better of him. Turning to Packet, he added, ' We are old friends, Mr. Bacon and I— or should I say me ?—do you know, I owe everything to him ! Believe me, I do not exaggerate, in spite of our national failing, I do not exaggerate.'

' But what do you owe to me, Salama ? '

' Literature ! ' the young man declaimed, a shade too emphatically for Athinoudis, perhaps. ' And what would Zaga-Zig be without Literature ! ' He took a large draught of beer and went on, very solemnly. ' But I owe you more than that—I owe you my life. Do you remember, sir, in my last year I was always wanting to commit suicide, I thought of it every day . . . '

' Yes, and I persuaded you to write poetry instead.' Salama was not the only young man for whom Bacon had done this little service.

' Yes—that was brilliant ! But which poet was it that you said my poems were like ? I cannot remember his name, but you were not fond of him, I think.'

' Ernest Dowson ? But yours were better than Dowson's, I always felt. You had more to complain of.'

Salama was pleased with this. ' Ah ! ' he glowed. He hailed a waiter.

' Let me offer my English friends some oysters. No, no, I insist ! It is not often I have the happiness to meet with you.'

Yes, Packet thought, Salama was the rather rare kind that you could really be friends with, all the way. Every year the department turned out one or two such men. Some of them went to Paris to paint or study the art and craft of cinema, and disappeared ; some of them went to Europe, whence they returned five years later, transformed to cautious and highly specialized dons, rigidly minding their own business. But what of the others, who found miserably paid jobs in schools or banks or the civil service, the young men like Salama ? They were slowly accumulating, one day they would do something. He suddenly felt that it was most important that they should not be allowed to commit suicide.

' So you are happy teaching girls ? ' he asked.

' After teaching boys, yes ! '

Packet asked him if he didn't sometimes find girls a little difficult. For instance, Packet had been giving a weekly course on the English Romantic Poets with the First Year (' Oh the First Year ! ' Salama condoled), and he had spent considerable time and energy on a little poem called *The Green Linnet* (' Wordsworth ! ' Salama exclaimed triumphantly), stressing the Romantics' predilection for birds. The following week he returned to the poem. ' Now you know *what* a green linnet is, don't you ? ' he addressed the class at large. The class remained silent. He repeated the question more urgently, but no reply was forthcoming. To reassure himself, he pointed to one of his favoured girls, a quiet little thing, something of a village maiden, but far from stupid.

' Now *you* know what a green linnet is, don't you, Leila ? ' She said nothing, she looked nothing. ' Could it be a kind of cow, do you think ? ' he burst out in anguish, ' a green cow ? " Fluttering in the bushes " ? '

' Very well, sir,' the words were almost inaudible, ' a cow.' And she hid her head and wept.

' You know,' he told them, ' it was at least six weeks before she would speak to me again, or even look at me.' The memory of it saddened him.

' Poof, she thought you were calling her a cow ! ' Salama brushed it aside. ' I expect she was in love with you. All

my pupils are in love with me ! ' He roared with amusement. Probably they were, Packet thought, he was a fetching
young man.

' But if you want an easy life,' Salama continued con-
fidentially, ' you must not ask them things, you must tell
them things.' He went on to remark that ingenuousness
and susceptibility were to be expected from Egyptian girls
in their present state of emancipation, rather nearer to the
veil than the lipstick.

' But there are the other kind, too,' Packet said, ' the
mature young women who seem to know everything.'
He lived in some terror of these few. ' They make me feel
dreadfully young and inexperienced.'

' Have you noticed,' put in Bacon, ' that they nearly always
specialize in French ? ' Smiling at his colleague, he continued, ' You're finding women difficult, then ? '

Yes, Packet admitted reluctantly. Of course there were
reasons for being difficult, in the case to which Bacon was
referring, and perhaps in many others. He could see that.
But, even so, their inability—or rather unwillingness—to
think straight, to begin thinking from scratch, so to speak . . .
However, he supposed that women were all difficult, all
the same.

' All difficult, yes,' Bacon replied, ' but not all the same,
the Creator be praised ! '

He rather envied his young colleague the years in which
he would discover the lively diversity of such difficulties,
and the unexpected and miraculous easinesses with which
they were interspersed. But he did not mention the matter :
it was a bad thing to make people self-conscious, he believed :
a good teacher should know when to put the chalk down.

The conversation turned to Marcel Haggernetti. No-one
had seen him for a couple of months, since the great scandal
in fact.

' What exactly was it that happened ? ' Packet asked.

He was thinking of looking Marcel up, and ought to prime himself in advance. It was so easy, where Marcel was concerned, to talk about the wrong things, or at the wrong times.

'I don't know the details,' Bacon replied, ' but Marcel was not in the least at fault, this time.'

Relations between the churches were cordial in the extreme, it seemed, at least in Alexandria where Marcel's contacts and influence were strongest. There were secret conclaves out at his desert home, and he was rumoured to be engaged on the composition of a Pan-Christian Manifesto which they were all to sign and promulgate. Then, without any warning, some little incident occurred—probably common enough, normally no-one would have given it a second thought. A Greek Orthodox priest denounced a Greek Catholic priest from the pulpit. A purely personal matter. But it clattered and reverberated all the way up the ecclesiastical ladder, with Marcel sweating away at every step to smooth things over, until it reached the very top, in a cataclysm. And that was the end of all his plans.

'Poor Marcel,' Packet tried to keep a straight face for he felt very sorry, after all. ' After working so hard ! '

'According to my bookseller, he went round the shops in a fearful pet and took away all the stocks of his hagiographic pamphlet. And then apparently retired to the desert to lick his wounds. But a few days back I noticed a newspaper article by him on native handicrafts—so perhaps he has found consolation.'

Bacon had known Marcel since his first coming to Egypt, and he had no fears that this latest blow would prostrate him.

'When I met him first, it was Marcel the Journalist. He then blossomed into Marcel the Poet—he was never quite as *raffiné* as El Hamama, however, and an unsuccessful publication induced him to follow in his father's footsteps for a short period. Marcel the *Homme d'Affaires*, in this case business.

Then came Marcel the Elegant—his collection of ties dates from this period . . .'

Packet glanced down at the tie he was wearing. It was one of Marcel's rejects, he remembered, a rather dowdy specimen, presumed suitable for an Englishman—'the only tie between us,' Marcel had tittered in presenting him with it.

'. . . and he even did his best to learn to dance, for the look of the thing. But elegance costs a lot to keep up, and you know how careful he is. So he changed his tack and Marcel the Philosopher emerged. It was then that he learnt German, quickly but very well. However, he never hit it off happily with the professionals, and he was rapidly losing friends. I believe it was about then that he set up as an Adviser in Antiques. He knew a lot of refugees with things to sell—it didn't take him long to pick up the jargon and, as you know, he has natural taste. But then he got mixed up in the sale of something—a Priapos, I think—that wasn't as old as it should have been ; and since the buyer turned out to be an agent of the King, Marcel thought fit to retire. He reappeared as Marcel the Novelist, but his novels were so long that with all his energy he could never manage to finish them. And you know the rest of the story. Marcel still has much to offer the world . . .'

Salama had listened with great interest but little understanding. At the end he shook his head slowly. It was another world which this strange man called Marcel inhabited—a world in which intellectuals could be even more intellectual, because they did not have to grind away in a school all day.

He told them that he was saving to get married. They both knew the girl ; she had studied English at the university, a pleasant and bright young lady. She too was teaching. But they estimated that it would take another six years before they had saved enough money to persuade her father to give his blessing. He was a strict old man, Salama grumbled, and very old-fashioned : the couple were allowed to meet once a week, in the paternal parlour, under the paternal eye. He suspected that the old man was looking round for a more acceptable son-in-law.

' Egyptian school-teachers come just a little higher than *fellahin* in the social scale,' he lamented.

And who, he asked of Packet, were the bright seniors of today ? Packet mentioned several names. Salama knew of them—weren't they rather wild, he asked ; not that that meant very much, any young Egyptian with spirit in him was a bit wild, it was either that or continual *tric-trac* and chatter with male companions in the Arab cafés. Life was hard for them.

Packet agreed that life was hard for them. Three weeks previously some of them had invited him to a little hashish party. He was feeling low at the time—Sylvie had just rejected a very serious proposal of marriage—and he accepted. The party took place in a kind of *garçonnière*, bare and un-lighted, occupied by one of the students. At first all went merrily. They consumed large chunks of stewed mutton and drank beer and related their more sensational experiences with women. Then they related their experiences with doctors. Afterwards the hashish was served, in a real *shih-shah* hired from a neighbouring café. The hashish, looking like hardened horse-dung, was crumbled into small pieces and placed strategically within a clot of coarse wet Turkish tobacco moulded into a little pyramid on top of the pipe. The apex of the pyramid was flattened to receive glowing charcoal, somewhat amateurishly prepared by means of a primus stove and toasting tray.

The *shih-shah* was set reverently in the centre of the room and they squatted round it, each of them taking a deep draught and then passing the rubber tube to his neighbour. This intrigued Packet—the eastern custom, the element of ritual, and the moderate criminality of it—but he sucked with all his might to very little effect. A wisp of tepid-tasting smoke drifted out of his panting lungs. After several rounds the pyramid stood as firm as ever, but Packet was wilting. Fresh charcoal was heaped on, he was allowed extra time.

His friends were very jolly by now : they had impelled each other into a state of intense excitement. How did he feel, they asked Packet ? Nothing, he wheezed at them, he felt nothing at all. This was a notorious aphrodisiac, he informed himself—but for him it had all the effect of a cross-country run. He could hardly walk across the room.

In the end they consulted together, and then broke open a cigarette, loaded it with the remains of the hashish, patched it together again, and gave it to him. Perhaps Englishmen needed a heavier dose.

They had prepared a little surprise for him, he was told. They had arranged for some girls to come to the flat. Oh, dancing girls ? he asked. Well, perhaps they could dance as well. But the girls would be very nice : in his honour they had insisted on having Jewesses. Jewesses were not only prettier but cleaner too, and they usually spoke some English. Packet expressed a cautious gratification. The flat was illuminated only by a paraffin lamp and two candles, and he was unable to make out the labels of the bottles which were then brought in. One contained gin, they said, and the other vermouth. The mixture tasted shocking—but possibly that was the effect of the hashish, and he couldn't hurt his hosts' feelings by complaining about it.

The Egyptians became merrier and merrier, and Packet sadder and sadder. He thought of Sylvie, first angrily and then yearningly. They were so close—and yet never really together : he had given himself entirely, at least more entirely than he had ever managed before—it was she who deliberately, at the last moment, withdrew. But what an awful guest he was ! In desperation he called out for a very large gin and vermouth ; he would have called for madder music, had there been any ; he intended to be jolly at all costs.

There was a loud whispering at the door, and the girls entered with an introductory giggle. It was at once clear, even in the dimness, that they were not one hundredth part Jewish. As they approached, Packet began to feel that he had met one of them before, though their faces were practically anonymous. As she shook hands with one of the youths, he was horrified to see that the back of her hand was covered with hair. She noticed him, yelled with amusement, slapped him on the shoulder and shouted out something in Arabic. What was she saying ? he asked nervously. ' Oh sir,' was the reply, ' she is saying that you are a terrible fellow and she had to throw a flaming stove at you in self-defence.' He relaxed. As soon as he got home, he would burn those worthless notes he had taken.

Which girl did he prefer ? As guest of honour, the first choice fell to him. By this time his head felt as ravaged as his lungs. He chose bed. Quite so, they said anxiously, but which girl ? An embarrassing situation, for he didn't wish to seem contemptuous of Egyptian womanhood or un-appreciative of his friends' efforts. Well, then—he looked around him—it had better be the one over there, a stout somnolent-looking woman of pale hue, who seemed likely to drink herself to sleep on gin.

He was directed to a bed, the best available : he fell upon it avidly—what a marvellous soporific this hashish was ! —and sank at once into a dreamless sleep. It seemed years later that he was awakened by a guttural yell in his ear and a dreadful weight on his chest. In the dim light a quivering mass of grey lard could be seen. His girl had come for him. He groaned at her, he pleaded weariness, sickness, he would even have admitted to disease but felt she might not find that a cogent excuse—she merely cooed the more savagely and even laid rude hands upon him—and in the end he pushed with all the strength he could muster. There was a crash, and she disappeared from sight. What had he done ? After all, she was human, she was only earning her living. But she reappeared at the foot of the bed, dancing and singing, a great naked blancmange.

Drawn by the noise, one of the Egyptians entered, summed up the situation, and pulled the woman away ; after all, there were other men available. Packet's feeling of masculine shame, his sense of the necessity for explanation and apology, was engulfed in his overwhelming weariness, and he was asleep again before the door had closed.

It was six o'clock in the morning when he recovered consciousness, a frail, dim sort of consciousness. The room was bare, except for two empty bottles, gin and vermouth, both bearing the name of the Cypriot who had poisoned the fleet. A short investigation revealed his friends, lying in uncomfortable postures on heaps of blankets. They staggered to their elbows and turned grey faces upon him. He thanked them politely for the party, told them how well he had slept. There was just one thing—was there an aspirin in the house ? Alas, they had thought of everything but that. He tucked them back in their blankets and walked home, feeling as fragile as china. Luckily he had no work that morning, so he could go back to sleep. Pyjamas were a great invention, he thought gratefully, also one's own bed, with no-one else in it.

However, Packet did not relate this incident to Bacon and Salama. He merely nodded and agreed warmly that the lot of young Egyptian males was indeed a hard one.

' By the way,' Bacon said, ' would you be willing to come out with me to the internment camp at Aboukir, Packet ? Batrawy, the fourth year specialist, is there on some charge of communist activity. He's to do the written papers under police supervision, but two of us will have to go there for his oral.'

'Oh certainly I'll come with you. Poor Batrawy !'

'He was at an English school, wasn't he ?' put in Salama, 'at Victoria College ? His English must be very good.'

Yes, it would be a mere formality ; but a little change for Batrawy. They all felt sorry for the boy, a sensitive, rather sentimental scion of a well-to-do family, who walked about with a French Life of Lenin in his pocket and talked rather too freely. He was a good student, though his habit of writing about the evils of capitalism instead of *Volpone* had irritated them at the time. Otherwise there was no harm in him ; he was only an intellectual, incapable of violence.

A party led by El Hamama now entered the bar. Among them was Brett, escorting an English girl whom Packet recognized as the daughter of an important official in the Eastern Telegraph. The two of them came over.

'We've just come from the *Romance*,' Brett complained, 'the place is packed out. I found a nice large table in the centre, free, and we were just settling down when five or six of the black boys rushed up in a fearful stew, shrieking "El Malek ! El Malek !" The table was reserved *in perpetuo* for the King—that fellow has a finger in every pie, damn him !'

Damn him by all means, thought Packet, glancing quickly at Salama, but he would have been damned and forgotten long ago if it hadn't been for tactless remarks of that kind. However, Salama seemed unmoved. Packet hastened to introduce him : a teacher from Zaga-Zig.

'A teacher from Zaga-Zig,' Brett repeated. 'Well now, I've never met a teacher from Zaga-Zig before . . . There really is such a place ? I always thought it was a joke.'

It was no joke, Salama informed him, and they summoned up the ghost of a smile between them. The young lady thought that they should rejoin El Hamama, who was waiting to order a meal. As they left Brett shouted, 'And where is your Syrian girl tonight? Let you down?'

'You have a Syrian friend?' Salama asked respectfully. 'Ah, that is very nice. They are very different from us Egyptians, the Syrians. They are really Europeans, I think.'

'I don't want to hear any more about Europeans,' he replied.

Salama had to catch the last train back, and they walked with him to the station. The sour smells of the day had gone, and the sky was alive with more stars than Packet had ever seen together at one time. From an open-air cinema in the distance came the sound of Arabic music, barbaric and melodramatic, over-emphatic and vulgar, but full of nervous vitality. He touched Salama's sleeve.

'You know, it's a wonderful country, really.'

Chapter 11

GOD HATH GIVEN YOU TENTS TO LIVE IN

THE beaches near the city were hopelessly crowded at this time of year. The lucky owners of bathing huts invited their friends and relatives and business acquaintances and the friends of acquaintances. And, in addition, the annual influx of rich and sweating Cairenes had commenced. But a friend of Sylvie's had offered to take them that Sunday in his car to Agamy, the celebrated silver sands along the edge of the western desert. Having propitiated the local peasants with the gift of a few piastres, they pitched a small tent and changed into bathing suits.

This was what England deserved, Packet reflected : a little of all this shocking excess—the immense white-blue sky and the thick purple sea and the pure white crumbling wave. He lay on his stomach, while Sylvie trickled warm pricking sand on to the small of his back, almost sleeping to the soft roar and the sibilant exhalation of the waves. On either side of them the sea carried in dozens of long-legged yellow crabs who chased madly after the retreating wave. Sometimes they waited on the damp, swiftly drying sands, still and tense, as nervous as deer. Packet and Sylvie had been running after them, but the little creatures were far too shrewd to be caught. And once they had dashed into the water, they vanished completely, leaving their shadows behind.

'Crabs,' murmured Packet.

'What are you saying?' she asked incuriously.

'Crabs,' he repeated. Then, after some moments of silence, 'Funny, isn't it?'

'Yes. Funny.'

He turned half over on his side and pulled her down on the sand.

'Crab. A little sour apple. Crabby. Crabbed Age . . . That's all they meant to me. Literary associations. Oh dear me! But the reality is quite different. The Creator be praised!'—where had he heard those words recently?— 'One has to learn for oneself . . .' He stroked her arm lazily, and apparently fell asleep. The crabs scuttled back into the sea, leaving a comic pattern of claw-prints on the sand, until the next wave pounced.

'How happy they are!' he added with an effort. 'What lively little beasts they are!'

'Are they happy?' she asked. 'Just because they run into the sea like Sunday bathers? Perhaps they live in agony, perhaps they are terrified each time that the sea is leaving them for ever . . .'

'I suppose I'm the one who is happy'—that was a great confession to make. He took refuge in a few minutes of unconsciousness. 'And I shall always remember these crabs, these happy crabs . . . And you too, of course. Like the frogs in the gardens of Ramleh. I hear them from the flat at nights, chattering for hours on end. They all pontificate, and every one of them is right and venerable, and every one is the boss, and every one is happy. And the crickets, too. I never heard them at home—I mean in England—so they're new to me, and so they've become what teachers of literature call symbols, I suppose . . .' He scratched his back, indicated that she should divert the sand to his shoulders, and added, 'Humble creatures, aren't they, to be symbols? Crabs and frogs and crickets . . .'

In a fit of energy he lifted himself on his elbow and frowned at her. 'I'm not interested in the noble animals—tiger, tiger, burning bright—or the king of the jungle—who wants to be king there ?—or the bull or the bear. Nor in the poetic beasts—the priggish unicorn or the conceited swan or the histrionic nightingale. In my next incarnation I should like to be part of the southern landscape, a music-maker in a nocturnal community—a frog or a cricket. Or else a crab —part of the Mediterranean seascape.'

'You are very modest,' Sylvie commented, ' or else you suffer from end-of-term fatigue. Now I should like to be a bird of paradise, or a parakeet, or perhaps a gazelle. No, not a gazelle—they are soft animals. A leopard, rather . . .'

'How difficult you are ! For my part, I wish you were a bottle of beer, and even colder than you are . . .' She fished a bottle out of the little tent and filled two glasses.

'Here's to us,' he proposed defiantly, and they touched glasses. 'Whatever happens . . .' she added. 'May you never be caught in a lobster pot, my dear.'

'How embarrassing it is, how quite impossible, in fact,' Packet propounded in a tone of mild surprise, 'to say that one is happy. Instead one says that the crabs are happy or that the frogs are in love. That's all very well in literature, but surely in life one could be less indirect ?'

'Most men can hardly be reproached with indirectness,' she scowled. 'But you are in the right. It is safer to say that the crabs are enjoying themselves or that the parakeets are young and beautiful—because you will never regret having said it, you will never be proved wrong.'

'What a little crab apple you are—dry and sour, in spite of that soft tasty skin ! You are driving me to despair. I shall go and drown myself.'

He picked himself up painfully, tottered towards the advancing sea and cast himself in. The sand and the sweat were washed away, the water was almost too warm, it rocked him gently to and fro, seducing him into sleep.

Sylvie was about to join him when she heard cries from bathers higher up the beach. Heads were emerging from the water, bodies were scrambling on to the sand. She shouted to him to come out.

'Can't you let me die in peace,' he complained.

'They say there's a shark coming, quite near land—of course it may only be a dolphin.'

'The dolphin is a good and kindly animal, and the protector of poets. In medieval art it was the symbol of social love.'

'The shark is the symbol of something else,' she said, ' and it has very sharp teeth.' They stood there looking into the sea. A dark shape came towards them, moving fairly quickly.

'It can't be a shark, they don't come so near to land,' Packet objected.

'Very well, go and find out what it is,' she replied. 'One has to learn for oneself, you say.'

'If it gambols then it's a dolphin—and I shall go and be social with it.'

But it performed nothing remotely resembling a gambol. On the contrary, it held a steady purposeful course, rolling over menacingly, like a giant drill. A fin cut the surface, as grim as the keel of an overturned boat. He shivered slightly. 'It's no friend to men—or even to poets. You were quite right.'

'It is part of the Mediterranean seascape—which you want to join.'

They had not realized that there were so many visitors at Agamy. The beach was spotted with them now, they would not venture back into the water yet. The crabs had all disappeared.

'You are sometimes rather simple, my dear boy,' she sighed.

In the late afternoon an agreeably fresh breeze began to blow. They decided that it would be a good idea to call on Marcel, whom neither of them had seen since the dissolution of the churches. His house was no more than twenty minutes' walk away.

'We really ought to ring him beforehand,' Packet said doubtfully. 'I know how Marcel detests having unexpected visitors.' The nearest phone box, however, was further away than Marcel's house.

But Marcel expressed great pleasure at the sight of them. He put away the book he was studying—it seemed to be a catalogue of agricultural implements, copiously illustrated—and clapped his hands sharply. The middle-aged Bedouin servant, a man of upright carriage and rather austere expression, appeared instantly, and tea was ordered. Their host apologized for having nothing stronger to offer them.

'The priests drank it all,' he explained bitterly.

Marcel kept a rather romantic establishment below stairs : the man, his wife and their daughter. The women were tall, buxom and obedient—Packet never knew which was the mother, which the daughter—and the man tall, lean and respectful. They were all three capable, quiet and respectable. So respectable, indeed, that Marcel was careful to dismiss them to their quarters, a small congregation of tents beyond the garden wall, whenever anything at all untoward seemed likely to happen. He even seemed terrified lest they should encounter one of his guests in a state of mild inebriation. 'They are strict people,' he had thought it necessary to warn Packet long ago, 'I have to observe the proprieties.' Packet had been all for that.

The only disadvantage attaching to these domestics—and it was confined to the women, and only really serious in the summer—lay in their bodily odour. Washing was not one of the proprieties which they observed. This had never worried Packet, who in any case was impressed beyond sensibility by the idea of one small plump man having a family of three tall and dignified beings to wait upon him.

Nor had it worried Marcel, until his house became the resort of Christian notables. And then he had spoken to the man, very gravely, bidding him see that his wife and daughter were entirely immersed in a large bath of warm and soapy water. ' He bowed his head,' Marcel told them, ' and said " So be it " and it was carried out forthwith.' Packet was once again impressed by his friend's authority. That was the proper way of tackling the problem, no doubt, but he couldn't have done it himself, in any way, in any language, or under any circumstances, not even for the sake of the Pope.

These particular circumstances had changed, however. ' I have returned to Man,' Marcel sniggered, with a bold amused look at Sylvie. ' That is my proper sphere.' Packet glanced round the room : true, the ikons of the last period had gone, and the Negro carvings had reappeared, together with some ferocious embroidery from Java or thereabouts.

' Man ? ' Packet queried a little nervously.

Here they were, Marcel elaborated, living in an Arab country, without taking the slightest interest in the Arabs as such. The Arabs could build as well as lay waste. And this cultural cold-shouldering was not good enough. (Here the old kindly, forgiving look came over his face : someone, Packet could tell, was going to receive benefits.) He, Marcel, enjoyed unique conditions—living in peace and quiet, unaffected by the stresses of fashionable society, well away from the debased Arabs of the town, with a small private income (' very small of course,' he warned them and the world at large), and a Bedouin encampment at the bottom of his garden, so to speak. They looked up to him, these Bedouins : he was the squire of their village, as it were. In short, he was the very man for the job.

' What job, exactly ? ' asked Packet.

' To find out what they can do, and persuade them to do it.' Sylvie poured out more tea. The new Marcellian era did not interest her much more than the last; she had no missionary instinct, either religious or social.

Marcel continued eagerly. They could make good practical baskets, *espadrilles* and sandals which were simple but strong, amusingly decorated slippers and leather bags. And the making of such articles would be healthier, more educative and more profitable than fiddling about with an old goat and three or four moth-eaten sheep. With a little application, they could raise their standard of living to unknown heights.

' *You* ought to find this enthralling,' he told Packet.

' How are they responding to this plan of yours ? ' Packet replied.

' Well, it's something completely new, of course. Revolutionary, even, for them.' A mad glint came into his eyes. A liberator of the people, he was thinking, fire from heaven, the flowering desert, the eagle of Zeus tearing at his liver. Hum, his father would have a word with Zeus.

' They're a terribly narrow, conservative people,' he went on, ' even when they have nothing to conserve. It will take time, and patience. But we have already accomplished a good deal—by beginning with the children.'

That sounded more interesting, Packet thought. He had spent most of this year finding out things about himself, instead of finding out what ought to be done for other people's good. Arty-crafty Arabs sounded like a waste of time—but all the same, something needed doing for the children, those little bags of bones, who attracted flies like carrion. He had seen them running in and out of the cramped shacks—made from squashed petrol tins left over from the war and hung with old skins—dragging a dead kid or a decaying cat or throwing huge stones at each other with alarming accuracy.

' In collaboration with several enlightened Egyptians,' Marcel took up a more formal stance, ' I have managed to establish a little school or training centre nearby. Not to teach arithmetic or geography or English literature—but simply to teach them to use their hands. They make shopping baskets and door-mats from osiers. Some of the older boys are working on wicker chairs. And next week we hope to make a start on carpentry, if the Ministry of Education will provide the tools . . .'

Would they care to look round the school? It was just across the railway line. Yes, of course, they would love to.

It was almost real desert outside the house. A few shabby palm-trees, an old man with some goats, a slope to slither down and another to scramble up, then the tracks to cross, and they were in the village. The indigenes, walking thoughtfully between the tents and shacks or squatting against bits of fencing which no longer had anything to fence in, were clearly pleased to see them. They did not exactly touch their forelocks to the squire, but they greeted him with immensely dignified salutations or enthusiastic grins, according to their ages. The women too, suckling their children or counting out beans for the evening meal, beamed at him. Marcel was obviously regarded as an acquisition to the community, and Packet could understand what balm this would lay to his newly wounded spirit.

The school was as yet rudimentary : a few sheds roughly arranged in a square, and in the shelter of them several little pens surrounded by rough wooden palings, which reminded Packet rather of the *caracol*. Within these pens were boys of varying age, engaged with slightly exaggerated docility in bending twigs or stamping leather. They looked up, greeting the visitors one by one, without the least shyness, and their first and warmest greeting was for their benefactor. ' I see ' the visitors were saying, and ' how interesting ', and Packet was wishing that he could talk to the boys in their language.

At this point a middle-aged man, of worried demeanour and wearing an apron, rushed up to Marcel and caught hold of him with little ceremony. The two began to chatter excitedly.

'The instructor is complaining that they have no material left to work with,' Sylvie translated in an undertone, 'and Marcel is complaining that he has no money left.'

They were then taken to what Marcel called the display room. Here, laid out on trestle tables, were the finished products of Man's industry : row on row of lumpish but honest sandals, of grim but immortal slippers, stretches of matting eminently suitable for gymnasia or reformatory messes.

'If you would care to patronize the establishment . . .' Marcel smiled and waved his hand towards these attractions.

'Can I offer you a shopping basket, Sylvie?'

'Why not buy yourself a pair of strong slippers?' she countered. The teacher was summoned to perform the vile act of trade while Marcel stood by with a benign look. The slippers turned out to be remarkably expensive, and they seemed to Packet to be oddly square in shape. But it was in a good cause, he felt, a better cause than the digging up of old and forgotten anchorites.

As they walked away from the school they came into a crowd of people gathered outside one of the small brick dwellings, their attention focused on two merry individuals who were rolling up their sleeves.

'This looks interesting,' Packet said. 'What's it all about?'

'A wedding,' Marcel replied loftily. He questioned a bystander. 'This is the fourth day—and the end of the ceremonies.' They were about to move on when Marcel exclaimed, 'Oh, but we must see this, my dears! the high point of the festivities.'

The two men had each taken an end of a long stick and

were tossing their bodies about in a curious fashion. 'Strictly speaking,' Marcel commented expertly, 'one of them should be a woman, but female dancers are always professionals and they have to be imported from the city at great expense. But never mind. We must make do.' He sniggered. Gradually the men came closer together, moving along the stick, and twisting their trunks voluptuously. Closer and closer they came, wriggling their bellies to the hand-clapping of the crowd. The symbolic nature of the dance was rather too obvious and, though Packet felt it a good thing to have witnessed this piece of ritual, he was relieved when the two men finally bumped together, slapped each other on the chest and roared with amusement.

'And now something for you two,' said Marcel in kindly tones. Towards the house came a group of people carrying the bridegroom, a youth clad in clean white robes, high above their heads in a kind of chair. It was an altogether haphazard procession, and the chair seemed likely to fall to the ground. When they reached the door of the house the youth dismounted and went in alone.

'The bride is waiting for him there,' Marcel hissed.

After the groom had closed the door the onlookers were completely silent for a whole minute. Then with a suddenness which took Sylvie and Packet by surprise, they burst into a protracted yell—not a song or a prayer, not chanting, not a salutation or congratulation, but just sheer noise, of any and every variety. The children reinforced their piping voices by clashing tins together. This they kept up for a good half-minute, stopping as suddenly as they had begun, and then most of them made off towards their dwellings. The party was unmistakably over, and Packet asked, 'But why that uproar?'

'Don't you see?' said Marcel, with his head on one side. 'The Bedouins live at close quarters, without privacy, and they cannot afford honeymoons. So they've invented rituals of this kind—and the yelling is a ritual for which the blushing bride must be very grateful.' He leered slightly.

' Shall we go now ? ' said Sylvie, beginning to walk away.

' If you wait a moment,' their guide suggested, ' you may see the sheet thrown out of the window by the lucky man. And if—as is always the case of course—the sheet . . .'

' Thank you, but no ! '

' Oh spare us the anthropology, Marcel, please,' requested Packet, feeling the need to mediate between his two difficult friends. He hurried them along before any such sheet should appear. The dance was in order, that was legitimately interesting, but to stand outside a bedroom window . . .

There was a period of silence between them, and then Marcel said something to Sylvie in Arabic. She replied curtly. Packet felt sad to think that in some ways Marcel could be nearer to her than he was.

' Bacon speaks Arabic well, doesn't he ? ' he remarked gloomily, for lack of anything better to say.

' Oh yes, how is our mutual friend ? ' asked Marcel.

' As ever. A little tired at the moment—he bears most of the burden of exams, you know.'

' Yes, he's a hard worker, a most conscientious man . . .' From the tone of his voice they could tell that Marcel was talking of himself. '. . . not appreciated at his true value, I fear, but certainly the power behind the scenes. Indomitable . . .'

Packet was tempted to tell the story of the Education symposium, but he reminded himself that Marcel would disapprove strongly of the incident and—except immediately —would not see anything humorous about it. Marcel had been in many a sorry scrape himself, but his withdrawals had always been carried out soberly, silently and without giving offence to anyone who counted. Only shoe-blacks and news-boys could point the finger at him.

' He is a very good man,' Packet stated, feeling that

his adjective, though vague enough, was less inapt than Marcel's.

' A good man, yes. Too good a man in some ways.' But Marcel remembered that he was talking about Bacon, not himself, and added, ' And yet, you know, stupid in other ways, utterly unreasonable.'

' Ah ? '

' Look. How long ago is it now ? Fifteen years, perhaps, or more,' he looked a little anxious. ' I was very young at the time, of course. And I told him, " Your wife has left you. Well, that's that, and good riddance. Now let me choose another for you—I promise you she will be a good woman, and a rich one." But he only smiled. Time and time again I invited him out to meet this lady or that lady —all of them from families I knew, good solid families. But no. And then he took Sourayah into the house to look after him . . .'

' But—— '

' Not that I have anything against Sourayah—on the con- trary, I admire her, she is a woman of character, a most unusual woman for her class. But think, just think, of the advantageous unions he could have made—he could have given up all that teaching. They would have been glad to have him, for an Englishman was quite a catch in those days . . .' Packet winked at Sylvie. '. . . but now it's too late,' Marcel concluded indignantly, ' Bacon is getting on, and he would never rid himself of Sourayah, and Sourayah could never tolerate a female overseer after all her years of power. And in any case, the British passport isn't as young and virile as it used to be.' He looked deeply distressed, as though he himself had invented the British passport. A long scroll of tangled history suddenly unrolled itself before his mind's eye, and for a moment he felt his age. They had walked too quickly, he complained, and his back was hurting.

Entering the house, however, the scene of so many passions and of so much convalescence, his spirits revived. ' A carpenter's saw, made in Sheffield,' he shrieked at them, ' do you know how much it costs in this country ? '

After Marcel had given them a thick and acrid liqueur made from coffee by the local Arabs—he apologized for it by describing it as the kind of drink he could offer only to his most constant friends—they walked down to the road and took a bus which by a circuitous route would eventually reach the city. It was not one of the main road pullman coaches, but a truly *baladi* contraption, rollicking and haphazard and very sociable, under the easy government of a garrulous old driver. They were agreeably tired after the long day in the sun and the sea, and they enjoyed the bumpy ride, rushing and swerving and hopping with open windows through the cooling air. Tough middle-aged men in *gallabiehs* held hands all round them, and so did they ; indeed, it was their only hope of staying in their seats. A light meal and a cool drink : that was all they could wish for now.

Sitting in the restaurant, a Greek *taverna* full of bustling waiters and demanding customers, Packet awoke to his responsibilities again. It wasn't fair to either of them, going on like this, not knowing what one was doing. So he informed her. She simply raised an eyebrow. A decision would have to be made, he continued, arranging the cutlery meticulously around his plate, which was heaped with rice and marine life.

It was the one hour of true and absolute content, Sylvie felt, the body for once a little more tired than the mind, and yet not so much tired as resting. This experience never palled, for all that she was a native of the Middle East, and it never failed her. Coolness after extreme heat, a soft yellow light after the rich glare of the sun, a good dish in front of a pleasantly empty stomach. A condition of the whole person which even the noisy waiters, the clinking dishes and a stout neighbour's pungent cigar could not impair. For it was as if one were under some mild and blessed anaesthetic, which softened the impact of everything, so that the iced beer was not cold enough to give rise to hiccups, the cigar smoke was not so rank as to cause coughing, and one did not mind in the least that one's hair was out of order and one's finger-nails full of sand. Certainly not the hour in which to take a decision, she ruminated—and yet it was an hour well calculated to soften the pain of decision.

Pointing lazily to the food, she remarked, 'The Greeks call it *fruits de mer*, the French prefer to think of it as *frutti di mare*. I wonder what the Italians call it? Watery fruits, do you think?'

'The menu in the Ristorante d'Italia down the road describes the dish as *frutti di mare*,' Packet stated decisively. He was in a mood to decapitate all red herrings at first sight.

Would she marry him—now—or at least as soon as possible? No, she regretted she could not. She had a strong feeling that she was not going to marry anyone, again. He would not ask her again, he affirmed. There was a pause. Then, she would miss being asked to marry him, she said quietly. Perhaps she would also miss *him*, he suggested, though his voice was not so steady as he had hoped it would be. There was a longer pause, and then she answered, yes, she *would* miss him, very much.

'Look, my dear,' she continued, 'there is no future for you here. Even if English teachers are allowed to stay on indefinitely, which, as you say, seems doubtful. You would become a melancholy expatriate, belonging to neither of your countries, and in the end not really wanted by either of them. And tied to a Syrian wife, getting fatter and more *difficile* as the years passed. I should not want to see that.'

'But if you came back with me, to England . . .' His

voice tailed off. He felt very miserable, already unwanted by everybody, his decisiveness had evaporated. There was a decision being taken after months of argument and shilly-shallying, as he had insisted, but it was not he who was taking it, he felt.

' Life would not be like that ? No, I can well believe it. Perhaps I should not get fat ! But it would be *too* different, I am afraid. We can only *adjust* ourselves, you know—we cannot create new instruments of ourselves, not at our age.' She had lost her hour of content, so it was best to wake up and do what apparently had to be done. ' English for me is not a way of living, but simply a language which I speak fairly well. It exists on paper, in print. That is all . . . But get on with your sea fruits—they are very good. True citizens of the world.'

There was silence for a few minutes while they ate. Then she said, ' To use your own words, neither life would be fair to either of us.' This, she thought, was a line of reasoning which he might find acceptable ; the others he would con-sider no reasons at all. But it was a strain on her ingenuity.

They went on talking, and they always reached the same conclusion. It did them good to talk, however. The give and take of argument, the sound of one's own voice, the odd witticism which could be enjoyed for its own sake— Packet began to feel that life had not yet come to a dead stop. He even began to suspect that it never did.

' Will you join me in some cognac ? ' Sylvie asked.

' To celebrate ? Why, yes, I suppose so.'

' I am treating you. That is understood.' And she asked the waiter to leave the bottle on the table.

A good deal later she remarked, ' What an intellectual you are, with your decisions ! Must you always be thinking and planning and working things out ? In business perhaps that is the secret of success. But you cannot run your life as if it were a business.'

That stung him. ' But I'm not a business man at all ! ' he protested.

' But you are—a business man without a business. You know, I come from a business family, but my relatives reserve their organizing gifts for the office.' They were both being slightly untruthful, to about the same degree.

' But Sylvie, you are the planning fiend—you've mapped out our two possible lives—and damned them both ! '

' Was it I who forced the decision ? Life very often makes its own decisions, if you wait a little while—and that saves us from the trouble of making them, and from the pain.'

Sadly they toasted each other in cognac. And Packet was reminded of their first meeting. He looked round the restaurant nervously—but it was not the sort of place that El Hamama or Brett or the monkey-faced man (whose name he still didn't know) would be likely to patronize.

A little later she suddenly said, ' And men in particular ought to tread slowly and speak softly, for they need so long to find out what it is they want. Whereas a decision is made so quickly, and often so easily, for there is a comfortable unreality about decisions which are not made by life itself.'

She emptied her glass with an abrupt movement. ' I think I must be slightly drunk, I am talking so much. You had better take me home.'

Chapter 12

THEIR WORKS ARE LIKE THE
VAPOUR IN A PLAIN

PACKET wandered in a melancholy half-sleep between the silent agonizing rows. Only the unevenness of the ground, he suspected, kept him awake at all—and of course the occasional large black ant, astonished at finding itself in the middle of a large marquee, that crept into his sandals.

He used to wear sandals when dancing with Sylvie, out of consideration for her feet, which seemed so little and vulnerable. Capable, nonetheless, of administering a firm kick in the pants. Having nothing to have to think about, he thought about Sylvie.

If only they knew, these unhappy young people here ! In spite of their sleepless nights, their racked brains, the hashish, the aspirin—sitting there, pens in sticky trembling hands, they were as near to being masters of their fate as he was. He hoped that his face wore the keen, alert look of a true invigilator, confident and stern, the look of a man who has set the questions and knows all the answers.

This would not do at all. He must go and restore his spirits at the expense of the Third and Fourth Year Subsidiary English. This paper was taken by students from other arts departments, who in theory spent two hours in the week studying some simple English text. They were those who were not considered quite bright enough to devote themselves entirely to Arabic, History, Philosophy or whatever their main subject was. And so, besides mastering Arabic or History or Philosophy, they were condemned to keep up English as well. The examination was not much more than a formality, however, and it was considered bad form to fail them, since it only led to trouble with their own departments.

They were over on his left, scribbling away busily, in an atmosphere comparatively untroubled, a mere chore. Walking along the rows he glanced down at what they were writing. Something caught his attention.

'Tennyson's ear was with the audience, but after he became a poet laureate both his eyes were upon the Queen.' Packet pointed to the sentence and looked enquiringly at the writer. 'Is it wrong, sir?' the latter asked, gazing innocently up at him. Packet shook his head and walked on. He had been reading some of the *Idylls of the King* with them—was it possible that *he* had made such a clever remark?

He squinted down at the next candidate's paper. 'Dickens' father was not successful in his marriage and he had ten children.' Presumably that was plain lack of practice in English. But what was this old man making of it, he wondered, as he approached a broad bent back and greying hair. Ah, he was tackling one of the general essay subjects, on Modern Warfare—that might be interesting, as long as it wasn't a catalogue of inaccurately described tanks and artillery. He looked over the writer's shoulder.

'. . . so in an international meeting a code was signed refusing gaz raids, and the reason is that gaz kills military forces as well as civilians.' Packet looked hopefully at the student: a wit, a philosopher, a cynic, a rebel? But the old fellow glanced up hastily, smiled weakly at him, murmured sadly, 'Ah sir, the time is short . . .' and reapplied himself to his feverish scribbling. Packet tried to console himself: after all, never trust the artist, trust the tale.

Through the flap of the great marquee he could glimpse

the sea, stiff and still, at this distance, with a hard whiteness about it that hurt his eyes. In the evening, late, it would be a lake of indigo, stirring musically under the kindly moon, and breathing a perceptible coolness which fell against the face like damp cobweb. When Packet had first come, he had studiously ignored the sea : it was a bit of nature, and he was interested in *man*—not in bosky dells and craggy steeps and dancing billows and all the rest of the picture postcard series. But this particular sea had turned out to be a power which made itself felt, and a very versatile power. It didn't merely lie alongside the city : he had begun to feel of late that the city just happened to be lying alongside the sea. Which seemed to indicate that Sylvie wasn't altogether correct in describing him as an intellectual, a rationalist.

Had he failed in understanding, with Sylvie ? If you understand something, then you can like it or you can dislike it. It is described, and it can be disposed of. How would he describe *her* ? Certainly he would never forget her. Any more than he would forget the Mediterranean, however far he might be from it. Was that a way of describing her ? That mixture of intelligence and intuition, of hardness and tenderness, of light and sudden darknesses ?

On summer afternoons the sea was really too much for him : it was well-nigh carnal, it smirked, it lapped like a great complaisant tongue around the bodies which sprawled almost naked along the shore ; vulgar among the vulgar, it swayed and glittered importuningly before the chalets of the rich ; only its size saved it from a suspicion of abjectness. And yet, how different a being at night, when the chalets were empty and locked, and there was no-one but a bored *shawish* or an anxious prostitute to watch it ! The street-lamps, reflected in the pulsing waters, danced and dilated, while the moon threw a broad path as far as the eye could see, fading somewhere on the horizon. And then again, this changeable deity, on an evening of *khamsin*, when a great veil of fine dust hung between the setting sun and the motionless sea—static, but altering its expression from moment to moment, till at last one was almost afraid to watch it any longer, it seemed the end of the world, a dull seething corruption, barely contained in a thin stretched skin—and the tainted sun eventually sank away, and the sea greyed and darkened and fell asleep. Indefinable, elusive, intangible. Sylvie was like—the Mediterranean . . .

A student snapped his fingers to attract attention. Could he please borrow the rubber of the girl sitting in front of him ?

Sylvie like the Mediterranean ? What arrant rot ! Bad poetry ! It was easy to understand people when one didn't know them. The notebook open, the pencil poised. ' And how does it feel to be the Mediterranean, Miss Sylvie ? ' He cleared his throat in disgust. The efficient pencil fell from the fingers, the notebook blurred over. And instead one sat, bowed like these figures between which he was passing, wondering what relation those half-remembered lectures could bear to the alien, contorted questions that lay before them.

He beckoned to a servant. ' *Ahwa, min fadlak.*' The kind of coffee they made here would have kept the Sleeping Beauty on her feet, let alone drag a sentimental invigilator out of his morbid ruminations.

He walked over to his friends, imperturbably taking their finals, at the far end of the tent. They grinned at him: it was not his fault that they were subjected to this adolescent humiliation. ' How are you getting along ? ' he asked. ' It's easy enough, sir. We've arranged to go for a bathe after another ten minutes. Shall we see you there later ? ' They expressed their regret that he should have to stay till the end.

A quivering young man in another part of the assembly

indicated in some or other language that he needed to be excused. Packet escorted him to the mouth of the tent and handed him over ceremoniously to a police officer in immaculate breeches, who marched the candidate off as if to gaol. That was always a diversion : one felt important and useful for the moment : one knew the rules.

He remembered the letter which had been waiting for him in the staff room and pulled it from his pocket. ' Dear Sir,' he read, ' I owe to you a great gratitude for the good effort you did, and still to do and for the easiness I feel when I read the literature books and for the delicacy you shown us during this year.' Oh yes, the usual little vote of thanks which arrived tactfully at examination time. It continued, ' Believe me I am ready to tell everyone that you are a good teacher and a gentleman in the same time. This a few lines coming from my heart and I cannot bear myself not to tell them. Your Sincere Student, Ramsis Moussa.'

That was generous—a good teacher and a gentleman in the same time. Who the devil was Ramsis Moussa anyway ? Somebody in the First Year, Packet fancied, though he couldn't summon up any precise features. Very likely this was the first piece of written work that Mr. Moussa had done in his career as an undergraduate. Did he really believe that his Dear Sir would be taken in ? But the phraseology of the letter pricked Packet's conscience. Delicacy was exactly the last thing he had shown the First Year, and he had given them precious little cause to suppose him a gentleman. They had led him a dance with their addled politics —and in return he had made them pay for his hurt pride and for Sylvie. Bacon's verses on school-teachers came into his head. How privately apt, if publicly unsuitable—and it was to him that they applied, not to Bacon. He tore the letter up : it would be fairer to forget the writer's name when it came to marking the papers.

A further diversion was caused by a student fainting. He

was handed over to the mysterious ministrations of one of
the servants, an old man with a vague reputation for wisdom.
The victim's neighbours broke into excited comment and
had to be quelled. In a far corner a girl was crying quietly.
She had cried steadily ever since first glancing at the question
paper. Packet had tried to console her once or twice, but
she only wept with less restraint. He would have helped
her, but the paper was in Persian. And she had written
nothing so far except her name and number. Would she
get a Pass Minus, he wondered cynically, or a Weak Plus?
Was it possible to be so completely without an answer?
He wished that someone would cheat arrantly enough to
provoke him into taking action : at least he could then be
indignant, and that would save him from slipping back into
these dim and painful half-dreams.

Some of his pupils left their desks and handed in their
scripts with sad, injured smiles and deprecatory remarks.
'It is too difficult, sir.' 'I fear that I have failed, sir.' 'Is
it possible to pass if one has answered half the questions, sir?'

'As Allah wills,' he replied with the dependable old tag.
But they were in no mood for *badinage* and crept quickly
away.

He flipped over the pages of a script, rather surreptitiously
as invigilators were not supposed to read while on duty and
he had no wish to be rebuked by one of the Control's smug
agents. Most of the students could be divided into three
categories : Bright, Banal and Bad. The Bright, faced with
a question on Milton, would write enthusiastically about
Salvador Dali and André Breton ; the Banal reproduced,
often with amazing accuracy, the less significant parts of
what they had been told or had read ; the Bad did the same
as the Banal, but with less accuracy.

These scripts were by Third Year General students with
whom he had spent most of the year on the more obvious,
more amenable aspects of modern literature. 'Discuss the

importance of T. S. Eliot '—that, he had thought, would give them plenty of scope. He read, ' Mr. Eliot writes a Lovesong of Prue Frock about a man and a woman getting into bed together and getting out again. This was never done in literature before. And that is why Mr. Eliot is important . . .'

The session drew to its close. The invigilators consulted their watches. Someone from Examination Control marched importantly into the tent and announced that there were four minutes left . . . three minutes . . . two minutes . . . And then the wise old servant appeared at the door and rang a bell. The invigilators ran madly down their rows, tearing the scripts from protesting candidates ; the gentler teachers, with a fearful eye on the agent from the Control, waited at elbows for an interminable sentence to be ended ; and then the piles of scripts were borne away, into Examination Control's safe-keeping, where they would be counted and placed in sealed envelopes to await collection by some responsible member of staff.

The hot weather had set in. A new rule laid down that scripts should be marked and returned to the Control within three days of the particular examination. As most of the examinations in any subject took place at the same time, and as the teachers of that subject were invigilating during that period, it became apparent very soon that the rule was impracticable. It remained on the statute book, it was even referred to with pride by the Control as a notable advance on their predecessors' practices ; but no attempt was made to enforce it.

Nerves were on edge. Bacon reminded his colleagues after one little outburst that they couldn't expect strikes all the year round. Finally, after mutual exhortation and encouragement, the First and Second Years were marked. And then, after some cooking on Bacon's part, the results were handed in. An average sixty-three per cent pass : it should be, under the circumstances, acceptable as an opening bid.

For the English Department were always under fire at the final Examiners' Meeting. What they did with their own specialists was their matter—but Egyptian professors complained bitterly that their brightest pupils had unaccountably failed in the compulsory English paper. The Dean suavely hoped that the esteemed English Department would reconsider their verdict ; and his hopes were rarely in vain. Examinee Number One Hundred and Seventy-Three had achieved Excellent in Philosophy, Excellent in History, Very Good in Geography, Good in Arabic, Good in French, Pass in Spoken French—and Weak in English. Did that sound feasible ? His script would be produced. The English staff would glance desperately through it, in a huddle, the blacklegs of the faculty. ' It really isn't very good, is it ? ' ' No-one said it was very good. Who marked this question ? ' ' I think I did.' ' Could you give him two marks more, do you think ?—that's all he needs.' ' Hum. We'ell.' ' After all he's got this bit of quotation almost right.' ' Look at the time ! Mark him up, do—we shan't be troubled with him next year, he's going to be a philosopher.' And so the question was marked up, the total was increased, the grade was changed from Weak to Pass. The French staff concealed their relief, the Egyptian staff did not bother to conceal their satisfaction. And after three or four hours of such bargaining the vast number of border-line fates were settled.

Packet had been most indignant on the occasion of his first Examiners' Meeting ; he had been ready to fight every single case, to stay in that sweltering muttering room till midnight if necessary.

' But damn it, if a student has failed, then he has failed ! Good God, we give them every chance to pass.'

' Don't forget that English is a foreign language in these parts,' Bacon had cautioned, ' and each year it gets more foreign. Isn't that what you young men want ? Gaelic for the Gaels, Arabic for the Arabs.'

'I see. So we have to adjust ourselves to changing conditions—and not only ourselves but also Mr. Shakespeare and Mr. Wordsworth and so on.'

'Yes, I wonder what they'd think ? . . . What we have to take into account is the background, the home life of our students—what little we know of it. As for Wordsworth —a shepherd for them is what their grandfathers often were —and what they don't intend to be. They begin by feeling towards shepherds much as you or I might feel towards a remote ancestor who burnt witches and never took a bath. With the important difference that their grandfathers are usually alive—and, indeed, kicking.'

'But they've asked for our world—they've made the decision to study English literature in their universities, and they must stand by it. We can't be expected to perform adjustments to reality for their sakes.' Packet was to feel very uncomfortable when he heard similar sentiments on Brett's lips several years later.

'Youth is hard,' Bacon had retorted. 'Adjustment—I only doubt whether we can make the right sort of adjustment. Anyway, if Wordsworth gets knocked about in the process, perhaps that doesn't matter so much after all. I'm afraid life has come to seem more important to me than literature : at least the flow should be in *that* direction. Reality, as you say, that's our job . . .'

Packet was impressed by a sincerity which he knew must have been put to the test, but his hurt pride still rankled.

'Yes but—I mean, we must teach literature for what it's worth—and doesn't that mean marking exam papers for what they're worth ?'

'Literature for what it's worth—yes. We agree, don't we, that whatever literature is worth, its worth has something to do with everyday life ?—pardon the banality . . . And

that is precisely what our students are only just beginning
to find out. An exciting discovery—difficult for us to
imagine. Their own literature hasn't had much to do with
their lives—can you blame them for not taking it very
seriously ?—just the perfumed rose in the rich man's garden.
Think, Packet, it's exactly as if English poetry consisted of
nothing but commendatory verses in Latin ! And then
suddenly there they are—listening to you and me talking
glibly about tradition and social background. No wonder
they get a bit flustered by Wordsworth's shepherds ! It's
like opening your mouth for a sip of liqueur and having
the sea pour into it, fish, ships and all ! Have you noticed
how they're forever writing something like " Milton is the
greatest epic poet in *our* literature ", or " We are proud of
our world-famous dramatist, Shakespeare " ? That kind of
thing used to irritate me immensely—there are of course
uncharitable explanations of the habit—but now it makes me
feel rather pleased.'

' Well I never,' Packet could only think to say, ' I do believe
you're a bit of a mystic ! '

' A mystic ! I thought I was a cynical old bloke.' Bacon
looked distinctly put out and made a gesture towards the
glass that wasn't there.

' Every now and then a cultural high-up comes from
London and tells us that we are doing good work and all
the rest of it. And to some extent he's right—though he
hasn't the right to be, for he knows precious little about it.
Unless someone works hard now, in another twenty years
or so this country will be suffering from a combination of
all the horrors of the past with all the horrors of the present
—and enjoying the pleasures of neither ! Violence is what
we're up against—various varieties of it—and you won't
fight it with pedagogic violence, even if you do come from
Cambridge.'

It was that same year, after the results had been published, that an unsuccessful candidate had killed himself. He was afraid to go home to his village, his friends explained, his father would have beaten him. Packet had the feeling that Bacon had won the argument, though not altogether by fair means.

The last straw, it was generally felt, was the oral examinations. They went on and on. One talked for five minutes on end, perhaps, in order to elicit three or four words from the examinee on which to base a mark. Packet was glad to find that Examination Control had allotted him to Bacon as a partner in this ordeal. Bacon was one of the few staff who could remember practically every student's name, and he knew in advance what each of them deserved.

But it was painful, all the same, for all concerned. The examiners ran out of questions by mid-morning. It seemed a waste of time asking the male students what career they intended to take up, for the great majority had the same ambition—journalism. The more articulate admitted, however, that they would probably end up as teachers—except for a few prize students who had their eyes on much better paid jobs in Coca-Cola publicity. The real difficulty for examiners, Bacon remarked when they broke off for coffee, was to remember that their victims were individual human beings ; the majority of students seemed tragic, under examination, but some of them really were.

The observation had been prompted by their last interview. The girl, who was perhaps twenty-five years old, had begun bravely, but then burst into tears. It turned out that she was a widow, with two young children and an old mother to support. Bacon moaned something about happy student days, while Packet chivalrously praised her command of English—it was well up to average—and gave her to understand pretty plainly—he had noticed Bacon entering the mark ' Good ' against her name—that she need have no fears about the English oral : another two years and she would be able (if Allah still willed) to take a teaching post and support her family.

'Oh but it is not English I am afraid of,' she said between sobs, and not very gratefully, Packet felt. 'It is the compulsory examination in Arabic, which everyone fears.'

The sad and thoughtful approach which this interview had induced proved unsuited to the next. It was a Coptic student, who, after a rather unsuccessful attempt to cope with Bacon's query about a set text, put all his cards on the table.

'Dear sirs,' he leant with both arms on the rickety desk and looked earnestly into their faces, 'you will be kind to me, I think. Because I am a Church-going like you. We are not like the others. They hate me. I am a friend of Christ, and you also are friends of Christ.'

'Well, of all the . . .' Packet was beginning, scandalized and tickled and making a mental note of it, when Bacon put in softly, 'Naughty boy telling naughty fib ! You know they do not hate you at all, and in any case you get all the best jobs in the Postal Service, you friends of Christ . . . And you haven't answered my question,' his cooing changed into a roar. '*Why did Macbeth murder Banquo ?*'

It was difficult, after that, not to fail him.

An army transport was waiting for them when Bacon and Packet arrived at the faculty early the next morning, and in three quarters of an hour they were at the gates of the internment camp. The camp, in spite of its long history of diverse usages, had the casual, makeshift and temporary appearance characteristic of such places. It consisted of huts, tents and enough wire to fence in all the chickens of the world. This was Packet's first visit to a concentration camp —as he preferred to call it—and he was feeling at the same time grave and hostile and rather excited. The guards at the gate waved at them in a jolly fashion—evidently their visit was something of an event. Inside, guards and internees stood about in attitudes of boredom. Supposed Zionists, supposed communists, supposed soldiers, all in indiscriminate shirts and shabby trousers—it was difficult to tell the oppressor from the oppressed.

An officer met them and escorted them to a large army hut. This hut, he explained affably, was normally used by the inmates as a recreation room, but it had been specially cleaned up for the occasion. There they would find the student, Mr. Batrawy. He opened the door and they walked in. A little desk, borrowed from the nearest primary school, stood in the middle of the room, along with three chairs. The officer shook hands with his prisoner, and left them. The examiners shook hands with their examinee and asked anxiously after his health.

'Shall we sit down?' the young man suggested, resolved to play the host. 'Would you like some coffee? You are sure?' In some slight embarrassment they took up examination positions. Would he like some cigarettes? No, he thanked them sincerely, but he was well supplied with cigarettes—and indeed with comforts of all kinds. The guards were no zealots, and they were poor : and so an occasional gift of a few shillings on the part of his parents kept the channels open.

But how was he treated, Packet asked solemnly. Well, it was all a question of how you got along with the camp personalities : luckily they were a mild lot, and the internees too were pacific and well-behaved. The place had much of the atmosphere of a cheap convalescent hospital : the inmates were waiting—waiting for something to pass, to get better or to get worse—and neither party wished to aggravate matters. Batrawy had no serious complaints to make on that score. And conditions, he admitted, were ideal for study : he had done much more work this year than would have been the case otherwise.

'But of course,' he added tactfully, 'I have been deprived of your lectures and discussions.'

'We can tell you,' Bacon said, 'quite illegally, you understand, that you've done excellently in all the written papers.'

The young man told them a little about his life in the camp. Not because he had much to tell or felt any urge to tell it, but simply because this was meant to be an oral examination, after all, even if the teachers had forgotten the fact.

No, he could not say that there was anything he wished for, except——

'Yes?' Packet pressed. 'What is it?'

'My liberty,' the boy said, pathetically. But in all their ears the word struck a false note : it echoed flatly between the faded walls, where other slogans hung, vestiges of the hut's earlier occupants—'Sergeants' Mess', 'Walls have Ears' with a picture of Hitler's distended ear in the luggage rack, 'Death to the Jews' in decorative Arabic script, and a painstaking amateur mural labelled 'Russian Rose'.

He continued, in some shame, 'I mean—my friends, my family, the university, the streets . . .' and now his voice was truly pathetic.

'Well, let's end *this* farce, at any rate,' Bacon grumbled, getting up from the little desk. 'Shall we give him "Excellent" for the oral? What do you say, Packet?'

So there was really nothing they could do for him, they asked in preparing to leave, nothing they could send him from the outside world? No, except—Batrawy pointed shyly to the local English-language paper sticking out of Bacon's pocket. Newspapers were banned from the camp, for some reason, until they were a fortnight old. Bacon handed it over and the boy concealed it, not particularly carefully, inside his shirt.

'There is another thing, sir, if I may ask it,' he said. 'I expect to be let out of here in a month or so. And then I

must find a job, something in business—I don't intend to
teach people. A testimonial from you would be of great
value, Mr. Bacon.'

' Certainly I'll give you a testimonial, for what it's worth,'
Bacon grinned. 'Do you want me to say that you have
never been in prison ? '

They shook hands with him, and rejoined the officer
outside. The latter asked anxiously as to how they had
found the young man. Bacon assured him that he seemed
fit and as cheerful as circumstances allowed, and the officer
showed his gratification. Their driver saluted and they
drove off.

' Anybody would think that we were inspecting the place,'
Packet grunted. The visit had not lived up to his expectations,
but he reminded himself that it could only have done so at
Batrawy's expense.

' Poor boy, he's bored to death,' Bacon remarked. ' He
entered the camp all keyed up for martyrdom. And now
he's about to leave it, all prepared for a respectable business
career. Egypt is not so simple as she seems . . .'

As the week wore on their spirits fell lower and lower.
They no longer chatted about their holiday plans in the
intervals. When they entered the examination room on
the last morning Bacon tried to make a little joke about
Packet's discarded notebooks, but neither of them found it
very funny.

So many of their dullest pupils had blossomed out, in the
most unnerving of ways. Was it their nervousness, their
terror of having nothing to say—Packet wondered—was it
a device to evade questions on the texts, or was it the result
of speaking in a language which had little to do with their
private lives, that led them into such painful intimacies ?
Grievances poured out. Stories of the injustices of employers ;
complaints against their Egyptian teachers ; stories of political

persecution ; abject confessions of poverty, and of fear of the future when, at the best, all that most of them could expect was twelve pounds a month teaching long and harassed hours in government schools. At times the shrinking examiners were appalled by gratuitous glimpses into their family lives, their difficulties with parents, and even their hopeless loves. Packet hoped that it was language ineptitude that gave these tormented monologues their nightmarish quality. Pass, pass, pass. Because they could not afford to marry their beloveds or because they had to support their sisters, crippled hopelessly in road accidents, or because they could speak English.

But it was even worse when nothing at all came out. A very dark, smooth-skinned youth sat tensely in front of them, and not a word emerged from his quivering lips. The examiners made encouraging speeches, to no effect, and they too fell silent ; there was no anger in them, but only something more intolerable than embarrassment. Packet became aware of a soft and regular tapping sound ; by an effort of concentration he traced it to the student—the sweat was rolling off his face, dripping on to the desk between them. Bacon attempted to dismiss him gently, with the promise of a second attempt in September, but he sat on, too terrified to speak, too terrified to leave, waiting rigidly for the inspiration that failed to come. In the end he was persuaded to yield up his seat, though not gently.

A plump jovial Egyptian professor of Egyptology bustled in and whispered in Bacon's ear. Would they be good enough to examine So-and-so now ?—he had recently suffered an attack of pneumonia which had left one side of his face paralysed, thus preventing him from speaking clearly, but he knew English very well—he, the Egyptian professor, could vouch for that—and perhaps they would allow him to write down the answers to their questions ? The professor smiled fatly and winked and nodded as if purveying some highly coveted and perverted delight. Bacon nodded coldly, and he ushered in a small thin youth with an intensely sad expression ; he spoke to him soothingly in Arabic, made further violently knowing gesticulations at the examiners, and hurried away.

' We hear that you have been ill,' said Packet in a friendly voice. Physical illness was unequivocal. ' What was the matter with you ? '

Nothing at all happened. The boy's expression remained precisely as it was ; he seemed quite relaxed.

' What illness have you been suffering from ? ' Packet asked again, pushing some paper and a pencil towards him. There was a short pause, and the reply came, perfectly articulated and distinct.

' Ten thousand tadpoles . . .' and the voice tailed off.

Not another word could they get from him, spoken or written, to reassure them. He made a weary, helpless gesture with his hands, and his deep eyes filled with tears. The tears of things, but certainly not of human things. Bacon went for a servant, and the boy was taken quietly away.

' He must have sat through the whole examination,' —but it did not bear thinking about, and a fresh candidate was already before them.

He was large and of sullen appearance. He looked as much like a mob as one man by himself can. They were both exhausted, gazing back at him with equal resentment, unable to conjure up anything to ask.

' Your pigeon,' said Bacon.

' Well, er . . . ' At last Packet thought to ask, ' Who was your teacher during the year ? '

' You, sir,' he answered promptly, indignation and long-suffering mixed in his voice, and he pointed to his interrogator.

' I have never seen you before in my life ! ' There was once again complete silence. The student accepted Packet's remark as a statement of fact, not as an accusation which might deserve a reply. Packet felt his temper getting out of control : it was even a pleasurable sensation.

'How often have you attended my lectures ? '

'Some times, sir.'

'Yes, but how many times ? ' Packet was near to bellowing. A simple straightforward case of inexcusable laziness and bare-faced impertinence. Bacon lit a cigarette and gazed out of the window, as if this were some private quarrel of his colleague's. A peanut vendor grinned broadly in at him and waved a paper bag enquiringly.

'Not always, sir,' with a sad, ingratiating and shifty smile.

'And why not always, may I ask ?   I have to come to my lectures, why the devil shouldn't you ? '

'Ah sir,' he lifted his heavy shoulders and let them fall with a suddenness that made Packet jump ; his voice was thick with a deeply forgiving and excessively mild regret, it shook slightly with the tears of human things. 'I have been in prison.'

Packet changed his tone. The young man had been in prison. It happens to the best of us. He thought of Andrea, and Batrawy, and Bunyan too. Well, one up to him.

'Dear me,' he said urbanely, kindly, 'and why were you in prison ? '

'The government, sir. They sent me in prison with my brother.' The youth realized that he was making up for his unfortunate outset. Everyone knew that Englishmen never loved the government of Egypt. After a fiercely furtive look at the closed door, he continued in a whisper, 'They are the enemy of my people. They do not wish democracy. I spoke against them——'

'Don't you mean,' Bacon suddenly woke up, 'that you shouted " Down with Britain " at the wrong time of year, knocked down an underfed *shawish*, and broke a Greek grocer's window without official permission ? '

The youth responded a little too swiftly for the role which he had adopted, of slow-witted but honest patriot. ' Oh sir, never ! I love Britain. I cry " Up with Britain ". She is the friend of the people, the land of liberties. I am an English student.'

' A student of English.' He looked annoyed with himself and added, ' A grammatical point I have warned you about before.'

' Yes sir. I love too much the language and the books of Britain,' he went on protesting. They dismissed him and looked glumly at each other.

' It had better be a Pass. After all, he did talk—a sort of English. Put a question mark against it—we'll check on how he did in the written papers—failed, I hope.'

A short search of the neighbouring corridors brought to light no further candidate. The long task was over. They shook hands solemnly. And then Bacon went upstairs to the Control to investigate the case of the sick boy and insist that he be sent to hospital.

Packet waited for him at the entrance, where, just out of the blazing sun, two police officers dozed, poised precariously on their chairs. At the side of the road were squatting three men, playing some enigmatic game with round stones. From time to time they stared at Packet. He had often wondered what the rules of the game were. But he couldn't very well ask them : they were already quarrelling among themselves : one of them, a tall wall-eyed fellow, suddenly snatched up the stones and threw them savagely at a tethered mule. ' Ten thousand tadpoles '—could they possibly not have heard correctly ? He devoutly hoped so.

' It seems,' Bacon reported, ' that there is no rule against sitting for an examination while of unsound mind.'

' That rule would debar too many,' said Packet, without a trace of malice.

Chapter 13

MAN PRAYETH FOR EVIL AS HE PRAYETH
FOR GOOD; FOR MAN IS HASTY

AND now the academic year was over at last. And
there was nothing more to be done. Except to
go on leave, or say good-bye to those who were
going on leave. The passport office, the consulates, the
travel agencies were full of hot and bothered teachers, avid
for Europe's cloudy skies.

Outside a leather shop Bacon bumped into Brett.

'Are you going on leave?' he asked.

'Yes. I'm off home at the beginning of next week,
thank the Lord. And you?' He glanced at the new
suitcase that Bacon was carrying. 'Are you going home?'

'No, I'm not going to England.'

'Oh, you're staying here then?' The young man's tone
conveyed a slight rebuke. But Bacon met him half-way.

'I'm thinking of spending a month in Cyprus—an old
pupil of mine owns a hotel there, in very agreeable surroundings. A few green trees, a breeze, good eating and good
sleeping—that's what makes a holiday when you're my age.'

Brett's regard brightened somewhat. Cyprus was at any
rate a colony: he expressed interest: he wouldn't mind
going to Cyprus himself one day.

It would be a notable change for Bacon to spend a summer
away from Alexandria. But a change, he felt, was what he
needed. He had not been at his best this last year. To lose

one's temper without achieving any useful result was a silly thing ; and, for instance, he had not been very pleasant to this young man, who after all was young, and new here, and belonged to a difficult generation. He ought to try to make amends, Bacon thought.

' Will you come to tea with me ? ' he asked. Sourayah was out for the day, so the young man would be safe and unembarrassed.

' Why yes. I'm not doing anything this afternoon. Yes, thank you.' For this was the beginning of the vacation, the short season of general forgiveness.

As they were finishing tea there came a knock at the door. First a hesitant tap, then some mumbling, and then vigorous thumping. Bacon opened the door and three men, wearing discoloured *gallabiehs* and gaping shoes, slouched into the hall. There was a moment's silence while Bacon looked at them enquiringly, and then the tallest of them began a loud harangue. He carried tribal scars on his cheeks and one of his pupils was clouded over, like an artificial eye in which the colours had run.

Disturbed by the tone, remembering the evening in Nicola's bar, Brett came to see what was the matter. Bacon signed to him to keep quiet while the Egyptian spoke. Afterwards, while the three men stood still, their eyes on the carpet, he explained reluctantly.

' They say they are relatives of Sourayah—my housekeeper —and that it is a dishonour to the family that she should live alone with me. A dishonour which can be wiped out only in blood. But of course they mean in money . . . '

Suddenly losing his nerve, the leader shouted out something in Arabic.

' I'm truly sorry that this should happen during your visit,' Bacon continued quietly, ' but don't be alarmed. Just go on with your tea. It's not really serious, you know. Honour doesn't begin to smart sixteen or seventeen years after a fatal wound. The truth is that they're miserably poor, and misery stimulates the imagination. All the same, keep quiet and don't try to do anything. And better stay away from the windows . . .'

He spoke to the intruders in their language, ' You are welcome, O lords ! May I offer you some coffee ?' They shuffled uneasily, and one of them gave a short strained laugh.

' It is vengeance we want . . .' They followed him into the living-room and therewith followed a lengthy and rather comic recital of the humiliations they had suffered in their village on account of their niece's or sister-in-law's or fifth cousin's shameless behaviour in the city, where she had been seduced by a foreign gentleman. Bacon could not help smiling, but he was careful not to laugh. Carried away by their imagined sorrows the three swayed back and forth, gesturing towards Allah, plucking their heavy miseries out of their mouths. It was as if the priests of some deity both violent and hard of hearing were engaged in their strained and painful rites. Factually, Bacon noted, their accounts didn't quite match.

Understanding nothing of what was said, Brett was appalled at the scene. He felt his mind contracting, smaller and smaller, while the sound of their rasping voices swelled and the smell of garlic on their breath filled his whole existence. He began to feel horribly disgusted, he was sickened by these animals, and above all he felt an intolerable anger, the same anger that had swept over him when watching the rioters from the window. Beat them, kick them down the stairs, give them money, give them whatever they ask for—he wanted to tell Bacon—but make them go at once.

' What you have said is not quite true,' Bacon replied, carrying on from their speech in almost identical tones, his shoulders hunched and his hands with open palms splayed outwards in front of him. Brett watched him with nauseated fascination. What was he doing? No Englishman ought to behave like that. How theatrical, how insincere his antics were! It was obvious that he was lying to them. That fat Egyptian woman had been his mistress, after all . . .

'. . . and the woman Sourayah would tell you so. But' —nodding his head wisely—'it is bad that your friends should have spat on you in the village . . . through seventeen long years. . . . He who is knocked down by a car in the public street is entitled to compensation.'

Convinced of their deserts, the three growled in fierce approval. They listened intently.

'Sourayah is a good cook. I am a good master. I am prepared to be your friend. Let us talk of a little compensation.'

'We are poor, O sir,' whined one of them, a thin little man with a twisted foot, 'and the railway was very expensive, and we have left our work. Twenty pounds is nothing to a teacher in the big school.'

'I will give you a pound each,' Bacon offered as an opening bid. He felt happier now that the bargaining had begun. Another ten minutes of fantastic oaths and pained ejaculations and simple witticisms and the silly business would be over. It would probably cost him six pounds, for he couldn't haggle at length with Brett standing by, so tense and thin-lipped. And brewing up Turkish coffee, at which he was a master, would take time. Poor Brett. A funny kind of amends to make the young man. And Sourayah would be furious, he thought, she would probably go after them, take back the money and leave them with broken heads.

'You are mocking us,' growled the biggest, thrusting his ugly head forward, 'the honour of a family costs more than three pounds . . .' Nervous lest the Englishman should have another visitor and the balance of power be disturbed, he too felt that the process of bargaining needed acceleration. And he was conscious of his comrades' waning courage. They had not anticipated this kind of opposition. '. . . It costs blood,' he roared desperately, and slipped a long bone-handled knife out of his sleeve, waving it strenuously in Bacon's direction. His fellows flinched ; they muttered discontentedly at him. The little man moved slightly towards the door.

But Bacon only smiled suavely and said, with that rather improper tenderness which only oriental languages are able to suggest, ' *Ya salaam !* You have brought me a curio from your village ? It is indeed a noble and manly weapon, and just what I require. But will it cut ? Will it sharpen this old pencil of mine ? '

The three of them, even the disgruntled fellow with the knife, smiled at this. They were really rather relieved : the *Inglisi* was a true man of spirit, he jested like an Egyptian, he spoke the language almost as well. They enjoyed a foretaste of the uproarious gatherings they would have at home, relating over and over again the events of this evening. And a good story was a kind of riches.

Bacon, too, felt rather pleased. It was an exercise in creative tact, and one hadn't so many opportunities for that exercise among Europeans these days. What a pity it was that Brett couldn't follow the little comedy.

But Brett was following a nightmare of his own. The skinny squirming figures in front of him, so close, with their twisted feet, the terrible melted eyeball, the filthy blood-stained bandage tied loosely round the hand of one of them —these were figures of absolute squalor ; and squalor for him was the same thing as evil. He was breathing a tainted air ; he shivered convulsively—it was not fear that made him shiver, he told himself, it was moral outrage, it was being involved, by no responsibility of his own, in this foul encounter.

It was not fear, he reassured himself; his nature shivered raw and naked in a blast of utter disgust.

The knife glinted in the light as the big Egyptian squinted along the blade, with an ugly affectionate smile. He put out his great leathery fist to take the pencil from Bacon, examined it carefully as if he suspected that it might be a piece of steel in disguise, stretched it out at arm's length and lifted his other arm, ready to slice the pencil in two at one stroke. He could do it, he knew; it was a good blade, he was used to it.

One of his companions, the timid little man with the twisted foot, moved hastily out of range. Knives he couldn't abide. He stumbled against Brett. The touch of him pre-cipitated Brett's horror, and with a shriek he pushed the man away with all his force, propelling him violently into the little group.

There was a short senseless skirmish, a moment of complete confusion, the pencil fell to the ground, the knife somehow rose and fell. Then a groan, and Bacon lurched against the wall and slipped awkwardly to the floor, a hand pressed to his breast. There was again silence, for a moment, while the Egyptians slowly became aware of what had happened. Blood was soaking into the carpet. Their little comedy was over. It was no longer their honour that was at stake, or their future wealth, but their lives. Cursing each other as the murderer, the murderer of an innocent and good man, they struggled savagely together, in an unthinking panic.

'Stupid, stupid!' came from Bacon in a kind of exasperated wail.

Brett automatically knelt down by his host. The blood ran on to his trousers, and yet he felt a kind of relief. The tension had broken. He could understand things now.

Bacon was trying to say something. 'Whisky—in the cupboard . . . You must learn to speak the same language as they, even if you only tell lies in it . . . But no, Brett, you're still alive . . . speak your own . . . a doctor below . . .'

As Brett ran out he heard Bacon's last words. 'Incredible —damnation !'

Chapter 14

BUT LET THY PACE BE MIDDLING;
AND LOWER THY VOICE

BACON was dead when the doctor arrived. The unhappy Egyptians were still struggling among themselves when the police arrived, a little later. They were taken to prison, and beaten, whereupon they continued each to blame the others, more and more vociferously.

Sourayah was interrogated on her return the next day, and it transpired that the would-be blackmailers were no relatives of hers. Her own relatives, she explained, were living quite contentedly on money which she sent them out of her earnings as Bacon's housekeeper. The prisoners were poor men from her village; she knew their wives, and they of course were acquainted with her situation. That the men should have attempted some such trickery did not surprise her; but that it should have ended so violently she could not understand. She was inconsolable.

'He was a good man. He was my father. . . . It was for a little money—he had so much of it—more than sixty pounds each month!—and he was generous . . .' Her sorrow was vocal but undeniably genuine, and she was soon released.

The Egyptians were eventually thrown into gaol for an indefinite period. But several years later, on the occasion of a change of government and a sharp outbreak of anti-

British feeling, they were given what was called their freedom: a touch which Bacon would have appreciated.

Packet had decided—though it seemed to him that events had done the deciding for him—to throw up his job and leave the country. In the afterglow of feeling that followed their old employee's death, the university agreed to pay Packet's fare home even though he hadn't given the prescribed amount of notice.

Bacon had been his closest friend, and he felt he could not stay on in Egypt after what had happened. The wrongness of it was too much for him, the awful illogic—he explained to Sylvie in making his final adieus—the utter perversity of Egyptian fate. And from the way he eyed her, she knew that he was speaking of her, too.

'And so I can't ask you again,' he added, 'because I'm out of work now.'

That was almost too much for her. 'You make it very difficult for me not to change my mind.' She found refuge in exasperation. 'And if we had married—*alors*? What would you do? You would stay on. In spite of every feeling you would stay on. And the bitterness would grow.'

He was about to point out bitterly that now he was to lose two friends instead of one, but she continued.

'Did I not tell you that life often makes its own decisions? You need to be free at this moment—I know you, my dear —and see, you are free. Happy man! But oh, you remind me of Simone's base Indian and his pearl!'

She had just heard that her husband was ready to give her a divorce. She too would be free. But she thought it better not to mention this news to her friend.

'Will you do two things for me?' he asked timidly.

'You know there is only one thing I will not do.'

'Firstly, write to me. Secondly,' he looked stern,

'keep away from that horrible fellow who looks like a monkey.'

'Yes, twice. And I am even better at keeping away from horrible fellows than at writing letters.'

Packet felt less tragic. He had great faith in the virtues of keeping up a correspondence.

'You may change your mind,' he pointed out, 'and then you can write and let me know.'

'You may change yours—and then you needn't write and let me know.'

She dropped a few tears, but not until he had left. Freedom was an expensive thing—it had cost her much already—but she would treasure it the more.

And that left Packet with absolutely no plans for the future. He would return to England in any case ; perhaps he could find work in adult education ; or perhaps he would try to write that novel which Bacon had talked about ; at the worst he could always turn to schoolmastering. The main thing at present was to get away. His state of mind resembled that of a schoolboy just before the examinations : he had learnt a lot, but he lacked the opportunity to find out what exactly he had learnt. Like Wilhelm Meister at the moment when he was told that his apprenticeship had ended, Packet felt more confused than ever. Yet there was something happy about his confusion : a hint of release from false gods. And even underneath the planlessness something exciting was stirring. His times, too, had been good times, and he would not cry them down, but now it was time that they should end, that he should go away, and go on.

Brett was leaving too, it seemed. He was to be transferred to a rather smart resort in the south of France, a much sought-after post, for which he had been destined all along. His service in Egypt was to be simply a sort of apprenticeship, but in view of the deplorable events in which he had been so painfully and innocently involved, his superiors decided to cut the process short.

The day before he was to sail, Packet visited Bacon's flat, partly to say goodbye to Sourayah, who was busy packing up Bacon's few possessions for his sister in England, and partly to look through the piles of manuscripts which filled the desk.

Sourayah opened the door to him, welcoming him with the conventional formula, from which all her old enthusiasm had drained away. She seemed deflated, and even thin. Complaining of complicated ailments, she told him that she intended to return to her family in the village, to wait for death. Alexandria was a bad city, full of people and noise and thieves. She would not take anything that did not belong to her—except a photograph of Bacon, for which she had already purchased a large chromium frame. It showed Bacon as a young man, as he was when he first came to Egypt: it had been taken for his future wife.

' Of course,' Packet assured her, ' of course you must keep it. It belongs to you.' He added hesitantly, ' But do you need money? I mean, the railway costs a lot, you know.' But she refused dully.

At this moment Marcel arrived, bustlingly busy and at the same time the incarnation of conscious grief.

' What did I say?' he moaned at Packet. 'I could have found him a score of impeccable wives. But now . . .' He peered about the room as if in search of his misguided friend. 'Tragic, tragic . . . And you are leaving, I hear? This is indeed the exodus! Ah well, you are right. There comes a time when, in all honour and without cowardice, one can do nothing else but leave.' He assumed a brave expression. 'I too am leaving. For Paris—where I have a post in the Egyptian Embassy, a rather important post,' he coughed modestly, ' as the first official Egyptian *attaché culturel.*' He beamed at Packet, and Packet smiled warmly back.

'But what about your poor Bedouins, Marcel? How will they get on without you?'

Marcel was thrown off his balance momentarily by this delving into ancient history. 'No funds,' he muttered, 'and the tools were disappearing as quickly as we bought them. A terrible thing, poverty . . . Ah well, every man to his trade.' He brightened up. 'Circumstances forbid sentiment—as so often with us,' he continued with a sad but indulgent smile, 'and so, *au revoir*, dear friend. I am sure that we shall meet again, in Paris or London.'

They shook hands as if wrestling. Then, remembering the purpose of his call, Marcel turned to Sourayah and launched into a considerable speech. All that Packet could gather was that he was praising their friend, 'a good man', 'a great man', 'a prince' and so forth. Sourayah nodded agreement vehemently; she began to weep afresh, and in a gingerly fashion Marcel reached up to pat her consolingly on her shoulder. Of course, he reflected wryly, Bacon and she had never—or not since their first days together, so long ago—lived together: his mind rested amusedly on the worldly euphemism: not even (and his own eccentric and painful passions persuaded him that it must be something) that. *Servante-maîtresse*—that was hardly Sourayah's role!

At the door Marcel carefully replaced his smart homburg, a new acquisition, and took up a large round parcel. To Packet's questioning look he replied, 'Oh, that's my tarbush, my very first tarbush, my maiden tarbush you might say!' He tittered. 'I am sure it will have a great success in Paris—but of course I wouldn't want to be seen dead in it here!'

'Good luck, then,' Packet said, 'in your new life.'

'Good luck to you, my dear,' he replied. A look of

sudden embarrassment came over his face, and he jumped into the waiting taxi. ' To the airport, quickly ! '

Packet opened the drawers. It had to be done, he told himself, and in that case he and he alone should do it. He pulled out papers of all sizes and shapes. Presumably they comprised a draft, or several drafts, of the great work on Education. But the writing was so small and so irregular that only a word emerged here and there. It might even have been written in some private code. What could he do with it all ? It was so heavy. And even if it could be deciphered, the fact remained that Bacon's name would hardly carry much weight among educational publishers.

Looking up, he saw Sourayah gazing proudly at the stacks of manuscript. Would she like to take it with her ? She nodded her head vigorously, scooped the papers into her lap, and piled them carefully on top of the photograph. What were they about, she asked him. Education, he told her, explaining it with some difficulty—it was all about Education. Ah, she replied lovingly, he was a clever man —clever and good as well.

A slip of paper fluttered out. Picking it up, Packet noticed something written on it in block letters. It was an extract from a student's answer to a comprehension test, apparently. ' The intellectual class : is dishonest people who make much trouble. Sometimes they can be educated and made useful to their country.'

OXFORD

MORE TWENTIETH CENTURY CLASSICS

Details of a selection of Twentieth-Century Classics follow. A complete list of Oxford Paperbacks, including The World's Classics, OPUS, Past Masters, Oxford Authors, Oxford Shakespeare, and Oxford Paperback Reference, as well as Twentieth-Century Classics, is available in the UK from the General Publicity Department, Oxford University Press, Walton Street, Oxford, OX2 6DP.

In the USA, complete lists are available from the Paperbacks Marketing Manager, Oxford University Press, 200 Madison Avenue, New York, NY 10016.

THE NOTEBOOK OF
MALTE LAURIDS BRIGGE

Rainer Maria Rilke

Translated by John Linton

Introduction by Stephen Spender

The Notebook of Malte Laurids Brigge, first published in 1910, is one of Rilke's few prose works. It has as its eponymous hero a young Danish poet, living in poverty in Paris, and is closely based on Rilke's bohemian years in the city at the turn of the century. In Malte's *Notebook* present and past intertwine. He is fascinated by squalor and observes the poor and sick of Paris, victims of fate like himself. Sickness intensifies his imagination, and he recreates the horrors of childhood, probing the many faces of death. It was in this novel that Rilke developed the precise, visual style which is largely associated with his writing.

MANSERVANT AND MAIDSERVANT

Ivy Compton-Burnett

Introduction by Penelope Lively

Ivy Compton-Burnett's novels are profound studies of family life; they are both immensely funny and completely original. *Manservant and Maidservant* describes the petty tyrannies to be found in an upper middle-class Edwardian household, and shows Dame Ivy's wit at its sharpest and her characterization at its most memorable.

'there is no doubt about her originality and the uniqueness of her world, and her mastery of a sinister comic vein, of which *Manservant and Maidservant* (1947) is a charateristic product' *Scotsman*

'There is nobody in all this writing world even remotely like her.' *Guardian*

THE SECRET BATTLE

A. P. Herbert

Introduction by John Terraine

First published in 1919, *The Secret Battle* is an account of the wartime experiences of an infantry officer, Harry Penrose, as he is tested and brought to breaking-point, first in Gallipoli, then with his young wife in London, and finally in the trenches of France. Without melodrama or sensationalism, Herbert conveys the full horror of war and its awful impact on the mind and body of an ordinary solider.

'This book should be read in each generation, so that men and women may rest under no illusion about what war means.' Winston Churchill